The Fisher Folk of Late Imperial and Modern China

Although most studies of rural society in China deal with land villages, in fact very substantial numbers of Chinese people lived by the sea, on the rivers and the lakes. In land villages, mostly given to farming, people lived in permanent houses, whereas on the margins of the waterways many people lived in boats and sheds and developed their own marked features, often being viewed as pariahs by the rest of Chinese society. This book examines these boat-and-shed living people. It takes a "historical anthropological" approach, combining research in official records with investigations among surviving boat-and-shed living people, their oral traditions and their personal records. Besides outlining the special features of the boat-and-shed living people, the book considers why pressures over time drove many to move to land villages, and how boat-and-shed living people were gradually marginalized, often losing their fishing rights to those who claimed imperial connections. The book covers the subject from Ming and Qing times up to the present.

He Xi is Assistant Professor at the Chinese University of Hong Kong, China.

David Faure is Research Professor at the Chinese University of Hong Kong, China.

The Historical Anthropology of Chinese Society series

Series editor: David Faure, *Chinese University of Hong Kong*

Historians are being increasingly attracted by the methodology of historical anthropology, an approach which combines observations in the field with documentary analysis, both of official documents and of documents collected from local society. In China, historians have been pursuing such local historical research for a generation, with very little of this work being available in English hitherto. This series makes available in English research undertaken by the Historical Anthropology of Chinese Society project based at the Chinese University of Hong Kong, and related work. The books argue that top-heavy, dynasty-centred history is incomplete without an understanding of how local communities were involved in the government process and in the creation of their own historical narratives. The books argue that Chinese social history needs to be rewritten from the bottom up.

The Fisher Folk of Later Imperial and Modern China
An Historical Anthropology of Boat-and-Shed Living
Xi He and David Faure

The Fisher Folk of Late Imperial and Modern China
An historical anthropology of boat-and-shed living

Edited by Xi He and David Faure

LONDON AND NEW YORK

First published 2016 by Routledge

2 Park Square, Milton Park, Abingdon, Oxfordshire OX14 4RN
711 Third Avenue, New York, NY 10017

Routledge is an imprint of the Taylor & Francis Group, an informa business

First issued in paperback 2017

Copyright © 2016 He Xi and David Faure

The right of He Xi and David Faure to be identified as the author of the editorial material, and of the authors for their individual chapters, has been asserted in accordance with sections 77 and 78 of the Copyright, Designs and Patents Act 1988.

All rights reserved. No part of this book may be reprinted or reproduced or utilised in any form or by any electronic, mechanical, or other means, now known or hereafter invented, including photocopying and recording, or in any information storage or retrieval system, without permission in writing from the publishers.

Notice:
Product or corporate names may be trademarks or registered trademarks, and are used only for identification and explanation without intent to infringe.

British Library Cataloguing in Publication Data
A catalogue record for this book is available from the British Library

Library of Congress Cataloguing in Publication Data
The fisher folk of late Imperial and Modern China : an historical anthropology of boat-and-shed living / edited by He Xi and David Faure.
   pages   cm–(Anthropology of Asia series)
Includes bibliographical references and index.
1. Fishers–China–Social conditions.   2. Fishing villages–China.
3. Rural population–China.   I. Faure, David, editor.
HD8039.F66C545   2016
307.72–dc23   2015023191

ISBN: 978-1-138-92406-2 (hbk)
ISBN: 978-1-138-47694-3 (pbk)

Typeset in Times New Roman
by Out of House Publishing

Contents

List of illustrations	viii
List of contributors	x
Acknowledgements	xiii
A note for the reader	xiv
Preface	xv

Introduction: boat-and-shed living in land-based society   1
HE XI AND DAVID FAURE

PART I
As seen from historical sources   **31**

1   Government registration in the fishing industry in south
China during the Ming and the Qing   33
YANG PEINA

2   Dispersal and regrouping in the Zhoushan islands from
the Ming to the Qing   45
XIE SHI

3   The right to fish on Poyang lake as seen in a local record   57
LIANG HONGSHENG

4   The complexities of property rights at Diaocha lake as
seen from litigation   67
ZHANG XIAOYE

vi *Contents*

PART II
As encountered in field research   **81**

5 Gods adrift: religious ritual and local society on
Naozhou island   83
HE XI

6 Incense associations among small-boat fishermen
on Tai lake   101
XIA YIHONG

7 Some examples of the responsibilities and succession
of "incense heads" (*xiangtou*) among the fishermen of
Tai lake   113
OTA IZURU

8 From respect for the gods to sacrifice to the ancestors,
creating lineage culture among the fishermen of
Weishan lake   120
DIAO TONGJU AND SHE KANGLUE

PART III
As contemporary stereotypes   **133**

9 Land supports fishing people: the fishermen of Dongting
lake from the 1930s to the 1950s   135
WONG WING-HO

10 Going beyond pariah status: the boat people of
Fuzhou in the Chinese People's Republic   142
HUANG XIANGCHUN

11 From sheds to houses: a Dan village in the Pearl river
delta in the twentieth century   159
ZENG HUIJUAN

Contents vii

12 The recent history of the fishing households of the nine
surnames, a survey from the counties of Jiande and
Tonglu, Zhejiang province   173
SATO YOSHIFUMI

Appendices

1   *The religious festival of the Liu-wang-wei, 19 May 1877,*
    North China Herald   183
2   *Mechanization, market and moving ashore*   186
    HE XI AND DAVID FAURE

    Glossary of Chinese characters   199
    Index   207

Illustrations

Map 0.1	Locations of major research sites.	xii

Plate I.1	Net fishermen's associations (*wangchuan hui*) celebration, *Dianshi zhai huabao*, 1886.	15
Plate I.2	Net fishermen's associations celebration in c. 2007.	16
Plate 5.1	A domestic altar on Naozhou.	89
Plate 5.2	Praying to a circulated god's statue at a domestic altar.	91
Plate 5.3	Ferrying the god's statue on motorbike on Naozhou island.	92
Plate 6.1	Entrance to Xu Family Hall.	108
Plate 6.2	Altar at Xu Family Hall.	109
Plate 7.1	Singing the "song of praise to the gods".	114
Plate 7.2	Scroll showing pictures of gods and ancestors.	115
Plate 8.1	Incense for the ancestors on board a house boat at Weishan lake.	121
Plate 8.2	Scrolls displayed in "continuing the genealogy" ceremony.	127
Plate 12.1	Fishing village of the "fishing households of the nine surnames", also providing for tourist leisure.	174

Figure 11.1	Houses near Mr Guo's big shed from the 1930s to 1950s.	163
Figure A2.1	Acreage under fish farms and number of mechanized boats in Leqing county, 1951–1990.	193

Table A2.1	Fishing population and boats	188
Table A2.2	Monetary value of fishing in 1917 (million yuan)	189
Table A2.3	Supply of aqua-products to Shanghai, 1933–1948 (000 tons)	192

List of illustrations ix

Table A2.4 Import and export of fish and sea food, 1912–1928   192
Table A2.5 Fishing districts, villages, households and population,
            all China, 1950–1988   194

Contributors

David Faure is Wei Lun Research Professor of History at the Chinese University of Hong Kong, China.

Liang Hongsheng is Professor of History and Director of the Research Centre for the Development and Preservation of Historical Towns and Villages in South China at Jiangxi Normal University, China.

Zeng Huijuan recently obtained her Master's degree from the History Department of Sun Yat-sen University.

Ota Izuru is an Associate Professor in the History Department of the Faculty of Letters, Hiroshima University, Japan.

She Kangle obtained his Master's degree in 2012 from the Research Centre of Folklore, Advanced Institute of Confucian Studies, Shandong University and currently works in a township government in Jiangsu province, China.

Yang Peina is a Lecturer at the Centre for Historical Anthropology at Sun Yat-sen University, China.

Xie Shi is Professor of History at Sung Yat-sen University and Executive Editor of the journal, *Lishi renlei xue* (*Historical Anthropology*), China.

Diao Tongju is an Associate Professor at the Research Centre of Folklore, Advanced Institute of Confucian Studies, Shandong University and a Deputy Editor of the journal *Minsu yanjiu* (*Folklore Studies*), China.

Wong Wing-ho is a Lecturer in the Division of Humanities at the Hong Kong University of Science and Technology, China.

He Xi is an Assistant Professor in the History Department at the Chinese University of Hong Kong, China.

Zhang Xiaoye is Professor of History at Shenzhen University, China.

Huang Xiangchun is an Associate Professor in the Department of Anthropology and Ethnology in Xiamen University, China.

List of contributors xi

Xia Yihong obtained her MPhil in Anthropology at Hong Kong University of Science and Technology, China, and is now a registered social worker.

Sato Yoshifumi is a Professor in the Graduate School of Social Sciences at Hitosubashi University, Japan.

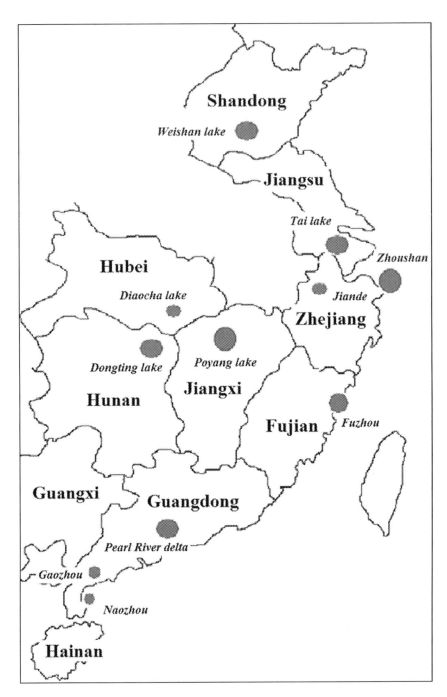

Map 0.1 Locations of major research sites.

Acknowledgements

The editors acknowledge with thanks the Hong Kong SAR University Grants Committee Areas of Excellence (Fifth Round) for funding the Historical Anthropology of Chinese Society project jointly managed by the Chinese University of Hong Kong, the Hong Kong University of Science and Technology and the Sun Yat-sen University. They are also grateful to the Toyo Bunko for permission to reprint the cover photograph.

A note for the reader

Registration of land and people goes back many centuries in China and comes into quite a few chapters in this book. The early Ming dynasty (1368–1644) introduced *lijia* for the purpose of taxation, registering households in units known as the *li* and the *jia*. By the sixteenth century, it was clear that *lijia* registration never worked effectively and so land registration was introduced in earnest. From approximately the same time, for the purpose of local defence, government officials implemented *baojia*. Households were registered in units known as *bao* and *jia* and were mutually responsible for law and order. *Baojia* was never implemented state-wise, but was revived periodically in the Qing dynasty (1644–1911) by local officials when they thought it was needed. As late as the 1930s, the Republican government supported *baojia*. By the 1950s, the People's Republic introduced universal household registration.

The Chinese land measure known as the *mu* can be taken to be approximately a sixth of an acre, but it should be noted that historically, land measures varied substantially even within a province and so conversion to standard measures should not convey a false sense of accuracy. Chinese age is reckoned in *sui* (year), counting from the beginning and not the end of the year. A Chinese person of 50 *sui*, therefore, is 49 years old by Western reckoning.

Preface

David Faure

This book brings together documentary and field research conducted by Chinese and Japanese scholars in different parts of China to reflect local experience under the monolithic unity that characterizes Chinese social history. Among the contributors, three have been trained as anthropologists, one as a folklorist and the remainder as historians. To understand the history of the people who lived on the margins of settled society, by the sea, on the lakes and on the rivers, most of whom were illiterate and left no written records, requires their combined expertise.

My co-editor, He Xi, came up with the initial research question. Maurice Freedman, the anthropologist who wrote the definitive account of the south China lineage, had pondered if the boat people known as the Dan would have adopted the lineage model of social organization if they moved ashore. Freedman believed that the lineage, not only designated by beliefs in common ancestry, but also buttressed by collective rituals and common ownership of property, was a product of the frontier society that he believed was south China. He had opined that the lineage had emerged as a social form in response to the institutional needs of land development. While working on her doctoral dissertation, He Xi had come across collective rituals carried out by boat people who had moved ashore, and she had drawn from that experience answers to Freedman inspired by Barbara Ward, the anthropologist who had studied the Hong Kong Dan boat people in the 1960s and 1970s. The ceremony that He witnessed indicated to her that the boat people, aware of the lineage ceremonies conducted by people on land, but having neither the ancestral hall to conduct the ceremonies in, nor the written genealogies that recorded descent from distant ancestors, had emulated land practices in ways that retained elements of their own indigenous boat-living customs. Moving ashore had, indeed, entailed their adapting to a lineage structure, but the manner by which they adapted highlighted how different the boat people's society was to the land villages: He Xi referred to boat living as constituting the house society, as opposed to the lineage structures focused on ancestral halls and landed estates as might be found on land villages. Her observations call for a comparison with other parts of China, and the result is this book.

xvi *Preface*

Documentary research has long been the mainstay of the China historian's craft. However, that is not to say that fieldwork is totally new to it. Collecting data in the field, especially of written documents recorded on steles, goes back at least a millennium in the writing of Chinese history. The recognition that much social and administrative history is recorded in ritual practices has a more recent origin from no earlier than the nineteenth century. In even more recent years, field observations on architecture, religion, rituals and folklore have been brought to bear on written records. The approach that combines fieldwork with documentary work in writing Chinese history, now often described as "historical anthropology", has gained increasing acceptance among China historians. We have organized this book to allow the documentary research to confront the fieldwork head-on. The reader will see that historical patterns emerged from the communities living on the water margins that mirrored but contrasted with social changes that have been described for long-settled land communities. Many of those communities were illiterate for much of their history, and the written record often embodies an outside view in contrast to the field ethnography that draws heavily on their religious practices.

The fieldwork approach demands such close knowledge of local communities that successful studies are achieved at the cost of considerable research commitment and time. Few researchers, therefore, ever master the history of more than one locality – or, at most, a few localities – in China through their lifetimes. Yet, local studies are of interest to non-locals only if they address questions that stretch across geographical boundaries. Local studies, therefore, have to be set in comparative frameworks, in terms of thematic variations over time and space. Although many Chinese historians work on local history, comparative studies are the exception rather than the rule; and, although many studies of Chinese history make implications that relate to local experience, few of those have looked at local experience in any detail. Bringing local research together in the light of generalizations that may bear meaningfully on an understanding of Chinese history is not easy. For the most part, the much-needed work to bridge the documentary and the fieldwork traditions has not yet been done.

With support from the Research Grants Council of the Hong Kong SAR government, the Area of Excellence project of the Historical Anthropology of Chinese Society is designed to contribute precisely to comparative local research. Through fieldwork, workshops and conferences, and short-term residence at the Chinese University of Hong Kong, China historians well-versed in the study of a locality are brought together to compare notes and raise questions. Of particular value are the opportunities for researchers to visit one another's research sites. The project has as its ambition no less an objective than rewriting China's history so that the local experience might be reflected in it. To that end, participants in the project are encouraged to explore the local experience that reveals regional or global trends. This book is the product of the working out of one such theme, namely how people who lived by the water margins, that is to say, the coast, the rivers and the lakes, interacted with land people and, in a very long process that lasted a millennium, gradually moved on land.

Certainly, ours is not the first effort to relate local experience to the larger whole of Chinese social history. The late G. William Skinner launched a major research effort in that direction with a focus on urban networks and it made a great deal of impact on scholarly research especially from the 1970s through the 1990s. Nevertheless, we now know that however important it might be to think about Chinese "macro-regions" in terms of urban hierarchies, in itself the urban network approach cannot be more than only one among many local variations that should breathe meaning into Chinese history. Some of us engaged in local studies, especially of south China, have opted for generalizations that relate the history of how local societies responded to changes in Chinese state practices, especially in matters related to tax and rituals. That is an alternative to, but not a replacement of the Skinnerian approach. No single theme exhausts the many variations of local experience in dynastic Chinese history, a history that covers four millennia in time, half a continent in space and possibly a quarter of the world's population. In as much as China as a nation must reflect the collective strengths of its varied populations, it must follow that Chinese history has to find a place for the many themes that make up the histories of local experience. To do that for marginal people is an objective of our research project and of this book.

How does the history of people living on boats or in makeshift sheds adapting to land-based lineage practices fit into the broad Chinese history that has yet to be written? The sheer scale of change and the numbers of people who must have been involved cry out for an understanding of what had happened in their history. Until possibly the twentieth century, the coasts, rivers and lakes were inhabited by people whose livelihood was very much tied to the foreshore. One might think of fishing and transport as their means of livelihood, but those bland terms cover tremendous variations ranging from habitation in boats to living in stilted sheds built on the foreshore and houses, some meant to be permanent and others deprived of the right to appear so. Just as massive land reclamations brought about settlement on land for some, the growth of cities until the middle years of the twentieth century created the slums that incorporated living on rivers into the urban environment. As some of the chapters of this book will illustrate, it was only in recent decades that the Chinese government acknowledged the right of boat-and-shed dwellers to live in permanent houses and created the housing programmes that actualized such right. The experience of water-margin-dwellers through the ages as is reconstructed in this book shows them pursuing social strategies that were not identical to the land villages, bringing about consequences that to this day leave sharp imprints on their communal practices. Contextualizing the social processes by which their communities have evolved puts on the map peoples who are otherwise barely visible and enriches the collective body of knowledge that makes up not only Chinese but all human history.

Introduction

Boat-and-shed living in land-based society

He Xi and David Faure

> A diminutive junk of 200 piculs capacity arrived here from Amoy, exactly built like the large trading junks of the place. She carried no cargo, but she had in her hold three idols, and her whole interior being fitted out like a pagan temple, she was called the "spiritual junk." The proprietors of the Tung-hing theatre made arrangements with the proprietor of this little floating temple to bring the idols on shore to the theatre, where there was a greater area, to enable people to come and worship, and admittance was fixed at 15 cash per head. The consequence was the people flocked, filling the place to suffocation, willingly paying their 15 cash for the privilege of worshipping these strange wooden gods.[1]

It was a strange episode in the early days of Hong Kong's history when a junk that served as a temple sailed into the harbour. Figures representing gods that were carried on the junk were brought to a theatre, where the owners charged worshippers 15 cash per head for entry. Junks, as we now know, routinely carried figures of gods and ancestors that were worshipped by the families operating them. It is a sign of our own ignorance as twentieth-century readers that we should be surprised by a floating temple. And we are not alone, for contemporary readers of the newspaper account reporting its presence were likewise surprised. We, the reading public, think of temples as structures built on land; whoever would have thought that a boat might serve as a roving temple.

The social boundaries of pariah status

Over a very long period of time measured in centuries, and nobody quite knows for how many centuries, many people lived on boats along the coast, rivers and lakes of China. In Guangdong province, by the Song dynasty, say the twelfth century, they came to be known as Dan people, and in some parts of central China, such as the provinces of Jiangxi and Zhejiang, in as late as the Ming dynasty in the sixteenth century, they were called the "fishing households of the nine surnames". Somewhat more is known of the Dan than the "fishing households of the nine surnames". The word "Dan" was

2 *He Xi and David Faure*

first used to refer to pearl-fishers off the coast of southern Guangdong. It was generalized, even during the early days of the Song, to apply loosely to people who lived by the water, but it was largely from the Ming dynasty that the term signified a status category of people living on the reclamations of the delta and who were said to have had no rights of permanent settlement. Because they had no rights to settle on land, even though they served as tenants to the landowners of the delta, it was said they were not allowed to wear shoes and could only live in sheds, not houses. Historians know of the "fishing households of the nine surnames" from the writings of Ming scholar-official Wang Yangming who encountered them in his suppression of the rebellion of imperial Prince Ning in 1519 in Jiangxi province. Wang did not leave a description of these people and, as historian Anders Hansson notes, it is not even clear if they lived on boats. The records are silent on these fishing households until the eighteenth century, when they were mentioned, along with the Dan, in what is often famously known to historians as the emancipation edict of the Yongzheng emperor in 1729 as pariahs who might not settle on shore and had been barred from the imperial examination. The Yongzheng edict freed them from some of those restrictions, but into the twentieth century it was well-known that these mean social statuses had by no means disappeared.[2]

Historians have every now and then written about the boat people but it is difficult to say very much about them as they lived on the margins of settled society, were illiterate and left no written records. Much of the source material that informs historians of society on the water margins had been filtered through the eyes of people who lived ashore, and who had a vested interest in keeping the boat people apart. Ethnography came only in the twentieth century, most of it, by far, conducted in southern China where the Dan social category characterized the boat population. The ethnographers, drawing from reports made by the people they interview, come to the conclusion that their living informants had been descended from the historical Dan. Were they, really? There is no certain way to tell. Moreover, did the discrimination that was applied to the south China Dan also apply to boat-and-shed living people in the rest of China? That would have been a very reasonable question that emerges from the south China research, but the answer to that is not known and, not likely to ever to be known, now that in the twenty-first century boat-and-shed living has all but disappeared.

Confronting the historical records that referred to boat living with the ethnographic accounts drawn from twentieth-century observations poses a predicament for the historian. Research work on the Pearl river delta shows that, over time, many people living on boats moved ashore, and some land-settlers possibly also took to boat living.[3] It follows, therefore, that the descendants of the Dan people were not to be found only among the boat-dwellers of the twentieth century but also among villagers now settled on the reclamations and, among boat-dwellers, not all would have been descended from them. Yet, all the while, boat-and-shed living continued to carry a pariah status. The

Introduction 3

ethnographic records, therefore, recall not the "remnant" of a historical Dan population, but, for whatever reason, the living tradition of the application of a derogatory term onto a selection of people. To rephrase this argument, one might say there is a mismatch between the historical record of mobility and the historical conception of the status term. Chinese history is full of examples of status terms, often masqueraded as ethnic terms, that had originated in ancient literature, which came to be applied on peoples who were totally unrelated to the context in which the terms had first appeared in ancient times. Indeed, ethnographic studies of the Dan report that they were popularly thought of as being distinguishable from the land population by their language and their physique, both of which turn out to be quite untrue upon examination.

Is it likely that the boundary between boat- and land-living was porous even as it was widely believed that boat-and-shed living carried a pariah status that was rigidly maintained? For several reasons, it is possible to argue that it was. First, despite popular impressions, boat people were not always poor. Fishing was highly commercialized even in the sixteenth century where its produce could be supplied to Ming-dynasty China's populous cities, and transport was associated with very lucrative trade that included many contrabands as defined by Ming and Qing imperial law. Second, periodic shifts in the political order provided opportunities for massive redefining of the social identity. That happened at the collapse of the Yuan and the establishment of the Ming dynasty in the fourteenth century, during rebellions in south China in the fifteenth, at the collapse of the Ming dynasty and the establishment of the Qing dynasty in the seventeenth, during the Taiping Rebellion in the nineteenth and the many shifts of government in the twentieth. Many boat people who moved onto land found that their landed status was recognized by the government even if not their neighbours during such varied incidents as the creation of the new county of Shunde after the Huang Xiaoyang rebellion in 1450 in Guangdong and the collapse of lineage power in the depression of the late 1930s.[4] Third, it was not always difficult to fudge social boundaries. Contrary to common belief, it took centuries for the examination system to take root in local society in many parts of China, and until that happened, local status was not differentiated into a degree-holding sector as against the non-degree-holding. For most parts of the Pearl river delta in Guangdong, for instance, that did not come about until the middle years of the Ming dynasty, say the late fifteenth to the early sixteenth century. That was when the lineage emerged as a status-defining institution, so that written genealogies and sacrifice to ancestors in sacrificial halls would define patriarchal descent from notable historical personages. By the sixteenth century, at least in the Pearl river delta, acquisition of a degree and demonstrated membership of a lineage would have qualified for a land-based status and indications are some boat-and-shed living people took that route as they settled on land.

Beyond south China, did boat-and-shed living always imply pariah status? Whether or not pariah status was implied, over long stretches of time,

4 He Xi and David Faure

were boat-dwellers in central and north China also looked upon as being set apart as socially distinct from the land population? These are questions that involve rights and privileges on the one hand, and lifestyles and customs on the other. In the Pearl river delta, by the sixteenth century, the boat-dweller was denied the right to settle on land and, thereby, the right to own land. Did boat-dwellers living elsewhere in China face similar denial to land rights? These are not easy questions to answer.

The written record: registration and privileges

Sometime between the twelfth and thirteenth centuries, the poet Gao Zhu (1170–1241) wrote:

> All his furniture he carries on his light boat,
> Spring to autumn back and forth on the Long River he goes,
> Three generations, sons and grandsons, live in the aft,
> Acquaintances from four directions he meets at the sandbar.
> Whither the wind? The old man wonders as he wakes at dawn.
> What pretty morning attire! The young woman says of her reflection in
> the running water.
> He laughs for having lived a life of much wandering,
> And loves the floating leisure that makes up his livelihood.[5]

Pastoral poems through the ages included the view of the leisurely boatman. The poet either did not know or, more likely, did not want to know that the same leisurely boatmen came under restrictions that related to where he could fish and where he could moor his boat.

The control of fishing rights by ownership of the foreshore may be found from the Song dynasty. Pan Lianggui (c. 1086–1142) who in 1125 was posted to Yangzhou just north of the Yangzi river, was confronted with the problem of "big surnames" (*daxing*) claiming rights to charge a rent on fishermen who wanted to fish in the lakes. He banned those rights.[6] The philosopher Zhu Xi's disciple and son-in-law, Huang Gan (1152–1221) while an official in Hanyang (Hubei province) in 1215, arguing for the need to continue such rights, left some revealing descriptions that rang true in different parts of China until the twentieth century. Hanyang was a small city of some 1,000 households. Outside the city along the river, 2,000 households who migrated annually with the ebb and flow of the river lived in "floating houses of reed" (*foju caowu*). In summer, they were located on the southern side of the city and in winter on the northern side. They were not the major fishing households: every winter, boats came from afar up and down the Yangzi river to fish at the many lakes in Hubei, and they had written contracts with the owners of the lakes to fish in them. These were not the poor people who lived in the "floating houses of reed", but "desperados" (*wangming bucheng zhi tu*) who were often engaged

Introduction 5

in fights among themselves and with the owners of the lakes. Huang Gan's superiors had ruled that fishing rights should be free to fishermen as an act of poor relief, but Huang Gan opted for a compromise: tax accrued from the lakes but not the river and so the lakes remained private property, lake owners could charge for fishing rights, but the Yangzi itself was thorough fare, and should be opened to all.[7]

It is well-known that the Song government practised household registration, and so the fact that officials such as Huang Gan found themselves at a loss trying to understand the boat people implies that they were not registered. However, if Huang Gan knew little about the "desperados" who sailed up and down the river in winter to fish in the lakes of Hubei, neither do we as historians. Of their presence, we can be quite certain because the boat people were engaged in numerous uprisings that were well recorded. One of those took place on Tai lake in Zhejiang province in 1225, when boat people were enticed to support the prince of Ji in the usurpation attempt that he was reluctantly drawn into.[8] During the Yuan dynasty, boat people were employed to convey tribute grain to the capital Dadu (Beijing) and the records speak of them as making up virtual private navies. By the end of the Yuan, the same private navies, engaged not only in transport but also salt smuggling, supported Fang Guozhen (1319–1374), who counted among his protégés, Zhu Yuanzhang, the future first Ming emperor. In the fifteenth century, Zhou Chen (1381–1453), the grand coordinator (*xunfu*) of Jiangnan, who had within his purview Tai lake and the lower Yangzi river, found as one of the seven loopholes in tax registration "living on boats and wandering" (*chunju fodang*). He described the boat people as "wandering people, carrying their families on the boats, under the guise of trading, obtaining false papers ... and travelling between Beijing and Nanjing, Hunan and Hubei, Honan and Huaian."[9] Successive governments looked upon boat people as the "poor", "desperados", "smugglers" or "pirates". Registration was meant to bring these people under control.[10]

There must have been status terms in use in Chinese local communities from time immemorial, but if currency was gained by some such term beyond the immediate locality in which it was used, there must have been reason associated with the broad social milieu in which boat-living was a part. The passage from Huang Gan cited above does not indicate that the boat-and-shed living people were ascribed a special status. Song texts often referred to the registration category known as "boat households" (*chuanhu*) even though the records are far from clear regarding how and where registration was enforced. Descriptions of boat-and-shed living people as "Dan" rather than "boat households" in southern China makes it amply clear that not all boat-and-shed living people were registered in the Song.

In tracking the continuity of institutions over long periods of time in China, say, for the millennium from the Song dynasty to the Qing, the historian would do well to consider the difference in scale and scope between successive dynasties. Not only did they not span the same geographical area, but

6   *He Xi and David Faure*

the Song state was organized much more haphazardly in many parts of China than the Ming state. The effective enforcement of registration over much of the geographic area that became China took place not in the Song, but in the Ming and Qing, and even in the Ming and Qing, registration was frequently ineffective. Registration of households as an administrative ideal had long been inherent in Chinese administrative thought, but in Chapter 1, with a focus on south China, that is to say, the provinces of Guangdong and Fujian, Yang Peina demonstrates that in practice, its implementation depended on local officials responding to perceived crises, all the while as the rudiments of state administration were being built up at the local level in the Ming and the Qing.

From the early years of the Ming dynasty in 1382, it was decreed that fishing households be registered at river mooring stations (*hebosuo*). The river mooring station registration had derived from the principles of *lijia* registration, which was to be implemented all over the Ming state, requiring all households to be registered under units of ten known as the *jia* to provide for corvee service. Households registered at river mooring stations were given fishing household (*yuhu*) status, and were responsible for paying a fish tax, payable in rice. In Guangdong, many of the people who registered were those that had been known as the Dan, even though that should not be taken to mean that many Dan actually registered.[11]

Obviously, households that were not registered for tax could not effectively be held liable for it. That was reason enough for many households not to want to register. In the century after household registration was imposed in the Ming dynasty, many river mooring stations became defunct, while the fish tax came to be allocated to registered households that might not be engaged in fishing. The breakdown of corvee service was endemic to the entire *lijia* registration structure, not only to fishing households, and by the sixteenth century, corvee service was rapidly being converted to payment in silver, while tax became increasingly based, not only on the registration of households, but on the registration of land. Registration of land, in its turn, created the conditions for large holdings. Studies of the reclamation of the sedimentary delta land (*shatian*) of the Pearl river have elaborated the consequence of that process. As Dan people settled in villages and reclaimed land, hiding their household status as they did so, taboos were imposed on them by the land settlers, whether or not they themselves had originally been Dan, to restrict settlement on shore so that vast areas of reclamation became out-of-bounds to new comers.

Failure in registering households might have provided impetus for local officials to consider registering their boats instead. Nevertheless, boat registration came from a different origin. It came in the first half of the sixteenth century as a response to the need for protection against the misnamed "Japanese pirates" (*wokou*). The so-called "Japanese pirates" consisted mostly of protection networks on the eastern coast that demanded payment from junk operators and robbed from settled villages. The government's answer to the networks was to establish similar networks of their own, under a policy of mutual responsibility known as *baojia*. In the sixteenth century, *baojia* headmen were appointed at the ports of Fujian and Guangdong who had charge of registering sailing junks. By the very last years of the Ming and the early Qing, the protection networks took a political turn, because the Zheng family, who headed possibly the largest protection network that governed the seas from the China coast to Japan, threw in its lot in support for the last Ming emperors. To quarantine Zheng Chenggong's regime in Taiwan, the newly established Qing dynasty ruthlessly enforced the policy known as the "coastal evacuation" (*qianhai*), under which coastal communities were moved inland, and no ships were to put to sea without a licence. When the coastal evacuation policy was rescinded in 1684, the licensing of boats had become accepted imperial policy. Boats were registered according to their sizes, and bonds of collective responsibility had to be produced for their sailors that showed the joint guarantee of the village community at which the boats were registered as well as the approval of the magistrate. Long-distance boats were now tied to the ports from which they originated. Numerous records are extant that document long-distance boats in the eighteenth and nineteenth centuries carrying official papers. Whether coastal fishing boats effectively registered is far less clear.[12]

It is fairly clear that during the Ming and the Qing dynasties, registration of land and boats, which was introduced as a comprehensive measure over the entire realm, was never really very successful. Yet, because official rulings came to dominate the language of rights and privileges, despite the failure in their implementation, they made some very definite impact on local society. As the local magistrate, appointed by the imperial government, collected tax with reference to imperial promulgations, and as he adjudicated disputes according to his knowledge of tax enforcement, local people learnt to build up their rights and privileges, over land, boats, animals and people, using the same language. In Chapters 2 to 4, through very careful reading of local sources, including documents that have only in recent years been collected from the field, Xie Shi, Liang Hongsheng and Zhang Xiaoye explore the implications of registration and ownership on the foreshore.

In Chapter 2, Xie's account of the Zhoushan islands details how, by the Ming dynasty, land registration became the cornerstone of long-term settlement. Yet, because the Ming government could barely assert control over the islands, aside from establishing some military stations there in the fourteenth century that were abandoned by the fifteenth, it simply denied the islands to settlement. The islands were, therefore, known as pirate hideouts for most of the Ming and became, indeed, sanctuaries for Ming loyalists when the Qing took over. The Qing government captured Zhoushan, evacuated its population and, after the coastal evacuation, by the end of the seventeenth century, established Dinghai county to govern the islands.

For centuries, the seas off Zhoushan had been the most important fishing grounds for the cities of the lower Yangzi. Also, the area was strategically

8 *He Xi and David Faure*

so important that, in the nineteenth century, at the time of the Opium War (1840–1842), the British preferred it to the island of Hong Kong as a trading station.[13] The British presence left some interesting contemporary accounts. The British diplomat Sir John Francis Davis estimated the population of Zhoushan island to be 200,000. They lived in villages that came to be settled from the end of the seventeenth century. By the reports of the British, most local inhabitants farmed, but some also made sea salt. They also fished, keeping their catches in ice storages before they were sold. The fishing industry was well-established from much earlier. Magistrate Miao Sui, posted to Zhoushan island as magistrate of Dinghai county from 1695 to 1715, noted that in the fishing season during summer and autumn, fishing fleets came from Zhejiang and Fujian, and "poor" people built sheds on the islands to trade with the fishermen. Military commander Wu Jun noted in 1708 that when thousands of boats appeared during the fishing season, many people dried their catches on shore. Also to note is the report of James Cunningham, a British naval surgeon who was in Zhoushan in 1701 and who noted the large mudbanks by the sea on which fishermen travelled by the "mud-ski". Together, these descriptions give the impression, once again, of the difference between the long-distance fishermen, undoubtedly well-capitalized in their boats, and the hangers-on on the water margin who depended on fishing as a subsistence rather than trade.

Liang Hongsheng's case study in Chapter 3 was located inland, at a small lake known as Knotweed pond (Liaohua *chi*) and nearby Long river (Chang *he*) near the Poyang lake in Jiangxi province. The case shows many similarities with the situation that Huang Gan found in Hubei in the thirteenth century. The Knotweed pond case is particularly interesting because Liang discovered documents held by owners of the pond that date from at least the last decades of the nineteenth century and incorporate claims that had been made much earlier. One document, which bears the title "Tax record of the river anchorages of Xingzi (county) in the Ming and the Qing periods" highlights the close linkages between registration (in this case, in the mutual-responsibility arrangement of the *baojia*), lineage organization and land rights to the lake foreshore. The entire holding as described in this document had, at one time, been registered under the name of a single ancestor of the Zhang surname, resident of the first *jia*, who – according to the local lineage genealogy – had lived in the fifteenth century. He was held liable for tax, but was described not as an owner but as a tenant. When his rights to the holdings were contested and he was taken to court, the magistrate, in his ruling, re-registered the holdings under the name of an ancestor who lived in the eighteenth century, resident of the sixth *jia*. The same eighteenth-century ancestor, moreover, also held lake properties by contract from another family located elsewhere.

The cross-holding of properties by different groups of people under the names of ancestors is well-known to students of Ming and Qing society. The ancestral name served as the focus of a lineage "trust" to which members of the group might lay claim through the tracing of descent. We do not know

Introduction 9

enough from the records regarding what obligations these corporate owners owed the fishermen who contracted from them the right to fish in their ponds. We also do not know who had responsibility for the maintenance of local projects such as dyke repairs. Until 1865, during the turmoil of the Taiping Rebellion, the term "pond headman" was not used in the records available to us, and occasional references to such headmen did not include the Zhang surname who were among the owners of the lakes. By the twentieth century, petitions to the magistrate were written under the name of a "manager", who was indeed a Zhang. By 1937, we have the very interesting description of fishing at the ponds in the area that included Knotweed. Only about a fifth of the fishermen lived by fishing full-time, the others farmed as well as fished. The most prominent of those worked in nine teams of 12 people, using nets provided by a "net owner" (*wangzhu*), who kept half the catch. The nets were hauled by two boats that had to undertake skilful manoeuvres to haul the nets in. The majority would have worked as "husband-and-wife" teams, in contrast to the larger-scale operations sponsored by the "net owners".

Whether the fishermen worked as a domestic "husband-and-wife" team, or whether they worked under the "net owners", some among those people would have had to pay the lake owners for the right to fish. Their anonymity in all our sources has been a very effective obliteration of their character. Yet, we must not forget the donor who gave the documents to Liang Hongsheng that became the substance of this chapter. In the 1950s, half the people in his village farmed and half of them fished. He considered his a fishing family, but he also held four *mu* of paddy and 13 *mu* of dry land, and was classed as upper-middle peasant. His father had obtained the documents recording his fishing rights by purchase in the few years leading up to 1949. He also recalled a ritual aspect in the management of the pond. On the property that belonged to his ancestors, he recalled: "there were no deeds, but nobody disputed", a statement that was obviously untrue in light of the documents he held in his possession. Yet, it is a statement that can be understood in the light of the feast held a week before the lunar New Year indicating the beginning of the fishing season for the year. We do not know if his family and others like him had been upwardly mobile in the 1940s. We do know that outside the relationships spelled out by contracts and litigation, there was the community that attended the pre-New Year feast who were engaged in fishing, as owners and fishermen.

In Chapter 4, Zhang Xiaoye produces more local documentation on fishing rights at the lakes. Her focus on the legal angles recorded in the documents reveal communities that were not only litigious but were also active in creating precisely the documents that were produced in litigation.

Diaocha lake, the locus of Zhang's research, is located precisely in the area in Hubei province that Huang Gan had written about in the thirteenth century. The text that illustrates lake rights forms a chapter by the title "lake records" included in the local Huang surname genealogy. Zhang supplements the text with interviews with local people of the Huang surname and their

10 *He Xi and David Faure*

neighbours, and finds that lineage stories relate to ownership of the lake are still remembered. Those stories tell of the ten "lake shares" owned by the Huang surname, portions of which had been brought into the lineage by a female ancestor as her dowry. They also tell of disputes with the ancestor of the Xiang surname who in the sixteenth century saved the life of an imperial prince's son and who, therefore, was recognized as a guest of honour in the prince's household. The involvement of princely families in claims to land in this area is well documented in Ming dynasty sources, but when the Huang family, said to be left in ruins from litigation with the Xiang family, finally had to appeal directly to the emperor, the story that the imperial ruling consisted of throwing the appellant on a piece of rope over the walls of the imperial palace suggests high drama in storytelling rather than historical reality. In other words, a substantial portion of the history noted in the text was fictional, but it was fiction that had meaning for the families living around the lakes.

Into the Qing dynasty, the "lake records" begin to be filled with documents from litigation. The technical language in which details are expressed suggests that the documents had genuinely been derived from court cases: owners on the lake shore had by now accumulated documents to prove ownership, and the documents presented in the text would have been among those they kept for the purpose. Were the documents genuine within their own terms; that is to say, if a deed of sale was produced bearing an earlier date than the occurrence of litigation, would that be evidence enough to argue that it was necessarily drawn up at the earlier date? The magistrate knew that they probably were not. One party to the litigation would have supported its claim with land deeds, and the other with tax registration records, none of which he could find among the archives of his office. Genuine or not, documents were written, produced, put away and kept, in the case of the "lake records", making up a chapter in the lineage genealogy. That tells us something about the society that was now evolving on the lake shore.

Many documents have in recent years been published bearing Ming dynasty dates to demonstrate the registration of fishing households from the early years of the dynasty. Xu Bin, who discovered some such documents among litigation records dating from 1948, has argued that they corroborate a passage describing the history of the fish tax recorded in the 1613 Hanyang prefectural gazetteer.[14] The registration document cited does not date from the early Ming, but from the early Qing in 1647, in which reference is made to the "crimson registries" (*chili ce*) of the Hongwu period in the Ming, that is to say, from 1368 to 1398. It records, first, the overall tax liabilities (in terms of fish, fish oil, tung oil, iron, hemp and other products) included in the Hongwu red registries; second, names of people registered within the ten-household *jia* units; third, separately from them, the names of people who were registered to deliver the different products in tax; and, fourth, desertions from the registration records. The 1613 prefectural gazetteer takes note of the economic importance of fishery in the area, and says that in the first 70 years of the Ming dynasty, lake properties were given to military households, who together with merchants and agents, allotted fishing rights to fishermen in return for a charge. Properties might consist of lake surface, which was recorded in the "crimson registries", but they might also consist of the foreshore, which fell into the hands of powerful people who succeeded in not registering, with the result that the tax fell upon a few people who did and were held liable for collecting and delivering the fish tax. Xu argues from the existence of such "crimson registries" and their references to Hongwu period tax records, that registration of fishing households from the early Ming was comprehensive.

There is an enormous abyss between the observation that in the early Ming, the mechanisms had been established for the registration of fishing households, and the inference that many people were, therefore, registered. According to Qing dynasty sources, which Xu also cites, the "crimson registers" were reports filed by tax payers that were meant to tally with records held in local government offices. Until 1679, when they were replaced by receipt books, they were a basis for compiling tax notices. Tax-paying households might have possessed copies of such tax returns, which they then produced in litigation as evidence of ownership and tax liabilities. It is unlikely that government offices would have retained copies of such tax returns during the transition from the Ming to the Qing even if they had ever possessed them, and so the early Qing reference to Ming "crimson registers" would have been more a formality than a reality. The early Qing, by instituting written records in place of the influence of powerful local households, generated the documents that are now being discovered by historians with an interest in local history. They underline the significance of the possession of a written record as demonstration of ownership, not that ownership necessarily accrued to people who fished. Possessors of such records might, in tax registration, be known as "fishing households", but they were, in reality, landlords.

Ethnography of community and identity as expressed in ritual

Where, then, were the fishermen? They are described from their religious practices in Chapters 5 to 8. Those four chapters summarize field research conducted in recent years, including observations of rituals and social practices that are part of an ongoing tradition. They reveal dynamics of community that are very different from observations made from historical records.

He Xi's Chapter 5 returns to life on an island. Tiny Naozhou island, studied in this chapter, lies off the coast of Leizhou in Guangdong. The villages He Xi found on it possibly resemble those on Zhoushan. The visitor to the island today still finds fishing nets everywhere, but the villagers are adamant that they are not fishermen (*yumin*). The people who are known as the fishermen are members of the fishermen's village, Hongwei. People of Hongwei agree. They are the fishing people as evidenced by their living in sheds until very recent years. The sheds were not scattered over a large area, but arranged in a row by the seaside and raised on stilts. Household registration since 1949

12 *He Xi and David Faure*

might account for some such recognition. Hongwei was registered as a fishing commune (*yumin gongshe*) by the late 1950s, but the other villages were not. People of Hongwei, moreover, were known as Dan. In case the distinction between Hongwei and the other villages gives rise to any easy hypothesis on the transition of fishing people to a land-based lifestyle, He's description of the land settlements should suggest a much more complex picture. During the Qing, troops had been stationed on the island. Where they were quartered, a school had been built. The land villagers might have had small boats that they used for fishing, but junks were anchored in two anchorages respectively on the north and the south of the island, and those anchorages had been set up by common agreement and official support. At the southern anchorage, a sizable market developed. We do not know who owned the boats that moored in the anchorages, but it is possibly not far-fetched to assume that people on Naozhou, land villagers or fishermen, owned and worked on some of them. At least from the eighteenth century, some fishing boats were registered, as evidenced in contemporary donation records left in the temples, and by the nineteenth century, some land households likewise. A few leading villagers had official titles, recognition so obtained being shared also by their descendants. Some of them were clearly organized in lineages, possessing written genealogies and practising ancestral sacrifice in halls and at graves.

By analogy, we can presume that Zhoushan had much the same social structure, consisting of small farming villages where villagers also put to sea, military settlements and makeshift sheds on the beaches. Fieldwork on Naozhou, however, adds an extra dimension, described in Chapter 5 as the "circulation of the gods". That feature is unlike what is usually found in areas dominated principally by land villages.

To describe the "circulation of the gods", reference should first be made to another practice He Xi had found near but not on Naozhou that was focused on what was described to her as ancestral sacrifice.[15] At a marketplace in Gaozhou city, periodically, people of the same surname who had formerly lived on boats, gathered on shore to set up a makeshift matshed (shed made of bamboo scaffolding covered by mattings) for the purpose of sacrificing to ancestors. At the matshed, they gather together statuettes representing the ancestors that they normally place on their domestic altars and, after hired daoist priests have performed ceremonies, they decide by drawing lots which statuette would return to which family. In other words, the ancestor whose image they produce for the celebration is not necessarily the one that they take home. She draws from that feature of the ceremony the conclusion that participants in the ceremony do not subscribe to single-line genealogies, as land villagers do when they portray themselves as lineages. Her surmise is, moreover, confirmed by the genealogy the participants produce, which shows recognition of descent lines only since their settlement on shore in the last two to three decades. In Naozhou, island-wide sacrifices are held not at ancestral shrines, but at temples, including some makeshift ones, on particular days of the year.

Introduction 13

Although some Naozhou deities are represented as statues and deposited at temples, most deities on the island are invited out of the temples and given daily sacrifice to on domestic altars. The practice is so common on the island that some tricycles have been fitted out with special compartments to ferry the statues around, and when a deity is received into one family, other families come over to "borrow" them for their own occasions. She explains the practices in Gaozhou city and Naozhou with reference to boat-and-shed living. In the days when the boat people lived on boats, most boats were small, accommodating no more than a family. They contained, nevertheless, domestic altars to which ancestors and deities were represented in statues, a practice that she shows is still maintained by the boat people who have moved ashore in the fishing markets around the Beibu *wan* area in which she researches.[16] The boat people believed that they belonged to larger networks, including lineages, and they would have re-enacted their conception of lineage practices in their own ancestral sacrifice. They would come upon the lineages of land people often enough to realize that ancestors were sacrificed to by descendants in common. Yet, not owning an ancestral hall built on land, and not owning land to serve as a focus of lineage organization, their efforts at common sacrifice would have resembled their practices at temples, such as she now describes for Naozhou. The collective ceremonial locus would have been temporary, and deities would have been housed on domestic altars, from where they may, in turn, be gathered for collective worship. Like temples in land villages, periodic sacrifice must be held but, unlike many land villages, the temples of seaside villages from which boat people invite their deities to their domestic altars serve a revolving clientele. Common worshipping provides for networking, but not enough of it for knowledge of lines of descent to make up a lineage in the land people's mode.

The same pattern of the assumed rather than demonstrated lineage can be seen again on the edge of Tai lake in Jiangsu province, central China, in Xia Yihong's Chapter 6 and Ota Izuru's Chapter 7. The two chapters describe some ceremonies that are essentially held by the same households. Xia gives the descriptions of the households and, in particular, their altars, and Ota provides details of the "incense heads", who are the local religious masters and officiants of the ceremonies.

The Tai lake area that Xia and Ota study falls within the delta of the Yangzi river, known at least for the last millennium for its prosperity. The catches from the fishing grounds near Zhoushan, that have been described in Chapter 2, were sold directly to some of the cities located in the area, and so were catches from Tai lake. The area is also known to historians and anthropologists of China through the work of anthropologist Fei Xiaotong (Fei Hsiao-tung). When Fei wrote his doctoral thesis for London University, completed in 1938, the farmers of Kaixiangong farmed on land harnessed from the rivers by polders surrounding their fields and travelled from village to market towns by boat.[17] That is a far cry from the motor-road-served

14 *He Xi and David Faure*

suburban scene that greeted Xia and Ota when they conducted their field research shortly after 2000. Fei did not talk about people living on boats but, had he gone two miles in a northwesterly direction, he would have reached Xia and Ota's field site, Temple Anchorage (Miao *gang*). There, Xia and Ota encountered fishing families that had lived on boats. They were net fishermen on Tai lake, grouped into fishery cooperatives in the early 1950s, a commune in 1958 and reverted to work teams by 1961. Under the household registration nomenclature of the People's Republic of China, they were not "peasant" (*nongmin*) but "fishing people" (*yumin*). By 1983, when the collective economy was abandoned, they became, administratively, "fishing villages" (*yuye cun*). The recent Temple Anchorage township gazetteer lays out rather clearly the social and economic transformation in the process. In 1965, there were 210 fishing boats at the anchorage, 30 households living in permanent houses and 60 in sheds. In 1978, there were 284 boats, 260 households living on shore and 404 single-storey houses. By 1995, there were 420 boats, 363 households living on shore, 320 single-storey and 360 multi-storey houses. In 1995, the villagers fished and farmed, ran enterprises related to fishing and owned a metalworks factory in addition. In 1995, there were, in the village, eight private motor cars, 200 bicycles, six motorcycles, 320 television sets (of which 120 were colour), 50 video recorders, 60 refrigerators and 160 washing machines.[18]

Xia and Ota refer to the villagers' attendance at the King Liu temple festivals. The Shanghai newspaper *North China Herald* in 1877 included a lengthy report of one such festival (Appendix 1), which gives some sense of the communal emotions exhibited on those occasions. This fascinating contemporary account provides the first glimpse of the encounter of a traditional village festival with the operation of modern transport. The two King Liu temples involved in the celebration were separated by the distance of half a mile. They were not located in the area studied by Xia and Ota, but in what became Jiangwan district in the vicinity of Shanghai (65 miles from Temple Anchorage). The first railway in China had just been completed in 1876, and this was the first time the procession between the two temples at Jiangwan was held after its completion. As the writer noted, two consequences were immediate. First, government officials banned the procession that went from one temple to the other as that required crossing the railway tracks. Second, the railway brought more participants to the festivities, adding to the crowds that had come from 30 to 40 miles by their own means. The writer noted that the people had come with offerings that were "tawdry but picturesque". One really has to have seen a temple festival to appreciate what that meant, for – unknown to the author of the newspaper article – those flags and pennants would have been carried by worshippers as organized groups coming from their home villages or anchorages. The offerings, according to a report in 1947, at the town of Wangjiangjing (16 miles to the east of Temple Anchorage), included papier mâché figures of two aeroplanes and a motor car, and participants in the procession dressed as in theatrical costumes, some walking on

Introduction 15

Plate I.1 Net fishermen's associations (*wangchuan hui*) celebration, *Dianshi zhai huabao*, 1886, pp. 49b–50a.

stilts, carrying incense burners (some of which were hooked through the flesh of the carriers' arms), musical instruments, all escorting ten sedan chairs carrying the images of King Liu from the temples.[19]

Many groups that gathered at King Liu celebrations in the web of waterways of the lower Yangzi, came from what Xia and Ota have studied as "incense associations" (*xiangshe*). To understand these associations, it is important to realize that they are rooted in local society and meshed into the networks that have built up around temple festivals spread all over the Yangzi delta. The association is led by the "incense head" (*xiangtou*) who conducts principal ceremonies at his domestic altar. In Chapter 6, Xia describes one such altar that she found located in a room attached to the incense head's house. On the altar were placed statues of gods, images of the incense head's masters, and also deceased relatives. Although the worship area in the house now occupies an entire room, as Xia explains, in times past when the family was living on a boat, some gods and spirits were recorded only as paper portraits that were produced as required at religious ceremonies. Aside from maintaining the altar, the incense head, as Ota finds in Chapter 7, leads the ceremonies that are held at the altar. Ota refers to that role as singing the "songs of praise

Plate I.2 Net fishermen's associations celebration in c. 2007 (credit: Zhang Juemin).

to the gods" (*chang shenge*), which requires the chanting of written texts as a small gong is struck by the chanting incense head. Incense heads need skill in performing the "songs of praise to the gods", but they also arrive at the position by succession. It is not clear if living masters designate their successors; the oral reports suggest that succession is the result of revelation, for example, by the posthumous appearance of deceased incense masters to the appointee. Incense heads are said to be able to cure illness, but it is not clear from the reports if they personally possess such powers, or if the powers derive from the ceremonies when properly conducted. They do not collect money for curing illnesses, but they do for maintaining the altar. As incense heads, they also lead processions from their altars to the temple festivals.

The reports from Xia and Ota indicate that succession as incense heads often but not necessarily passes along family lines, for instance, from father to son. Incense heads intermarry, but relationships built up during lifetimes can also be augmented by posthumous relationships ascribed to the dead. The incense heads have their followers who take part in ceremonies and in temple processions, but commitment to the incense association is apparently stable, although not permanent. It should be clear that neither the association nor the incense head's family maintain very clear descent genealogies. Despite frequent references to previous masters as "ancestors", they are looked upon as religious authorities rather than procreators of descendants.

Introduction 17

Such master–disciple relationships have always been common among religious groups in China and are very distinct from the lineage relationships built upon the compilation of written genealogies and the maintenance of ancestral halls among land villages.

In Chapter 8, Diao Tongju and She Kanglue show that similar practices are found also far north of the Tai lake area into the surroundings of Weishan lake in Shandong province. Tai lake, it should be noted, is connected to Weishan lake by the Grand Canal and so, although further evidence needs to be adduced, it may be hypothesized that the geographic linkage provided by the canal promoted common practices. Diao and She report that families possess picture scrolls of ancestors and deities that are produced for religious occasions. Such scrolls are passed by elderly parents to their eldest sons, even though there does not seem to be any prohibition against younger sons also holding them or their duplicates. They cite a scroll that records portraits and tablets of ancestors of three generations and so they find it reasonable to argue that sacrifice in front of the scroll, for example at the lunar New Year, may be looked upon as an acknowledgement of lineage connections. They state also that during New Year, "junior members of the lineage", presumably younger sons and their descendants, also gather at the ceremonies held in front of the scrolls. Every five or ten years, families of the same surname gather together to hold the ceremony known as "continuing the genealogy" (*xu jiapu*) in which sacrifice is offered to ancestors, represented by rice bushels in which incense sticks are placed. Nevertheless, the ceremony sacrifices not only to ancestors but also to the gods to which the families pledge respect, as represented on the scrolls they have inherited.

Elsewhere, She Kanglue has supplied greater detail about the ceremony conducted in the household at New Year.[20] His study focuses on a single multi-surname village of 2,100 people who had moved from living on boats to living in houses on shore only in the 1970s. Aside from the change of residence, She also recounts a measure imposed by the local government from about the same time, that fishing families might fish only in the lake on which they had settled, when previously, they had moved frequently between the four adjoined lakes in the area. In other words, from the mid-1970s, the fishing households on the Weishan lake had become localized to a much greater degree than they had previously. She Kanglue states very specifically that, although both the New Year ceremony and "continuing the genealogy" (*xu jiapu*) involve ancestors, ancestors are not the only spirits to which offerings are made but, rather, they are present as part of the set of household deities held by worshippers' families through paper portraits. Thus, on both occasions, not only are ancestors received and despatched but so are many deities.

She Kanglue in his more detailed study also describes the "continuing the genealogy" ceremony, but an even fuller account is available from Lin Ching-chih's recent doctoral dissertation. The two accounts agree on the essential features, that is, that the ceremony is held periodically every five to ten years, that it is officiated by spirit masters known as *duangong*, who both

18   *He Xi and David Faure*

perform according to texts and, at particular moments during the ceremony, act as mediums for ancestral spirits. Again, ancestral spirits are invited to the ceremony, but not exclusively, for a good many other deities are likewise invited. A distinction is made between the two in that the ancestors are installed on rice bushels on the altar during the first day's celebrations, and only thereafter are the deity scrolls introduced into the ceremony. Those scrolls and the bushels to hold the ancestral spirits have been supplied by such family units as would have conducted sacrifice to the ancestors and the gods at New Year. According to She, although in recent years, the ceremony has resulted in the compilation of written genealogies that are distributed to participating families, no genealogies were compiled in the past.

A very informative analysis of the personnel involved in the rituals among the fishing families of Weishan lake is included in Lin Ching-chih's study of the "continuing the genealogy" ceremony.[21] Lin highlights the *duangong* mediums as "masters of association" (*huizhu*).[22] They are adept at a style of chanting and dancing to the accompaniment of small gongs characterized by their thinness and attachment to a handle (in recognition of their fan-like appearance, Lin calls them "fan drums"). These associations hold multi-day ceremonies every five years or at times of bad fortune and are "structurally similar to the continuation of genealogy". The associations have their own fee-paying followers, who may take part in more than one association. Although the *duangong* serves as the master of the association, he is not necessarily its organizer, who is known as the "association head" (*huitou*). The master of the association does not even necessarily officiate at the ceremony, for other *duangong* can be hired to perform the ceremonies. Lin's examples show that deceased masters achieve godly statuses and are recorded as such in scrolls. Lin considers the family to be the basic unit of the association, for when one family member joins, the entire family become members.

The sacrificial associations of the Weishan lake bear striking similarities to the associations of the Tai lake. They are both engaged in ceremonies in which the officiator is occasionally possessed by spirits, and chants and dances to music accompanied by small gongs. In the ceremonies in both places, not only is there participation from family groups but the representations of the gods to which sacrifice is offered are normally held in the family rather than in temples and, although at Tai lake the example reported by Xia and Ota shows that they are now represented as statues, informants recall that paper images had been formerly used. Moreover, in both places, the ancestors are singled out as a significant category among the spirits to which sacrifice is offered.

On the history of genealogy compilation, Lin is silent. Neither She nor Lin seems to have examined any genealogy resulting from the "continuing the genealogy" ceremony. One suspects that despite Lin's use of the term "lineage" to describe the activity, there is little evidence of written genealogies having been compiled among participants of the festival in the past.

The use of the term "lineage" raises some serious questions about the extrapolation of contemporary ritual observations onto a historical

Introduction 19

context. The issue does not lie in terminology. The word is sufficiently general to suggest different understandings: a group of people may have some idea of common ancestry, knowledge of some line of descent that is orally passed down from generation to generation, or be in possession of written genealogies that link them to people in other lines of descent than their own. The same people may or may not conduct ceremonies in common, hold common rights or privileges, or interact as a single community. The ethnography on Weishan lake suggests that the people who together hold the "continuing the genealogy" ceremony claim common descent, but not agreement on the lines of descent or, indeed, have knowledge of such lines until recent years. In any case, the ethnography suggests that the active tracing of ancestry is conducted by family groups and genealogical knowledge does not go beyond several generations. It is conceivable that before the 1970s, when fishing was not confined to the vicinity of the family's designated abode, fishing families of the several lakes connected by waterways could have been in frequent touch and that some sense of community might have been built up, which underpinned the "continuing the genealogies" ceremonies. It is also conceivable that from the late 1940s to the early 1970s, the local governments had been sensitive towards collective religious sacrifice. Not only was local religion looked upon as superstition but also in some parts of China, membership of religious associations was looked upon as potentially seditious.[23] Therefore, it would have been reasonable for the *duangong* ritualists to veer towards an emphasis on ancestral sacrifice when religious celebrations were revived from the 1980s. However attractive the appeal to politics as an explanation for the current emphasis on genealogies in communal celebrations, it should be supplemented with She Kanglue's contention that tracing ancestry – rather than preserving a vague sense of some ancestry – is simply more strongly associated with settlement on land than living on boats. Why that is so has to be a matter of surmise. It could be due to greater stability or, even more likely, the indirect result of the many other changes that have come with land settlement in recently years, including a more comfortable livelihood, more education and hence higher literacy, and an awareness of written genealogies that, after all, are very much in the common knowledge broadcasted in the popular media. Like the former fishermen at Gaozhou or the islanders at Naozhou, the stress on lineage and genealogy had resulted from a process of emulating land practices. We must not rule out that some boat communities might have taken the process to completion and, thereby, totally discarded their boat-and-shed origin, but equally we must not assume that the process must necessarily run full course before participants legitimize their rituals as traditions with which they identify. Labels without history are tale-telling signs of the creation of new traditions. "Continuing the genealogy" would seem in every respect to be a label without a history.

The contrast between the issue of administrative control over land and boats, summed up in the imposition of registration at different times in history as detailed in Chapters 1 to 4, and the fluid religious gatherings among local people who still live on the water margins, as described in Chapters 5 to 8, illustrates the institutional division that, over time, has come to characterize two different populations. The landowners, that is to say, the people who came to assert their rights and privileges on the understanding that they held the foreshore and paid tax on it, whether or not they paid, adopted the lineage model as was common among the land population. The boat-and-shed living population, being largely illiterate for long periods of time, and not owning the land on which they might build an ancestral hall, gathered at religious festivals around their gods, and were associated through established but fluid contributory associations. Their mobility allowed substantial geographic extant for their celebrations. As the boat-and-shed living population migrated to land, they modelled their contributory associations on the lineage. Some might, in time, become quite successful in adopting that model. All the while, the distinction of a boat-and-shed living pattern from the land-living pattern kept alive the conceptualization of boat-and-shed living as an aberration of the landed ideal.

The boat people of Guangdong and Guangxi have been found to be speakers of a common language (Cantonese).[24] It is not clear if a common spoken language characterizes the fishing people on the lakes that are linked by the Grand Canal. That is a subject that should prove highly fruitful for a social history of the boat-and-shed living people when more is known about it.

Aberrations of the landed ideal in recent years

The nineteenth and twentieth centuries introduced technological changes that fundamentally altered the nature of fishing and transport as ways of life. A brief account of those changes may be found in Appendix 2. Equally important were political changes. The imperial government was overthrown in 1911 and from then on, China was effectively a republic. Through the first half of the twentieth century, China was devastated by war, and since the establishment of the People's Republic in 1949, there had been sharp changes in political theory and practice that totally redefined Chinese society. Such changes intervened between the documentary studies of Chapters 1 to 4 and the ethnography of Chapters 5 to 8. Chapters 9 to 12, therefore, explore what they implied for an understanding of people living on the water margins. In brief, it may be said that through the twentieth century, water-margin life as it had been known earlier was all but totally displaced.

In Chapter 9, Wong Wing-ho describes the unwitting absorption of fishing people into the emerging sociological language of social classes by the 1940s. He notes a description of fishing on Dongting lake in the 1930s, which says it was made up of three different kinds of people who lived on the edges of the lake: people who fished in shallow waters, people who fished with nets and lived on boats, and half-fishing and half-farming people. On top of those, there were also people who sailed into the lake during the fishing season.

Introduction 21

Wong argues that the categories are quite misleading. There were not three different sorts of people, but the same people pursuing their livelihoods in three different sorts of ways in the context of the fishing season at different times of the year. During some months of the year, the lake teamed with fish that had come to spawn, and those were much sought by boat-fishermen using nets. During those months, the lake came to life, according to the report cited by Wong, for merchants followed the fishermen to purchase their catches, and an entertainment industry made up of teahouses and sing-song girls courted fishermen enriched by the sale of their fish. For reasons that would have had to do with the landscape, fishing boats gathered toward the deeper southern edge of the lake, but a different sort of fishing was conducted on the mudbanks located more to the silted north. The silted foreshore of the north, however, was also good for land reclamation. One has to see in the mind's eye the geography of land reclamation as mudbanks continued into cultivated land, which in this area was commonly enclosed within dykes. As the lake overflowed, sizable ponds formed within the dyked area, which would have been linked by rivulets into the lake – all of which made rich fishing ground. In late spring and summer, the lake flooded and so traps might be laid on the mudbanks, and they would have been laid not only by the people known as the shallow-water fishermen, but also villagers who, but for the interlude of the fishing season, would have worked on the land. The casual reporter would not have noticed the difference; he or she would only have seen temporary sheds built on the dykes during the fishing season, occupied by people who might have come from far or near, who drifted away when the season was over, back to the land that provided work in the fishing off-season.

Anthropologist, Fei Xiaotong, writing about the village barely up-river from Xia Yihong and Ota Izuru's fishermen in Chapters 6 and 7 noted that the fishing rights in the village pond were considered to be owned by the villagers and were leased by the village headman to "people from Hunan".[25] After the lease was made, the headman banned villagers from fishing in the lake. Not won over by a class analysis of village society, Fei stated very clearly that a distinction was drawn between the "inhabitants of the village" and "people from other villages". Inhabitants were said collectively to have rights over the lake, and they continued to trap shrimps there after the lake was let to outsider fishermen, despite the outsiders charging the villagers of theft. Likewise, outsiders were not allowed to gather reeds in the stream. Fei's villagers, as he shows, worked constantly to keep the rivers navigable and the dykes resistant to flooding. Seen in the light of Fei's description, the settled fishermen and the half-fishing and half-farming people on Dongting lake would have been distinguishable precisely not by their occupation but by right of access. The writers of the reports in 1930s and 1940s, outsiders to the village, left out the most important question: whose dyke was it? They noted that land and water rights were owned by landlords, and by that definition they assumed that charges applied to all who camped thereon. When it is

22   *He Xi and David Faure*

taken into consideration that villagers and outsiders might have enjoyed different rights to land and water, the question has to be asked if they were both charged, not only for fishing, but for camping on the dykes. That question was not asked and so we do not know.

What we do know is that through the 1930s and 1940s, in the innumerable studies of the conditions of what increasingly came to be referred to as the "peasants", hardly any referred to fishing or boat-and-shed living, Fei Xiaotong being the exception (even though his famous book was billed as "peasant life in China"). On the Pearl river delta, where attention had been drawn to the Dan population, specialist studies on the Dan referred to their moving ashore, but in the very influential monograph by Chen Hansheng on the peasants of Guangdong in which the system of multiple tenancy was described in detail, not a word was written about the boat people.[26] The single example of the shift in terminology that Wong documents in Chapter 9 can be repeated through many other examples from contemporary sources in the 1930s and 1940s. At the water margin, many peasants were boat people, but they did not fit into the landlord–tenant distinction and were left out of the literature.

The encounter of boat-and-shed living with the socialist state post-1949 was yet even more complicated than its encounter with social class theory, as Huang Xiangchun explains in Chapter 10. Huang's research, using a combination of interviewing and archival records, is focused on the city of Fuzhou in Fujian province from the 1930s to the 1950s. The boat people there had traditionally been known by the name "*keti*", the origin of which is not known, nor what Chinese characters might stand for it. Like the Danjia of Guangdong, it was thought in Fuzhou that the "*keti*" were a different sort of people and, under twentieth-century ideas of race, it was thought they might have been a minority ethnic group. Fuzhou was an ancient city. It was the seat of the Fujian provincial government and, since the Treaty of Nanjing in the aftermath of the Opium War in 1842, a designated port for maritime trade with the West. For a century before the establishment of the People's Republic in 1949, the city had expanded under the impact of trade and, as it did so, taken away reclamations on the river banks from settlement by boat people while providing work in plenty for the same people as fishermen and transporters. The city government – both imperial up to 1911 and Republican subsequent to revolution in that year – imposed *baojia* household registration and extended that to include boat households. Suspicious that registration might imply tax and corvee service, boat households avoided it. The nineteenth-century urban expansion along with trade produced two more consequences. The boat people regarded themselves as being local to Fuzhou and, under their trade associations, defended their turf against outsiders, for example, as transport workers. As an underprivileged population, they were also target for missionary conversion. The marine district, as the boat population was defined under Republican household registration, made up 45 per cent of all Roman Catholics in Fuzhou.

Introduction   23

Household status, land, religion and ethnicity all came back on the agenda when the People's Republic introduced socialism to Fuzhou in the 1950s, but perhaps no one was prepared for the mass hysteria that emerged in 1953 and 1954 when it was rumoured that "monkey spirits" and the "frog general" were about and that ghosts had been sighted. It was believed that the presence of those spirits would bring pestilence, and propaganda campaigns and exorcism ceremonies were carried out in response.[27] Even though the origins of such strange tales cannot be documented, it is not hard to tell where the tension might have come from. Similar stories, some involving the fear of castration among men, were reported in other cities in China as well around the same time. There must have been a broad feeling that government control was tightening as household registration was imposed almost as soon as the People's Republican government was set up. Yet, household registration among boat-and-shed living people was, as always, complicated by their mobility and the apparent standoff between themselves and the new government, as evidenced by their lack of enthusiasm to serve on precinct committees that were set up on the urban model. By 1951–1952, land reform was introduced to the countryside. While landlords were purged and their land was distributed to their tenants and hired hands, the boat people who were registered in the city were excluded from land distribution. Even in the countryside, boat-and-shed living people who had, prior to land reform, been working on land were designated peasants and received land, but the ones who lived on boats were excluded. The geographic divide did not always work, because some boat people could be registered in Fuzhou city even as they held land in the nearby countryside. It was also around the same time that the question was raised if the boat people should be registered as an ethnic minority. Scholarly reports adopted by the city government decided otherwise, on grounds that the boat people had similar customs to the land people. Finally there was the question of religion: distrust of what was considered "foreign" and "secret" by the government characterized the treatment of religious assemblies among the Roman Catholic communities of boat-and-shed living people.

While Chapter 10 skips over subsequent events that would have included the Great Leap Forward and the Great Proletarian Cultural Revolution to contrast an impression of boat people's tradition in the early 1950s with the author's personal impression in 2001, Fuzhou boat people had, since the 1980s, gradually been housed ashore.[28] Yet, distinction was maintained between the people who had moved ashore from boats and the long-settled land populations. They continued to be regarded as the downtrodden in society. As an inverse expression of their downtroddeness, it was said they embodied sturdiness that might protect children from evil forces and were sought out by land people to ritually "adopt" their children, much as children might be "adopted" by local gods. The chapter concludes with an account of a festival organized by land people in 2001 in which boat people had no part. The boat people, after all, were Roman Catholics and had no place in traditional Chinese religions. On land or boats, the boat people were regarded

24   *He Xi and David Faure*

as outsiders. There was no animosity with the insiders, but they were not one of them.

To conclude this account, now some centuries since brief descriptions of the Dan and the "fishing people of the nine surnames" had created the images that made up the boat-and-shed living population, what had happened to them by the twenty-first century? In Chapter 11, Zeng Huijuan returned to the "sands" (*shatian*) of the Pearl river delta and spoke to some of them. An 86-year-old man recalled that he had heard from his elders that the village where Zeng found him had been abandoned by nearby Shawan people who had come annually to farm, but he and other elders thought that they had always lived on land.[29] Yes, there were seine-net fishing people who lived on boats but they came from afar from the county next door. The people Zeng spoke to used to live in sheds but by the time of her visits boat-and-shed living had become a memory. Although they recalled vividly the social life from the shed-living days, they were now living in permanent houses.

In Chapter 12, Sato Yoshifumi looked up the "fishing people of the nine surnames" on the Fuchun river, which flows down to historic Hangzhou city in Zhejiang province. There, he found fishing people who still fished with cormorants and recalled that their elders had told them they were descended from the "fishing households of the nine surnames". Sato had some lingering doubts, because he was also told that someone knew about that ancestry only after he heard stories about it in a Hangzhou teahouse. There certainly was a tradition in this area of people being recalled as descendants of the nine surnames but, as always, how might one know if any particular group was really descended from ancestors born centuries ago?

Probably only the most discerning reader would have noticed that although Sato found people who had stories about descent from the "fishing households of the nine surnames" and could trace the claims to the nineteenth century, the Fuchun river on which he found them is located quite some distance from Jiangxi province where Wang Yangming first reported coming into touch with them in the sixteenth century. No less an authority in social history than Fu Yiling accepted the reports from two very separate locations made four centuries apart as merely another example of the same pariah status.[30] Terms of address can be very elusive as subjects of study. The question has to be asked how a term that was applied locally in one locality might come to be applied four centuries later in another locality. The dissemination of terms of reference by written texts would seem an obvious answer. Wang Yangming's essays were well-known and widely read. The local term, the "fishing households of the nine surnames" that he recorded found its way into the imperial edicts of emancipation in the eighteenth century. Only thereafter are found instances of the application of the term, primarily to the cormorant fishermen and the boat brothels in the vicinity of Hangzhou. Sato's informants were not descended from the sixteenth-century Jiangxi nine surnames. They were descended from people

Introduction 25

to whom the earlier term was applied in the late eighteenth century and mostly nineteenth century.

Conclusion

This book begins with two problems that are rooted in Chinese history. At various times between the Song and the Ming dynasties, pariah status had been noted about some people living on boats. The terms that were used to describe them gained sufficient currency for them to be noted in an imperial emancipation edict by the eighteenth century. In the twentieth century, ethnographers could describe them from first-hand fieldwork. In what sense might the people described by the ethnographers be said to have been descended from the people described in the historical texts of early centuries? Moreover, was pariah status associated with boat-and-shed living per se, or was it localized to the areas in which historical observations had been made?

The chapters included in this book argue that registration of household and land by the imperial government had much to do with polarizing land- and boat-living, and the rituals the boat people adopted in sacrifice to gods and ancestors with how they might portray their social relationships, both among themselves and in relation to other people. In turn, registration and rituals had a great deal to do with the building of the imperial state.

Although in the Song dynasty, the idea that fishing rights might be governed from the foreshore had been mooted, it was in the Ming dynasty, first through household registration in the *lijia*, and then through land tax registration, that local groups over much of the realm acquired rights to the foreshore. As registration was conducted at the magistrate's office (*yamen*), the groups that had acquired rights through registration tended to be attuned to the magistrate's administrative procedures. Settlement of disputes by litigation at the magistrate's office, or the threat that litigation might be conducted, provided incentive for connections and respectability that might be established through the scholarly tradition that became the backbone to the imperial examination system. Hence, landowning groups were motivated to sit for the imperial examination, to establish schools for their young and to steer in the direction of respectability, which in the Ming dynasty meant adherence to lineage sacrifice not only at grave sites but also in ancestral halls. People who lived on boats – who were far less exposed to schooling, who might attend temple festivals but were unable to set up their own on land – followed a different route in their communal organization. Spirits of gods and ancestors were represented by statuettes on boat domestic altars, and represented in groups through scrolls that were domestically held but displayed collectively at festivals. As affinity between the land tradition and state orthodoxy converged, the practices of the boat people appeared heterodox to the land people. The inherent bias towards the land population as opposed to the boat-living population seeped via the written records into

26   *He Xi and David Faure*

the historian's commentaries with the result that written histories presented boat-living as being marginal to imperial society. Marginality, of course, was not the view of the boat-living. To the boat population, their practices did not necessarily depart significantly from the dictates of the state or the moral codes of wider society.[31]

Between settlement on land and living on boats was a vast arena of an intermediate sphere characterized by sheds built on stilts located on shore. Sheds were commonly reported in a language that suggested that they were meant to be temporary structures. Some must indeed have been temporary, put up during the fishing season and abandoned thereafter. Others might have been built and rebuilt on the same locations year in and year out, whether or not they were necessarily inhabited for the entire year. The conduit between land and boat-and-shed living provided by the sheds must have been quite fluid. Fishing and transport (call some of it piracy if you will) must have been sufficiently lucrative at times to provide for social mobility. Where status terms had been employed, some of them perhaps only locally, the contest over their application would have become politically charged, supported by stories, customs, written documents, genealogies and rituals. Such politics provided the bulk of the historian's documentation. There would have been rituals that established the prestige of groups of people who had differential rights of access to resources, just as there would have been customary guarantees for foraging. Guided by their records, China historians have concentrated more on differential rights than on access to "commons" rights with the result that they have only a hazy notion of village life, not only in the intermediate zone of boat-and-shed living but also in land villages.

One might argue, drawing an analogy from Louis Dumont's *Homo Hierarchicus* that notions of purity were at the heart of the boat-living status distinction.[32] To qualify to sit for the imperial examination, it was necessary to produce a genealogy of three generations none of whom occupied menial status, which included the Dan and the "fishing households of the nine surnames".[33] The status terms were real in law, in ritual and in the popular imagination. But were the people assigned such terms encased in them by descent?

It is far from clear from the studies presented in this book that boat-living in many parts of China necessarily carried pariah statuses within their own communities or even among their neighbours. Without a doubt, living on the water margins was subject to hierarchical differences in the same way as living on land anywhere would have been. Yet, social boundaries were sufficiently porous to imply that status changes were possible with geographic or social mobility. There was no underclass that could not have escaped from the trappings of the terms, but over time, as the terms persisted, they were continuously applied to the underclasses. Examples of Dan and "fishing households of the nine surnames" might always be found as long as it was believed that the categories were real. State orthodoxy did not describe society; it prescribed what should be society. Our studies in this book have shown

Introduction   27

no evidence that boat-and-shed living outside Guangdong, or even in Jiangxi and Zhejiang where the term "fishing households of the nine surnames" was recorded to have been in circulation, might have been associated necessarily with pariah status. They do show that where the term had been applied, it became a factor to be reckoned with and manipulated in local definitions of hierarchy. As long as the social category lived on in the popular imagination, living people could always be found to fit the bill.

Notes

1 *Hong Kong Daily Press*, 22 January 1874, p. 2.
2 Anders Hansson, *Chinese Outcasts, Discrimination and Emancipation in Late Imperial China*, Leiden: Brill, 1996, pp. 107–132, 163–170.
3 Ye Xianen, "Notes on the territorial connections of the Dan", in David Faure and Helen F. Siu (eds.), *Down to Earth: The Territorial Bond in South China*, Stanford: Stanford University Press, 1995, pp. 83–88; Helen F. Siu, "Lineage, market, pirate, and Dan ethnicity in the Pearl river delta of south China", in Pamela Kyle Crossley, Helen F. Siu and Donald Sutton (eds.) *Empire at the Margins: Culture, Ethnicity, and Frontier in Early Modern China*, Berkeley: University of California Press, 2005, pp. 285–310.
4 David Faure, *Emperor and Ancestor: State and Lineage in South China*, Stanford: Stanford University Press 2007, pp. 79–92; Helen F. Siu, *Agents and Victims in South China, Accomplices in Rural Revolution*, New Haven: Yale University Press, 1989, pp. 88–115.
5 Gao Zhu, *Jujian ji* (Collection of the Sunflower Creek), *Siku quanshu* (Complete books of the four treasuries), no date or publisher, p. 13a.
6 Pan Lianggui, *Pan Mocheng gong wenji* (Pan Lianggui's collected writings), 1697 edition, reprinted in *Songji zhenben congkan*, Beijing: Xianzhuang shuju, 2004, p. 2/2b.
7 Huang Gan, *Mianzhai ji* (Huang Gan's collected writings), *Siku quanshu*, no date or publisher, pp. 10/3b–4a and 28/14a–16a.
8 He Zhuqi, *Liang Song nongmin zhanzheng shiliao huibian* (A collection of historical documents on peasant wars in the Song dynasty), Vol. 2, Beijing: Zhonghua, 1976, pp. 549–559.
9 Zhou Chen, *Shuangya wenji* (The collected works of Zhou Chen), no date or publisher, p. 3/6b.
10 Chen Bo, "Haiyun chuanhu yu Yuanmo haikou de shengcheng" (Maritime grain transport boat households and the formation of pirates at the end of the Yuan dynasty), *Shilin*, 2010, 2, pp. 105–111; Zhou Yunzhong, "Fang Guozhen juqi de dili beijing yanjiu" (A study of the geographical background to Fang Guozhen's rise to power), *Yuanshi ji minzu yu bianjiang yanjiu jikan*, 2013, pp. 115–127.
11 Ray Huang, *Taxation and Governmental Finance in Sixteenth-century Ming China*, Cambridge: Cambridge University Press, 1974, pp. 243–244.
12 On the coastal evacuation, see Xie Guozhen, *Ming Qing zhi ji dangshe yundong kao* (Factional movements in the Ming Qing transition), Beijing: Zhonghua, 1963, pp. 237–278.
13 For a recent study in English, see Christine Moll-Murata, "Sundry notes on the Zhoushan Archipelago: topographical notation and comparison to the Braudelian Islands", in Angela Schottenhammer and Roderich Ptak (eds.), *The Perception of Maritime Space in Traditional Chinese Sources*, Wiesbaden: Harrassowitz Verlag, 2006, pp. 109–123.

28   *He Xi and David Faure*

14 Xu Bin, "Mingdai hebosuo de bianqian yu yuhu guanli – yi Huguang diqu wei zhongxin" (Changes in the river mooring stations and the management of fishing households – with a focus on the Hubei-Hunan region), *Jiang-Han luntan*, 2008, 12, pp. 84–88; Xu Bin, "Ming Qing hebosuo chilice yanjiu – yi Hubei diqu wei zhongxin" (A study of the crimson registers of the Ming and Qing river mooring stations – with a focus on areas in Hubei), *Zhongguo nongshi*, 2011, 2, pp. 65–77.

15 He Xi, *Yishen yizu: Yue xi'nan xinyang jiangou de shehui shi* (Ancestor and deity: a social history of the construction of local religion in southwestern Guangdong), Beijing: Sanlian, 2011, pp. 222–247.

16 For comparable examples, see Qian Jian and Liang Chu'an, "Da'ao yumin jiating de shenzhi" (Gods in the homes of Da'ao fishermen), in Qiao Jian (ed.), *Zhongguo jiating jiqi bianqian* (Chinese families and their changes), Hong Kong: Hong Kong Asia-Pacific Research Institute, 1991, pp. 223–231; Zhou Chen and Fu Wenwei, "Zhejiang sheng haidao minsu" (Folk customs on the islands of Zhejiang province), in Lingmu Mannan (Suzuki Mitsuo) (ed.), *Zhejiang minsu yanjiu* (Studies of Zhejiang folk cultures), Hangzhou: Zhejiang renmin, 1992, pp. 221–242.

17 Fei Hsiao-tung, *Peasant Life in China, a Field Study of Country Life in the Yangtze Valley*, London: Routledge & Kegan Paul, 1939.

18 www.dfzb.suzhou.gov.cn/zsbl/1515927.htm (accessed 28 February, 2014).

19 Hong (pseud.), "Wangjiangjing de Liuwang hui" (The King Liu celebration at Wang Jiangjing), *Shuican yuekan*, 1947, 2, pp. 90–91. Wangjiangjing town is located on the Liansi marshes, and Xia in Chapter 6 reports that a statue of King Liu from that area is also found on the altar maintained by the incense head of the Xu Family Hall.

20 She Kangle, "Weishan hu yumin zongzu de dangxia shijian" (The present lineage practices of Weishan lake fishing people), unpublished Master's dissertation, Shandong University, 2012.

21 Lin Ching-chih, "The life and religious culture of the freshwater boat people of north China, 1700–present", unpublished PhD dissertation, University of California, Berkeley, 2012.

22 The translation is ours; Lin refers to the position as the "host" of the "assembly".

23 Wang Haiyan and Wu Dongsheng, "Jianguo chuqi Jiangsu qudi huidaomen gong-zuo shulun" (An account of the work to abolish secret societies in the early years of the People's Republic in Jiangsu), *Nanjing yike daxue xuebao (shehui kexue-ban)*, 2002, 7. pp. 122–127; Shao Yong, *Mimi shehui yu Zhongguo geming* (Secret societies and Chinese revolutions), Beijing: Shangwu, 2010, pp. 479–526; Cai Qinyu, "Huidaomen shili de fuzha fanqi" (Revival of the dregs of secret society influence), *Tansuo yu zhengming*, 1998, 12, pp. 30–31, 34.

24 John McCoy, "The dialects of the Hong Kong boat people: Kau Sai", *Journal of the Hong Kong Branch of the Royal Asiatic Society*, 5, 1965, pp. 46–64; Zhuang Chusheng, "Lingnan diqu shuishang jumin (danjia) de fangyan" (The dialect of the boat residents (Danjia) of the Lingnan region), *Wenhua yichan*, 2009, 3, pp. 126–132.

25 Fei, *Peasant Life in China*, p. 176.

26 Chen Hansheng, *Landlord and Peasant in China: a Study of the Agrarian Crisis in South China*, New York: International Publishers, 1936.

27 Similar rumours appeared in other places as well. See Li Ruojian, "Shehui bian-qian de zheshe: 20 shiji 50 niandai de 'maoren shuiguai' yaoyan chutan" (A reflection of social changes: first study into the rumours of "hairy people and water monsters" in the 1950s), *Shehuixue yanjiu*, 2005, 5, pp. 182–201; Li Ruojian, "Yaoyan de jiangou: 'maoren shuiguai' yaoyan zai fenxi" (The construction of

rumour: another analysis of the "hairy people water monster" rumour), *Kaifang shidai*, 2010, 3, pp. 105–125; Li Ruojian, "Shui lai 'gedan': 1950 nian huabei 'gedan' yaoyan zai fenxi" (Who castrates? Another analysis of the castration rumour in north China in 1950), *Guangdong shehui kexue*, 2011, 2, pp. 193–199.

28 *Fuzhou shi zhi* (Local history of Fuzhou municipality), Beijing: Fangzhi chuban she, 1998, 1, pp. 346, 460; 2, pp. 304–305; 8, pp. 8–9.

29 Liu Zhiwei, "Zongzu yu shatian kaifa – Panyu Shawan He zu de ge'an yanjiu" (Lineages and the reclamation of the "sands" – case study of the He lineage in Shawan, Panyu county), *Zhongguo nongshi*, 1992, 4, pp. 34–41.

30 Fu Yiling, *Ming-Qing shehui jingjishi lunwenji* (Essays on Ming and Qing social and economic history), Beijing: Renmin, 1982, pp. 317–326.

31 Barbara E. Ward, "Varieties of the conscious model: the fishermen of south China", in Michael Banton (ed.), *The Relevance of Models for Social Anthropology*, London: Tavistock Publications, 1965, pp. 113–137; and Barbara E. Ward, "Sociological self-awareness: some uses of the conscious models", *Man*, 1966, 1(2), pp. 201–215.

32 Louis Dumont, *Homo Hierarchicus, the Caste System and Its Implications*, trans. Mark Sainsbury, Chicago: University of Chicago Press, 1970.

33 The requirement was the subject of an edict in 1771 and discussed as a partial reversion of the policy of 1729 in Jing Junjian, *Qingdai shehui de jianmin dengji* (Classes of menial people in Qing society), Beijing: Zhongguo renmin daxue, 2009, pp. 189–191. Ye, "Notes on the territorial connections of the Dan", p. 87, includes a case of a Dan who was punished by beating for having purchased a degree only three generations after leaving the Dan lifestyle.

Part I

As seen from historical sources

1 Government registration in the fishing industry in south China during the Ming and the Qing

Yang Peina

The people who lived on boats had always given the impression that they lived adrift, following their catch where the waves took them, mooring wherever they pleased. Yet, life at sea was never very far from land. Land provided the drinking water, the markets, the temples and even the landmarks for any boat population living by the shoreline, and many more lived not only on boats but also on land, going to sea only as their livelihood took them. This chapter deals with one aspect of the sea–land relationship. Governments saw the chance for tax among boat people, and the threat to social and political order if they were ganged up as "pirates". In the Ming and the Qing dynasties, an interest to tax and to maintain law and order brought on administrative measures that defined and shaped the boat population. A major part of those policies had to do with registration of households, of land and of boats.

Registration of households via river mooring stations

At the founding of the Ming dynasty in the fourteenth century, the imperial government had realized that the coastal population were gathered in bands, which were divided by the manner by which they fished or were engaged in various other economic activities. Coastal resources consisted of salt, fish and transport routes, and they were tightly guarded. As the Ming government established its rule, it applied household registration (*lijia*) to the coastal population, dividing them into units of tens and hundreds of households according to the occupations that they followed, primarily as commoners (*min*), salterns (*zao*) or fishing people (*yu*). The imperial government also ensured a military presence by the establishment of military colonies (*weisuo*) that were manned by military (*jun*) households. Each category of household was held responsible for labour service peculiar to the nature of its manner of living.[1]

Ming dynasty law was quite clear on the registration of fishing people. In 1382, it was decreed that people who resided on boats and were known as the Dan were to be registered for tax at offices known as river mooring stations (*hebosuo*). In Xiangshan county, where the 1548 edition of the gazetteer has left a description of how such an office functioned, registration was set up in

34   *Yang Peina*

1391. In that county, the fishing people made up a substantial portion of the county population, and were grouped into six of the 39 *lijia* divisions known as *du* or *tu*. According to the manner by which the Dan households fished – that is to say, whether they fished with large or small nets or baskets of various types – they were further subdivided into 19 groups. Every year, one among the 2,620 households so registered was to be responsible for delivering the fish tax (*yuke*) of some 2,000 piculs of rice, 3,000 catties of fish oil and 68 catties of fish glue to the river mooring station. A single official supported by a clerk manned that station. The fishing people were obliged to volunteer household information on pain of confiscation of their fishing equipment.[2] Between 1381 and 1383, in Fujian province, 28 river mooring stations were set up, and 46 in Guangdong.[3]

As Liu Zhiwei has pointed out, it must be understood that, despite the wording of the law, the river mooring stations did not ever register all the fishing people, and that, even then, many were registered, not for labour service as fishing households but for military service as military households.[4] Registration under neither category succeeded. The description from the 1548 Xiangshan county gazetteer notes that towards the open sea to the northwest of the county, the Dan were not registered, paid no tax and the government had no means of registering them.[5] In Danzhou (Hainan), the demand for military service simply gave the local official the excuse for tax default, because, as they claimed, military exaction had caused massive exodus and, therefore, the river mooring taxes were left unpaid.[6] As the exodus of fishing people from the river mooring stations continued into the second half of the fifteenth century, the government began to close some of the stations.

Closing the stations implied the removal of the officials in charge, but not the removal of the tax quotas, which remained on the books for the whole of the Ming dynasty. In effect, it simply meant that the county magistrate now took direct charge of taxation accruing from the fishing people. In some places, changes might have been made to the *lijia* divisions into which they were classed, as in Xingning county in Guangdong, for instance. There, in one of the *du* divisions, as the foreshore was brought under cultivation, cultivators were brought together into two separate *tu*, and the tax-paying Dan were grouped with tax-paying Yao people to make up a new division.[7] In Lingshui county (Hainan), the 1618 prefectural gazetteer notes that four villages belonging to the river mooring station located near the present-day Sanya city were tenants on land held by commoners even though they remained to be held responsible for the fish tax.[8]

The reference to fishing people being tenants on land opens up a totally different aspect of complications in Ming dynasty taxation. The 1691 Chengxiang county gazetteer notes that after the river mooring station there was closed in 1532, the boat people were not only held liable for the fish tax but were also saddled with other taxes that had been transferred to them by the incumbents in the registration division they had joined. In 1671, the magistrate transferred the responsibility for those other taxes back onto the

Government registration in the fishing industry 35

land population so that the fishing people were held liable only for the fish tax.[9] Just as likely as the fishing people being held liable for taxes imposed on land was the shifting of the uncollected fish tax to the land population, or the farming of taxes to people who were powerful enough to profit from excess charges or who suffered from being bound to taxes that they could not collect. Those developments had to do with long-term changes in land taxation in the Ming dynasty and needs to be carefully considered below.

Registration of the foreshore

The failure of household registration for tax purposes was written over all of Ming China by the fifteenth century, and the long process began that culminated in what historians refer to as the single-whip reform. Two processes were central to that transformation: the conversion of corvee to a tax paid in silver, and the registration of land, not people, as the basis of taxation. Both processes were apparent in taxation imposed on coastal populations, including fishing people. They came to completion only by the early seventeenth century.[10]

Throughout the Ming dynasty, tax reform on the fishing people was a thorny problem because, as they lived on boats and did not hold land, obviously fishing people could not be taxed on the basis of land held. Yet, as more and more people deserted household registration, the tax burden fell increasingly and excessively upon people who remained on the registers. Although on occasion the Ming government granted tax amnesty, in the long term, tax remission did not solve the problem of how fishing people might be fairly taxed. Some officials advocated re-registration.[11] In other places, such as Xinxing county in Guangdong, the tax remitted from fishing people was absorbed by the rest of the county population, and, as the gazetteer noted "many people were implicated".[12]

The early Qing scholar Gu Yanwu recorded a vivid account of the change that came over ownership of the foreshore, which resulted by the seventeenth century. In Changpu county in Fujian, he said, tidal land could be divided into two types. On one type, nets could be set up at high tide, a distinction being made, even then, between deep-netting and shallow-netting locations. On the other type of tidal land, it was possible to catch fish by hand at low tide, and a distinction was made on that type between mud flats and sandy flats. All such land was privately owned. He noted that a century before his time, ownership accrued to people who worked on the land, but by the time he was writing, the land was bought and sold by powerful families.[13] A similar description of Guangdong province might be found in the writings of author Qu Dajun, who lamented that "although profit from the sea was bounteous, it had to be sought from man and not from heaven".[14] How that came about may be illustrated by a dispute over the foreshore in nearby Chao'an county.

In the 1691 Chao'an county gazetteer, the county magistrate, who himself had compiled the gazetteer, presented the case as the encroachment of

36   Yang Peina

poor people's foraging rights on the foreshore by the wealthy and powerful who were not necessarily living by the coast. He noted that back in the Ming dynasty, in 1624, as a result of litigation brought by the people registered in the *lijia*, an official notice had been issued and carved on stone to ban such encroachment. He also noted that since 1688, there had been continuous litigation and so he sought a similar injunction from the provincial governor on the encroachment of the foreshore. The provincial governor acceded to the request, with the provision that details of tax distribution in the *lijia* needed to be examined. Reference to the *lijia* suggests that the details of the litigation were far from trivial and that at stake was not really a case of rich versus poor, but the supersession of one institution of tax collection by another, exactly what one would expect when corvee service gave way to land registration during the Ming.

The magistrate, in his presentation, described the rich as having used the profit from controlling the foreshore – in one case, the foreshore owner charged 30 cash from fishing people as they went out to fish – to defray litigation costs, and that, because they won their case, the previous magistrate had accepted their plea and given them licences for their claims. Thereupon, in bringing suit against people registered in the *lijia*, the rich were able to produce documents to prove that they had been held liable for tax on the disputed land. The current magistrate retorted by arguing that tax had been charged not on land but on registered males (*ding*) and that, therefore, if registration for tax was the basis of the claim, the fishing people had equal claim.[15] That very interesting remark harked back to registration of boat people, and suggested that registration had continued, not necessarily thoroughly or practically, over the number of males each household reported. Whether or not the governor might accept the case as the current magistrate had presented it, therefore, the chance of tax collection was doomed from the start. It would have been as difficult to keep track of household males in the floating population as it was of households. The *lijia* that had not been delivering in the Ming made short shift of any effort to reassert its authority in the early Qing.

As time went on, the records become abundant that the foreshore had been registered for tax in various forms. Reclamation went on in earnest in Guangdong and Fujian, absorbing large numbers of coastal people, among whom many would have lived on boats as tenants and labourers for generations. In the Pearl river delta, Helen Siu and Liu Zhiwei have described in detail the redefinition of the Dan status in the reclamation process.[16] Along parts of the coast, salt fields had also been registered from the early Ming, and as the registration of saltern households collapsed like all household registration did, a similar process of encroachment by the wealthy and powerful was in place in those areas. Yet, certainly enough, many people continued to live on boats and maintain their living through fishing and transport, and through circumstances not totally connected with tax collection, the government found it increasingly attractive to register boats.

Boat registration

In the sixteenth century, piracy on the coast posed a very serious threat to the Ming government. The pirates were more than buccaneers, they were marauding bands that preyed on coastal settlements, including the cities. They were known to contemporaries as "Japanese pirates" (*wokou*), even though many had no connection with Japan. There were also the collectors of protection money, such as Xu Chaoguang, who surrendered to the government in 1545, who had sent out "huge junks" (*jujian*) to demand payment in return for tickets in proof that payment had been made.[17] Many followed in Xu's footsteps, the most well-known to historians is probably the family of Zheng Chenggong, who at the end of the Ming dynasty held out against the Qing. His family owned salt fields in Guangdong and controlled the sea beyond Chaozhou in the name of "master of the sea" (*haizhu*).[18] The registration of boats for tax was proposed as a source of income for naval forces to be deployed in fighting the pirates.

Local officials, of their own accord, experimented with different approaches to registering the boat people outside the *lijia*. One of the earliest to do so must have been Guangdong regional inspector Dai Jing, who held office in c. 1535. Dai's method fell short of registering boats, but he imposed *baojia*, that is registering of households, for the purpose of policing seamen. His method was to appoint a headman at the port for each ship's crew. Each crew came under the boat headman and deputy headman, but the port headman was to keep a register of all the names of the crew, organized in units of ten, and each boat was to have written on its stern in large characters the name of a member of the *jia* unit of ten, the name of the *jia* and the county from which it originated.[19] In Fujian, officials also discussed registering boat households at the ports in which they resided along with the land population in *baojia* policing units and appointing the wealthy people to serve as port headmen.[20]

A memorial from Wang Shu, who was appointed censor-in-chief for the inspection of Zhejiang and Fujian and given charge of fighting the pirates in the 1550s, shows the nature of the argument in favour of registering boats. A busy economy had grown on the sixteenth-century coastline at the heart of the piracy that he had to deal with. The threat at sea came from well-armed large junks of two masts that were fitted out by rich families on the coast for trade with the "barbarians", a term that could cover the Japanese as well as the Portuguese who were beginning to appear on the scene. This was a time when Chinese junks were plying not only the Southeast Asian peninsular, but also sailing to Manila and Nagasaki, when silver was transported to Chinese cities in exchange for Chinese goods in such large quantities that within the century it became the medium by which taxes might be paid. However, besides the junk trade, there was also a lucrative fishing business, the most profitable of which was the annual expedition for the yellow croaker season at a fishing ground located off the mouth of the Yangzi river in the East China Sea. The yellow croaker was one of the most common fishes consumed by

38   *Yang Peina*

the Lower Yangzi population, and the fishing season had been observed by fishermen from Shandong, Zhejiang and Fujian consistently at least from the Southern Song dynasty. The fishing fleets that set out for those grounds were well-organized and financed.[21] Despite the flourishing of profitable activities at a distance from the coast, the government's naval forces were capable only of policing the foreshore and its inlets. In those circumstances, boat registration was looked upon as a means of control from a land base.[22]

The proposal to register boats was but one of numerous measures that censor-in-chief Wang wanted to implement. Those measures included rebuilding the coastal military, appointing capable officials to coastal stations and encouraging defection among the pirates. Registration was proposed as a means to increase tax to provide for military expenditures. He summed up the history of the imperial maritime policy that was relevant to his proposal. In the early Ming, he said, no boat was allowed to put out to sea. As a result, for 180 years up to the time of his writing, the thousands of junks that went in pursuit of the yellow croaker had put out to sea illegally. He proposed, in effect, that the ban should be lifted and that fishing boats be taxed according to their size, and he added as an afterthought that registration itself might also counter illegal activities.[23]

We know from available records pertaining to Zhejiang province that registration came to be carried out among fishing people and their boats. Comprehensive enforcement came only in the early Qing dynasty, and that was after the enforcement of coastal evacuation imposed as a measure against Zheng Chenggong who held out as a remnant Ming force on Taiwan. The coastal evacuation policy brought momentous changes to coastal areas in southern provinces such as Guangdong and Fujian, for it wiped out overnight all imperial backing for rights to the foreshore in return for taxation. A decree of 1655 banned all transport junks putting out to sea without a licence but allowed licensed fishing boats of one mast if they fished in nearby waters.[24] The coastal evacuation policy was designed to block all supplies to the Ming rebels and, translated into action, that meant massive forced migration inland, laying fallow cultivated land and suspending periodic markets. The sufferings that policy brought about are well documented.

Coastal evacuation was lifted in 1684 but the lifting of the ban was accompanied by a series of legal controls that were put in place over the next two decades. Fundamental to those measures was that a licence had to be obtained before a boat might put to sea. By 1703, a decree specified the height of the single mast permitted, the number of sailors any ship might carry, the banning of saltpetre transport and, for the first time, the requirement that to obtain a licence for building the boat, a bond of collective responsibility had to be produced that was issued by lineage or village heads at the port. The bond was to cover all sailors on board and was to be stamped by the magistrate's seal. On completion of the boat construction, the bond was to be examined in the presence of the sailors before the licence to put out to sea might be granted. The term that was used for the parties that might offer the

Government registration in the fishing industry   39

collective guarantee for the bond was *"aojia"* (port headman), a term that suggests the law assumed that the *baojia* system of collective responsibility was to be established at every fishing port. A separate decree carrying the same terms applied to transport junks but, in contrast to the fishing junks, allowed them two masts reaching a greater height.[25]

Refinements in the law came later. In 1707, in recognition of the role of Fujian junks in the trade with Taiwan, they were allowed two masts.[26] In the same year, Fujian junks were to be registered in mutually responsible fleets of ten junks each, and in 1714 the ruling was applied to Guangdong.[27] Also in 1714, it was decreed that shipping masters, coxswains, sailors and even travelling merchants be given identity papers to carry on their persons (*yaopai*).[28] In 1731, it became a requirement to write on the cabin the name of the county of registration and the name of the ship master. In 1818, the limitations imposed on the size of the masts were rescinded for all boats.[29]

Throughout the eighteenth century, government reports indicated the port headmen system was in operation in Fujian and Guangdong, although little is known of their effectiveness in implementing boat registration. In a memorial of 1724, the Guangdong-Guangxi governor general expected the "ship captain" (*chuanchang*) of the port to know how many ships there were associated with the port and how many sailors each ship carried, and masters and men were to enter into bonds guaranteeing collective responsibility over their conduct. The captain was to inspect all ships as they left port to ensure that they did not carry armament or food rations beyond the allowed quota, and as they entered to see if they had carried merchandise.[30] In 1766, the then Guangdong-Guangxi governor general ordered that all fishing boats be registered, along with the names of their sailors, and to implement collective responsibility, so that "if one ship committed an offence, ten ships would be implicated".[31] In Fujian, by 1799, the provincial governor memorialized that of the 360 ports in Fujian, each port had several dozen to several hundred boats and sailors numbering in the tens of thousands – hundreds of thousands if their families were included. Each port had an honest port headman, every ten households had a *jia* headman who was responsible for catching robbers.[32] The general statement corroborates isolated references in the county gazetteers, such as the one for Jinmen, which records for the eighteenth century that at the ports of Large and Small Deng Islands (Da-Xiao Deng, on the outskirts of Xiamen), there was a port headman each who was responsible for inspecting ships. The trading junks and small boats in the ports all possessed licences and were registered under the character *"sheng"*.[33] Nevertheless, as late as 1782, the Guangdong governor was still issuing an order to demand that counties enforce registration of ships and boatmen.[34] That is not itself a statement that many boats were not registered but an indication that registration could only be as effective as its enforcement. In 1730, a coastal military station intercepted a fishing boat and found that the boatmen carried papers permitting them to make their living in the port issued not by the county, but by a powerful local family. That one incident says much

40 Yang Peina

about the likely enforcement of registration, especially insofar as local powerful families might take over when governments failed.[35]

Taxation of fishing people in the Qing dynasty

In 1684, when the coastal evacuation policy was rescinded and the coastal population could, once again, legally take to sea, the Qing government set up two customs stations separately in Fujian and Guangdong for the purpose of collecting duties from transport junks.[36] In 1689, the government decreed that fishing boats that were engaged in what amounted to "trade in common food" (*hukou maoyi*) were not liable to customs duty.[37] Nevertheless, these measures did not mean that fishing was not taxed. The fish tax quota that was set up in the Ming dynasty had to be fulfilled, either by distributing it to fishing households or to their fishing boats.[38]

Because the law allowed transport junks to be built much larger than fishing boats, it can be understood that in practical terms, what counted as one or the other was indicated by size. It is not surprising, therefore, that with the connivance of local officials, the size of fishing junks expanded, as measured by the length of their beams (that is, the width of the vessel), after the law was promulgated without their being classed as transport junks. Throughout the eighteenth century, county governments increasingly recognized that the restriction on boat sizes had to be relaxed because fishing junks were taking their catches from fishing grounds further afield.[39] In Changpu county, in 1705, the magistrate had had to distinguish between the different types of junks to which tax might be applied. He noted that only junks that could not leave port should be untaxed. Junks that fished at sea, big or small, should pay the fish tax, and transport junks should pay the transport tax (referred to as the Tonglu, standing for Tongshan and Lu'ao, two settlements located on the tip of the peninsulas embracing the harbours outside Changpu).[40] In 1736, the Fujian-Zhejiang governor general accepted the distinction, and ordered that junks be divided into three classes according to size for tax purposes.[41] The Guangdong provincial administration similarly struggled with a definition of a tax rate for junks. A tax was briefly imposed between 1730 to 1736, but reverted to a distribution of the earlier fish tax quota, the regulations of the Guangdong customs noting that junks that were engaged in the "trade in common food" were tax-exempt.[42]

Although the fish tax did not prove an additional burden, tax increase was, nevertheless, introduced surreptitiously through the salt monopoly. Salt was a necessity for preserving fish and was carried by fishing junks for that purpose. As early as 1552, in Zhejiang province, the payment of the fish tax by fishing junks had been linked to the issue of a salt certificate, a requirement under the government salt monopoly for dealing in salt.[43] As happened often in the salt monopoly, government monopoly salt had to face competition from illegal ("smuggled") salt, and the government monopoly was defended by its being enforced as a quota allocated to registered households so that it became more

Government registration in the fishing industry 41

like a tax. In 1680, the Fujian-Zhejiang governor general resorted to such an imposition in order to raise revenue while the coastal evacuation was still in place.[44] Subsequently, in the early eighteenth century, Fujian introduced various modifications to salt certificates, but it was in Guangdong that they became a routine tax: Guangdong fishing people, having bought their salt from private salt fields that were everywhere on the coast, paid a separate charge for salt certificates at the fishing ports. The emperor Yongzheng was so impressed when he learnt of the simplicity of this manner of charging a levy that he sanctioned incorporating it into the regular tax, a move in line with the tax policy he had been championing in streamlining taxation and increasing local government incomes. The provincial officialdom was very willing to oblige and so, from 1733, the local salt certificate offices at the fishing ports were ordered to close and certificates were henceforth issued directly by the provincial authorities.[45] By 1737, that manner of charging the salt surcharge was altered by allocating different rates to boats of different sizes. It was becoming routine that the bigger the fishing boat, the more it paid in tax.[46]

Territorial boundaries and fishing people's communities

Like so much in government administration in the Ming and the Qing dynasties, government rulings were a long way from social reality, but they imposed a norm that came to be reflected in language and social structure, not always in the way that the government had intended. By the fifteenth century, it was clear that household registration never really worked. In the Ming, efforts for change had come from local officials and in the Qing, after the coastal evacuation, as a concerted centrally directed effort. Either way, the impetus of reform was to tie boat people to the shore, partly because local officials, for convenience of taxation, recognized the claims that were made of the foreshore or, in response to the needs of policing, imposed registration for the sake of collective responsibility at the ports at which boats were berthed. This is a process that was similarly experienced by the land population. In the ports and military stations that grew up on the Guangdong and Fujian coast, when household registration gave way to land registration for tax, and education made its inroad with a small segment of the local population sitting for the imperial examinations, lineages emerged with all the pretensions needed for claims to the literati status. The absorption of the local population into the state was never complete and, therefore, there was always the suspicion that banditry or piracy and the failure of registration went together.[47]

A genealogy of the Lin surname in Wulong village at Dongshan on the Zhangzhou coast in Fujian attests to this process. The 1996 genealogy makes the claim that ancestors of the lineage had held the right to the management not only of the foreshore but also the sea beyond it for three centuries. Villagers at Wulong fished, made salt and traded. In the eighteenth century, they fought people of the Zhang surname in a nearby village for their rights to the foreshore. One of their ancestors wrote a book to record 99 peaks and 36

42 *Yang Peina*

caves in the area to demonstrate their rights to them. He also found that there was a stele in the Buddha Mother temple (Fomu *miao*) nearby that said: "In the second year of Qianlong [1787] Lin the vegetarian had succeeded Zhang the vegetarian, the Buddha Mother temple on Su Peak serves as the boundary." On the strength of that line, the local police chief awarded the rights to the Lin surname.[48] What version of those events might have been told by the Zhang surname is not known. Rights to land and sea had to be claimed through the rules that had been set up by a land-based government. The boat people might drift, but the rights they claimed and the reasoning that supported them did not.

Notes

1 Ray Huang, *Taxation and Governmental Finance in Sixteenth-century Ming China*, Cambridge: Cambridge University Press, 1974, pp 32–38.
2 *Xiangshan xianzhi* (Gazetteer of Xiangshan county), 1548, 3/19a–20b, 5/3b.
3 Author's own estimate, slightly different from Yin Lingling, "Lun Mingdai Fujian diqu de yuye fenbu" (The distribution of fishery in Fujian in the Ming dynasty), *Zhongguo nongshi*, 2006, 1, pp. 50–51, and Yin Lingling and Fu Yu, "Lun Mingdai Guangdong diqu de yuye fenbu" (The distribution of fishery in Guangdong in the Ming dynasty), in Ni Genjin (ed.), *Shengwu shi yu nongye xintan* (New approaches in the history of biology and agriculture), Taibei: Wanren, 2005, pp. 493–505.
4 Liu Zhiwei, *Zai guojia yu shehui zhi jian, Ming-Qing Guangdong lijia fuyi zhidu yanjiu* (Between state and society, a study of *lijia* service in Guangdong in the Ming and Qing dynasties), Guangzhou: Zhongshan daxue chubanshe, 1997, pp. 42–45, 65.
5 *Xiangshan xianzhi* (Gazetteer of Xiangshan county), 1548, 3/20a.
6 *Ming Yingzong shilu* (Veritable records of the emperor Yingzong in the Ming dynasty), Nangang: Institute of History and Philology, Academia Sinica, 1962–1968, 161/1a.
7 *Xingning xianzhi* (Gazetteer of Xingning county), 1552, 2/2b and 4/26a.
8 *Qiongzhou fuzhi* (Gazetteer of Qiongzhou prefecture), 1618, 3/61a.
9 *Chengxiang xianzhi* (Gazetteer of Chengxiang county), 1691, 1/9a.
10 Liang Fang-chung, *The Single-whip Method (I-t'iao-pien fa) of Taxation in China*, trans. Wang Yu-Ch'uan, Cambridge, MA: Chinese Economic and Political Studies, Harvard University, 1956.
11 He Qiaoyuan, *Minshu* (A work on Fujian), 1631, 45/32a–b.
12 *Zhaoqing fuzhi* (Gazetteer of Zhaoqing prefecture) 1588, 11/42a.
13 Gu Yanwu, *Tianxia junguo libingshu* (Book of gains and failings of the realm), c. 1662, reprinted and included in *Sibu congkan*, Shanghai: Shangwu, 1936, 26/119b–120a, citing *Changpu zhi* (Gazetteer of Changpu county) which is no longer extant.
14 Qu Dajun, *Guangdong xinyu* (New miscellany of Guangdong), c. 1700, j 14, reprinted Beijing: Zhonghuo, 1985, p. 395.
15 *Chao'an xianzhi* (Gazetteer of Chao'an county) 1691, 3/43b–53a.
16 Helen Siu and Liu Zhiwei, "Lineage, market, pirate, and Dan: ethnicity in the Pearl river delta of south China", in Pamela Kyle Crossley, Helen F. Siu and Donald S. Sutton (eds.), *Empire at the Margins, Culture, Ethnicity, and Frontier in Early Modern China*, Berkeley: University of California Press, 2005, pp. 285–310.
17 *Chenghai xianzhi* (Gazetteer of Chenghai county), 1686, 19/4a–5a.

Government registration in the fishing industry   43

18 Lin Renchuan, *Mingmo Qingchu siren haishang maoyi* (Private sea trade in the late Ming and early Qing), Shanghai: Huadong shifan, 1987, pp. 85–130.

19 *Guangdong tongzhi chugao* (Gazetteer of Guangdong province, first draft) 1535, 35/11b–12a.

20 Geng Dingxiang, *Geng Tiantai xiansheng wenji* (Collected essays of Geng Dingxiang), 1598, 18/16a–b: Wang Zaijin, *Haifang zhuanyao* (Essentials of maritime defense), 1613, 8/27b–36b.

21 Wang Shixing, *Guang zhi yi* (Selections from broad travels), Beijing: Zhonghua, 1981 (first published 1597), pp. 75–76 describes the fishing fleets from Zhejiang, which might have applied also to those from Fujian.

22 A detailed discussion of coastal defense from the Ming to the Qing may be found in Yang Peina, "Binhai shengji yu wangchao zhixu – Ming Qing Min-Yue yanhai defang shehui bianqian yanjiu" (Coastal livelihood and dynastic order: social changes of the coastal regions in Fujian and Guangdong from the Ming to the Qing dynasty), unpublished PhD dissertation, Sun Yat-sen University, 2009.

23 Chen Zilong, et al. *Ming jingshi wenbian* (Essays on state craft in the Ming dynasty), 1962, (first published c. 1638), pp. 2993–2998.

24 *Qinding Da Qing huidian zeli* (Sub-statutes of the collected institutes of the Great Qing dynasty), 1847, j. 114, no pagination, item under "*haijin*" (maritime ban).

25 Liu Xufeng, "Qing zhengfu dui chuyang chuanji de guanli zhengce (1684–1842)" (The Qing government's policy on sea-going shipping (1684–1842)) in Liu Xufeng (ed.), *Zhongguo haiyang fazhan shi lunwenji* (Essays in Chinese Maritime History), Vol. 9, Nankang, Taibei: Research Centre for Hmanities and Social Sciences, Academia Sinica, 2005, pp. 331–376.

26 *Shengzu renhuangdi shilu* (Veritable records of the Kangxi emperor), 1937, 229/5a–b.

27 *Qinding Da Qing huidian shili* (Regulations of the institutes of the Great Qing dynasty), 1904, j. 629, no pagination, item under "*haijin*".

28 *Shengzu renhuangdi shilu*, 258/8b–9a; *Gongzhong dang Yongzheng chao zouzhe* (Secret palace memorials of the Yongzheng period), Taibei: Palace Museum, 1977, Vol. 1, pp. 525–532.

29 *Qinding Da Qing huidian shili*, "*haijin*"; *Renzhong Ruihuangdi shilu* (The veritable records of the Jiaqing emperor), 1937, 347/11b–12a.

30 *Gongzhong dang Yongzheng chao zouzhe*, Vol. 2, p. 798.

31 *Guangdong Qingdai dang'an lu* (Archives of Guangdong from the Qing dynasty), no date or pagination, Puban Collection #694, University of British Columbia Library, under "*daxiao yuchuan bianhao liece jiaoying cun'an*" (Numbering and registering big and small fishing boats for record) in "*shangyu*" (commerce and fishery) chapter.

32 He Changling (ed.), *Huangchao jingshi wenbian* (State-craft essays of imperial government), 1872 (first published 1826), 85/11a–12b.

33 *Jinmen zhi* (Gazetteer of Jinmen), in *Taiwan wenxian congkan* (collection of Taiwan document), Taibei: Taiwan yinhang jingji yanjiushi, 1960 (first published 1882), pp. 46–47, citing *Tong'an xianzhi* (Gazetteer of Tong'an county), 1768.

34 *Guangdong Qingdai dang'an lu*, under "*biancha baojia shiyi*," (matters relating to *baojia* registration) in "*huyi*" (household corvee) chapter.

35 *Shizu Xianzong huangdi zhupi yuzhi* (Vermillion rescripts of the Yongzheng emperor), no date or pagination, in the *Siku quanshu* (Complete books of the four treasuries), 1782, j. 179, part 9, no pagination, under memorial by Fujian governor general Gao Qizhuo.

36 *Qinding Da Qing huidian shili*, 1904, j. 236, not paginated, under "*guanshui*" (customs charges). There were also two customs stations in Jiangsu and Zhejiang.

44   *Yang Peina*

37 *Qingchao wenxian tongkao* (Comprehensive investigations of the documents of the Qing period), Shanghai: Shangwu, 1936 (first compiled 1762), pp. 5078–5079.

38 *Gaozong chunhuangdi shilu* (Veritable records of the Qianlong emperor), 1937, 251/14a–b; *Huilai xianzhi* (Gazetteer of Huilai county), 1930 (first published 1731), 17/44a–b; *Chenghai xianzhi* (Gazetteer of Chenghai county), 1815, 14/26a–28a; *Guangdong Qingdai dang'an lu*, no pagination, under "*haichuan bianhao gezhao: youshi touwai zhaoguan yuan gongfei zhizhao, neigang jiashi chuanji shang bianhao geizhao, wuyong youshi touwei*" (Numbering of and issuing licenses to sea-going junks: paint head mast to completion according to official work rates, for junks restricted to harbour do not paint head mast) in "*shangyu*" chapter.

39 He, *Huangchao jingshi wenbian*, 50/21b–22b; *Guangdong Qingdai dang'an lu*, no pagination, under "*caibu yuchuan fenbie guigang riqi zeling paijia jicha, tingzhi lingjiao muqian*" (dates for return to ports of fishing vessels: order headmen to stop the practice of collecting wooden markers) in volume entitled "*shangyu, duchuan, guanshui*," (merchant and fishing, ferries, duties).

40 *Changpu xianzhi* (Gazetteer of Changpu county), 1885, 20/12a–b.

41 *Qingchao wenxian tongkao*, p. 5085.

42 *Qingchao wenxian tongkao*, p. 5136; *Gaozong chunhuangdi shilu*, 15/9a–10a; *Qinding Da Qing huidian zeli*, no pagination, j. 47, under "Guangdong *haiguan*" (Guangdong customs stations).

43 *Shaoxing fuzhi* (Gazetteer of Shaoxing prefecture), 1587, 23/17b–19a.

44 *Zhangzhou fuzhi* (Gazetteer of Zhangzhou prefecture), 1877, 15/30b.

45 *Qingchao wenxian tongkao*, p. 5108.

46 *Guangdong Qingdai dang'an lu*, under "*fuzou jinge ganbiao tieguo tieqi chuyang qingxing*" (memorial in reply to the ban on "dry markers", and the export of iron frying pans and iron implements) in "*haifang*" (sea defense) chapter; *Yuedong shengli xinzuan* (New compilation on the regulations of Guangdong province), Guangzhou, 1846, 6/7a–b.

47 The history of the major military stations that evolved into coastal towns may be found in Yang, "Binhai shengji yu wangchao zhixu".

48 *Wulong Linshi zupu* (Genealogy of the Lin surname of Wulong), no pagination, 1996, p. 37.

2 Dispersal and regrouping in the Zhoushan islands from the Ming to the Qing

Xie Shi

The Zhoushan archipelago, made up of some 1,390 islands lying off the coast of Zhejiang province, is now administratively designated a municipality and is home to a population of approximately one million people. In the Ming dynasty, it was well-known as a hideout used by the *wokou* (Japanese pirates) and, subsequent to them, the Portuguese. In the Qing dynasty, in 1692, eight years after the coastal evacuation order was rescinded (see Chapter 1), Zhoushan island, the largest in the archipelago, became the chosen location for the Zhejiang customs station, one of four customs stations opened to overseas trade. For a few years from 1698, ships from the British East India Company called at the island. It was long known to have occupied a crucial position on the China coast. Nevertheless, what might be said about the local population from historical records?

Under the Ming dynasty's settlement ban

As reconstructed by the historian Chen Bo, the Yuan dynasty innovation of transporting grain by the sea route to the newly founded capital of Beijing brought the islanders into service as boatmen on the imperial grain convoys. In compensation for their service, the government permitted the boatmen to carry salt for private trade.[1] Towards the end of the Yuan dynasty, the boatmen made up the bulk of the supporters of Fang Guozhen, who led the rebellion that eventually was to overthrow it. Fang was defeated by another Yuan rebel, Zhu Yuanzhang, the future Ming dynasty founding Hongwu emperor, and was thought to have hidden on the islands after his defeat. His followers were not wiped out until 1371, four years into the Ming dynasty, when the new dynasty declared a moratorium on boats putting out to sea without government permission and, at the same time, designated the boatmen who had been followers of Fang as military households. The sixteenth-century writer Zheng Xiao (1499–1566) rightly noted that from Jiangsu to Guangdong on the China coast, in the early years of the Ming, the "fierce young people of the seas" (*haishang eshao*) whom he described as "dan, islanders, fishing people and petty tradesmen" were thus recruited into military households.[2]

46 *Xie Shi*

The Ming dynasty denied the islands to settlement but maintained some military stations on them. Out of this policy, the story came about that the local population was forced to migrate to the mainland.[3] It was unlikely that any such forced migration, even if implemented, was successful. A sixteenth-century account reported that the first emperor of the dynasty, Hongwu, had granted a certain Wang Guozuo's petition to exempt his neighbourhood from evacuation, implying that there were settlements on the islands by then.[4] Another sixteenth-century account of coastal defence, written by Zhang Shiche, who was to become minister of war, described how fertile the land was on the islands and that 3,000 people lived there in some prosperity, while the military households had, by that time, largely deserted. He thought a county might be set up to administer the islands so that the produce thereon might be better used to supply the troops.[5] In any case, whatever government policies might imply, during the fishing season in the late spring, thousands of fishing boats converged on the seas outside the Zhoushan archipelago. For centuries, the richest fishing grounds on the China coast were found there.[6]

During the sixteenth century, Wang Shu, who was responsible for fighting the pirates in 1553, reported that the pirates followed the monsoon and needed hideouts among the islands all along the coast.[7] Official discussions on defence against the *wokou* Japanese pirates often referred to military weaknesses in Zhoushan. In the 1580s and 1620s, proposals were made to attract settlers to Jintang and Daxie, the two islands closest to the mainland where it was said 31,000 *mu* of land could be made available for cultivation. Such proposals, building on the fiction that the islands were unoccupied, effectively called for taxing their cultivated land. Opponents apparently understood the fiction for what it was when they remonstrated that such measures would have been disturbing to the local people and thus add to the turmoil caused by the Japanese pirates.[8]

From the late Ming into the Qing dynasty

It was only by the seventeenth century that senior officials memorialized the emperor on what they knew of the strategic importance of Zhoushan. The Fujian governor, Nan Juyi (d. 1644), reported in 1625 the clearest description of the complicated situation building up on the coastal routes. He said there were many fishing boats and the big boats belonged to merchants. He said that in Fujian, Zhejiang and Jiangsu, thousands of families had intermarried with the "Japanese". The networks that had been built up facilitated the traffic. He correctly identified the boats with the name contemporary Japanese records had given them, that is, "boats from the Tang" (Tang *chuan*). He said they carried goods from China that they traded with Japan. Troops did not dare ask too many questions. Of late, the Western barbarians (*yi*) had also appeared, and the people who had been helping the Japanese also worked with them. It was becoming as difficult to deal with the collaborators as it was with the pirates.[9]

Dispersal and regrouping in the Zhoushan islands 47

Zheng Chenggong, the Ming loyalist who held out in Taiwan after the fall of the Ming dynasty to the Qing came from exactly such a family as described by Nan. His father, who had married a Japanese woman, headed the maritime protection network that had stretched from Japan to Fujian. As Beijing fell to the armies of Li Zicheng and the Ming court broke up in 1644, the newly invested prince of Lu set himself up as a regent for the remnants of the Ming dynasty and held out very briefly in Shaoxing, on the mainland near Zhoushan. In 1646 he retreated to Zhoushan and stayed there until Zhoushan was taken after a bloody battle by Qing forces in 1651. The very reputable contemporary scholar Huang Zongxi's account of Zhoushan around this time described the local commander as a virtual warlord who drew support from islanders and pirates and who could mobilize war junks for battle. After its conquest of Zhoushan, the Qing government set up a military command on the main island in 1652, but lost its control to pirates in 1655. When it reconquered the island in 1656, the commander leading the conquest petitioned that all settlers be evacuated to the mainland. Huang Zongxi added that while they were being evacuated, many drowned.[10]

The early Qing experience became a repeat performance of the early Ming. When faced with the impossible task of defending the islands, the imperial government decided to evacuate their populations. The policy brought similar petitions for them to return. In 1658, a petition from one Xie Taijiao of Ningbo prefecture made a fitting case for the times. He said the coastal population, including "islanders, *dan* households, fishing people and petty tradesmen" had all served as guides for the imperial fleets. If their properties were not destroyed, these people could remain loyal to imperial defence, but if they were, those living close to the sea would join the bandits and the ones living further away would serve as their guides. Proponents of coastal evacuation might argue, Xie Taijiao said, that if coastal evacuation was relaxed, these people would supply the pirates with wine, rice and saltpetre, but he believed that the more stringently coastal evacuation was enforced, the more they would be driven to supply the pirates.[11] In 1668, Hao Liangtong, magistrate of Dinghai county (later renamed Zhenhai county), whose purview included the islands, also reported in a petition that when imperial forces retook Zhoushan in 1651, the powerful local men who controlled the different islands were at least segregated, but once the troops were withdrawn, they had joined forces and the islands were now infested with bandit lairs.[12]

The petitions all pointed to the same direction: it was more beneficial for the imperial cause to recruit the local population into its service than to drive them towards the pirates. The implicit common ground in these proposals was that coastal evacuation could not, by any means, be complete. Arguing from sources relating to the Guangdong coast, Wei Qingyuan has shown that to have been the case. Drawing on the very valuable contemporary Japanese reports as culled from Chinese seamen shipwrecked in Japan, Zhu Delan has also shown that during the coastal evacuation, the island of Putuoshan served as a centre of smuggling. She also shows that according to reports from the

48 *Xie Shi*

British East India Company, Zheng Chenggong's son, Zheng Jing, dispatched his men from Taiwan to conduct business at Putuoshan, for fishing boats from Putuoshan were able to collect goods from the mainland, including silk, which they could supply to the Dutch, who had appeared on the scene after the Portuguese.[13] One of the prince of Lu's staunchest supporters, the Ming loyalist Zhang Huangyan, went into hiding on one of the islands in 1663 and was caught by Qing forces that intercepted the boat with which he purchased his food supply.[14] All these reports point to continued habitation of the islands throughout the coastal evacuation, however much a stage of siege was imposed by it. In any case, coastal evacuation was lifted after the Zheng regime on Taiwan surrendered in 1683. In 1686, the imperial government took the islands out of the jurisdiction of the existing Dinghai county that was located on the mainland, set up a new Dinghai county and located its seat on Zhoushan island, renaming the former Dinghai as Zhenhai in the process.

Zhoushan under county administration

The first magistrate appointed to the new Dinghai was Li Tong (in office 1688–1690). The Dinghai gazetteer, which was compiled by his successor Zhou Shenghua (in office 1690–1695), said of him that in his three years of service, he encouraged agriculture and "he taught anyone whom he found was able to write", which does not indicate very widespread scholarship on Zhoushan. Li Tong's experience also shows that the civil and military administrations did not necessarily get on with each other. It is interesting that his successor, who would have had a vested interest in maintaining the supremacy of the civil administration, praised him for taking charge of an incident in which a soldier was said to have been disturbing the local people, much to the opposition of the local commander Huang Dalai.[15] That opposition might also explain Zhou Shenghua's efforts in cultivating the local literati, as is evident from the gazetteer he started to compile. His gazetteer gives their biographies:

> Xia Shidong, styled Longji, from Zhiwei, interested in public affairs and respected by the officials. At the time coastal evacuation concluded, he drew a map to present, and he served as guide. He contributed towards many things. Magistrate Zhou Shenghua wrote a plaque for his house, bearing the characters, "Contribution to Zhoushan". He petitioned for the removal of excess charges on foreshore land and his petition was granted. People of Dinghai to this day have benefited from his virtues.

> Wu Yun, styled Youwen, from Luhua. He stood up for justice and would settle for nothing less. When coastal evacuation was rescinded, a tax was levied on salt and surcharges were levied on foreshore land. The people suffered much from them. Yun petitioned for them to be lifted. While living in the village, he set up the Pavilion for Promoting the Examination

Dispersal and regrouping in the Zhoushan islands   49

and the communal granary with county students Miao Cheng and Wu Shiyang. His contributions to the village were many.

Zhou Changzhuo, styled Luxiang, lived outside the city. He was a determined person and his scholarship crowned the county school. He was devoted to education. Half of the fine scholars from the county came from his teaching. He was responsible for the thriving literary spirit in the county.

Xia Weizhuo, styled Moucan, from Cengang valley, generous and righteous, willing to help people in need, knowledgeable about local history and was often called upon by senior officials after the coastal evacuation.

Sun Hongye, whose family lived for generations to the north of the city, took care of people who were dislodged when settlement on the islands was again permitted in the Kangxi period (1662–1722). At the time, when the building of the Literary Temple and the Imperial Library was suggested, land owned by him was to be purchased for the purpose. He readily donated the land without charge. The magistrate Zhou Shenghua referred to him as a righteous person. In the spirit of his forebear, his grandson, Renjie, was also tirelessly engaged in acts of charity. When the magistrate Miao Sui built the Martyrs' Temple, he depended somewhat on his support.[16]

None of those people had an official title. Living on an island on which the imperial government had never been set up until 1683, they would not have sat for the imperial examination unless they did so somewhere else. But if they did not have titles, they, nonetheless, showed the pretensions that they might want to be counted among the literati. It should be apparent from these biographies how county officials were setting up the new administration. The gazetteer includes an account that describes how they sought out islanders who might draw maps to indicate the whereabouts of former military posts, taxes and the sizes of local populations. There were not many who could do so. However, they found Xia Shidong who was knowledgeable about such matters of the past, and he was presented to senior officials, who asked him to draw those maps and serve himself as their guide. The plaque that the magistrate gave him to hang up in his house would have been acknowledgement that he had access to the magistrate.

The people who stayed during the coastal evacuation would have been refugees and few would have left any records. The gazetteer that magistrate Zhou Shenghua started to compile contains the story of one Liu Zhensheng who would have been among them. Liu came from a military household on Zhoushan. His family was destroyed when the Qing army attacked the island in 1651. He hid up the hills. His mother, however, was away in Ningbo at the time and, upon hearing what had happened to the family, became a Buddhist nun. In 1656, the Qing naval commander found him in Zhoushan and brought him to Ningbo. Liu escaped and miraculously met

50   *Xie Shi*

his mother in the Puguang monastery of Ningbo. Thereupon, he lived near the monastery to look after her. His filial piety was noticed by a Fujianese merchant at Ningbo, who took him into his business like he might a son, and entrusted all his properties to him. When the merchant died, young Liu – being the upright person he was – notified and returned all his properties to his surviving relatives.[17]

The authenticity of a story such as Liu Zhensheng's might be questioned but the elements that made it up would have been readily recognized by contemporaries. Lan Li, military commander on Zhoushan after Huang Dalai, himself came from Changpu county of Fujian province, and his biography in Zhou's gazetteer notes that because there were many Fujianese merchants when the county was founded, he helped set up a Tianhou temple and even built next to it the Fujianese guildhall.[18]

The presence of the merchants notwithstanding, magistrates understood that the bulk of taxation had to come from land, and land taxation went hand-in-hand with repopulating the islands. Miao Sui, the third magistrate appointed to Zhoushan (in office 1695–1715), described the problem and its solution very clearly in one of his essays. He said that when the county was set up, the scholarly tradition had been so poorly developed that the county did not fill its full quota of county students, a status that had to be won through the first rung of the imperial examinations. People from other counties, therefore, had registered for the examination in Dinghai under false pretense of household registration in order to take advantage of the unfilled quota. Xia Shidong, the local man who presented a map of the island to the officials, had petitioned for tax relief for the islanders on the ground that the sea walls that held back salt water had been damaged during the evacuation and the people lacked the capital for their rebuilding. Miao Sui, taking the poverty of the local people into account, proposed that household registration be allowed in Dinghai in return for pledges to reclaim land for cultivation. Land reclamation, he noted, required the building of the sea walls, and that activity provided employment for the local people. The few locals holding "student" status, in what must have been an act of ingenuity, proposed to magistrate Miao that they could donate the money that they were paid – not for hauling mud over the sea wall but for supervising other people to do so – towards the building of a county school. Magistrate Miao was so pleased with the proposal that he delegated the right of reclaiming land for cultivation to students Huang Hao and Yang Hanzhao. The thinly veiled tax farming arrangement was very successful. The donations provided not only for the county school, but also for the Hall of Local Notables (*xiangxian ci*) and Hall of Reputable Officials (*minghuan ci*), the standard monuments in commemoration of county administration throughout the empire. Magistrate Miao led the leading members of Zhoushan in a ceremony to sacrifice to the spirits of the loyalists of the Ming dynasty who died on the island as soon as he arrived in 1695, and built a temple to house them in later years. The carnage of the wars of 1651 was annually remembered at the Ghost Festival in the seventh

Dispersal and regrouping in the Zhoushan islands   51

month, and, so, the magistrate's temple to pacify the souls of their conquerors was probably meant for more than a ritual purpose. Religion and state authority probably combined to pacify both living and dead.[19]

The exertion of patronage by the civil government in an area that had essentially been administered by the military garrison was precisely why magistrate Li Tong fell out with commander Huang Dalai. Miao Sui, who completed the gazetteer that Zhou Shenghua had started to compile, put the difference bluntly:

> In the past, the land had been taken surreptitiously by the troops. The people say, "This is land that used to belong to me." The troops say, "This is land that I brought into cultivation." It is impossible to distinguish owner and tenant in these cases. As a result, the taxable quota became less than half of what it used to be.[20]

He obviously favoured the claims of the civilian population, and, as he went on to say, a few years into his term as magistrate, they became wealthier and taxation improved. In outlining his own achievements, he took pride in obtaining permission to tax only as much land on the foreshore as was brought into cultivation, in his policy of allowing outsiders to register for the examination in return for investing in sea wall construction, in tying the taxation on the local production of salt to the locally registered population, and in removing daily necessities from the list of items on which duties were charged at the customs station. Salt was a major production on Zhoushan and the complexities of taxation on salt in relation to essentially a government monopoly had become burdensome. As for levying duties on goods in transit, that had become unavoidable when a customs station was set up on Zhoushan. The troops manning the station cut some corners when they imposed a fee on ships and people, regardless of what they carried. It was to magistrate Miao's credit that he persuaded his superiors to seek restraint over taxing Zhoushan islanders' daily necessities and, at the same time, abolished the levies on persons and ships.[21]

Magistrate Miao's description of what these daily necessities consisted of which had to be imported from the mainland makes interesting reading. The islanders took the following items for sale to the mainland: oil, candles, wine, rice, cloth, candies and paper. They imported from the mainland the following: umbrellas, wooden clogs, plates and bowls, lanterns and straw sandals.

The policy of repopulation applied also to islands nearer the mainland than Zhoushan itself, including Jintang, Fenglai and Anqi. The settlement of these islands had been an issue since the sixteenth century and the records indicate that they were settled even though the Ming dynasty government maintained its settlement ban. In 1690, the ban on these islands was lifted, even though the policy relaxation did not apply to islands further out in the China Sea. When it was suggested that Daqu *shan*, one of larger outer islands, might yield some 20,000 *mu* of land to cultivation,

52 *Xie Shi*

magistrate Miao Sui objected on the grounds that its distance from the mainland was conducive to producing communities that might support piracy. According to the magistrate, in the summer and autumn, when the fishing fleets from Fujian and Zhejiang appeared, poor people would come to the island and build sheds in which they would live as they farmed and traded with the fishing people. As long as settlement was banned on the islands, when found, those sheds were burnt by the troops so that the settlers might be driven away.[22] Magistrate Miao had his way and the status quo was left as it was, and it was not until 1878 that settlement of the outer islands was allowed.

The vivid description of makeshift sheds on the beach during the fishing season gives a sense of the roving populations that periodically visited the islands. The magistrate's contemporary, military commander Wu Jun wrote in 1708 that thousands of boats appeared during the season and many people dried their catches on the shores away from the sight of most people. Providing an explanation as to why he knew, he said the boat people were uneducated, as educated people did not take to the sea, and only the likes of himself who patrolled those waters would have witnessed those teaming people going about their livelihood.[23] Magistrate Miao in objecting to allowing land settlement realized the best fishing grounds were located off Daqu *shan* but he said the people who came to those areas as fishermen neither ploughed nor fertilized the land they occupied, unlike long-term settlers. He had also written another report to argue that they were not amenable to *baojia* policing, which combined household registration with the enforcement of collective responsibility and was looked upon as standard measure for maintaining law and order. They came in the name of fishing, but stole when opportunities arose, and people who were stolen from had little choice but to also turn to theft.[24]

Neither Magistrate Miao nor Commander Wu realized that almost as they were writing, the physician attached to the British East India Company's ships visiting Zhoushan was making a similar description to the Royal Asiatic Society in England. James Cunningham, writing in 1701 from Zhoushan island, realized that not until "about fourteen years ago, the island [was] beginning to be peopled". Cunningham was not very impressed with Zhoushan. He saw Dinghai city, "3/4 of a mile further from the shore, environed with a fine stone wall, about 3 miles in circumference, mounted with 22 square bastions placed at irregular distances, besides 4 great gates, on which are planted a few old iron guns, seldom or never used". He added, "the houses within are very meanly built: here the chumpeen or governor of the island lives, and betwist 3 and 4 thousand beggarly inhabitants, most part soldiers and fishermen, for the trade of this place being newly granted, has not as yet brought any considerable merchants hither".[25]

Of manufactures, Cunningham reported that the islanders made some lacquerware (possibly only varnished wooden furniture) but gave no details.

Dispersal and regrouping in the Zhoushan islands 53

He said they began to plant mulberry and to raise silkworms, and they also planted tea, but chiefly for their own use. He left details of fishing, farming and salt-making. His description of fishing on the mudbanks gave a clear eye-witness statement of the use of the mud-ski:

> In fishing, they use several sorts of nets and lines as we do; but because they have large banks of mud in some places, the fisherman, to go more easily thereon, has contrived a small frame about 3 or 4 foot long, not much larger than a hen-trough, elevated a little at each end, in which he rests upon one knee, leaning his arms on a cross stick, raised so high as his breast, and putting out the other foot often upon the mud, he pushes forward his frame thereon, and so carries himself along in it.[26]

In preparing land for farming, the local people used the cow or buffalo and took great care in weeding and watering. Cunningham found that provisions were plentiful, but nobody seemed to have come from the upper classes.

Almost a century and a half later, in 1853, Sir John Francis Davis, who visited Zhoushan in connection with the English expedition that arose from the Opium War, described Dinghai as a city of 27,500 inhabitants, and the whole island of 200,000. His report gives the impression of a bustling economy built upon agriculture, fishing and salt, where people were poor but not wanting. Fishing the yellow croaker attracted "a thousand boats". It was a thriving business: "When caught, it [yellow croaker] is immediately sold to merchants who are on the spot, with large boats filled with ice, in which, being carefully packed, it is taken over to the main[land], and thus sold all over the country." Most people could neither read nor write, but when the British took Zhoushan, they found islanders who had passed the imperial examination, even several among them holding the *juren* degree and one had been appointed a county magistrate.[27]

In 1882, a gazetteer was compiled that provides an impression of Dinghai being administered like all counties within the imperial realm. Magistrate Miao Sui had founded the essential institutions – the school, the temples for the officials and notables, and the granary – and long-established custom took care of the rest. The temples were reported in the gazetteers into the eighteenth century, and by the early twentieth century the gazetteers noted the presence of many trade associations that probably offered as much strong-arm protection as financial support. There is no need to assume that voluntary associations, financial or religious, were entirely new developments since the Qing, but it would have been difficult to craft the sense of community on architecture, such as by the building of a highly decorated temple, until the government recognized that settlement was legal and ended the state of siege that would have been produced by periodic raiding by the military on the grounds that settlers might be equated with bandits and smugglers.

54 *Xie Shi*

Reference must also be made to the well-known underclass known as the "fallen people" (*duomin*) that persisted all around Zhejiang province through the Ming and the Qing dynasties. A reference in the 1882 gazetteer notes that they were given the task of donning a red beard and wearing a daoist cap to exorcise ghosts towards the end of the year.[28] They would have served in other menial capacities in ceremonies such as weddings. There is no indication that they were associated with fishing or living on boats or sheds.

Conclusion

The history of Zhoushan has provided an excellent record of what happened to an area as it was brought under imperial administration. Despite the Ming government's denial that there might be settlement on Zhoushan, it would not be accurate to suppose that there had not been. Yet, the ban on settlement that was imposed on the islands gave the islanders liminal status. The stationing of military garrisons on the islands unquestionably established the claims of the state, yet the civil population being denied recognition was put in limbo with regards to the establishment of claims of landownership or participation in the imperial examination, the two facets of social life that most defined status in the Ming. The enormous change that came over Zhoushan as county government was established there highlights the stamp of respectability that the state could grant to local society, even at its remote corners.

A single event of 1716 stood out to earmark the new society that had been ushered in. Magistrate Miao died in that year while still in office, although he did not die in Zhoushan but in nearby Zhenhai county. His lengthy term of office on Zhoushan allowed him to do more for the islanders than his two predecessors. The gentry of Zhoushan, led by Huang Hao, organized a procession of several hundred people to go to Zhenhai to bring back his coffin. Fifty-nine people co-signed a petition to ask that he be buried in Dinghai. They won the support of the Ningbo prefect, the administrative circuit intendant and even the Zhejiang provincial governor. Magistrate Miao's son, however, thought otherwise. He wanted his father buried in his home county in Fujian and decided to take the corpse away. Finally, with much negotiation, it was decided that his body be buried at home but that his gown and his cap be buried in Dinghai. The magistrate's spirit tablet came to be housed in the school that he had established and that, during his lifetime, the local people had wanted to be designated his memorial. He had installed in the school the god of literary affairs, known as Wenchang, and so his spirit graced a side hall. Land properties had been donated to provide for regular sacrifice. Like all village temples, the estate was not constantly maintained and so, in 1805, ownership of some land was disputed and the then magistrate made a record of existing holdings. Interestingly, descendants of the donors of 1716 continued to maintain an interest in the management of the temple. Magistrate Miao, in his death, had created the ritual locus of the county gentry. He had indeed built a community that integrated into the state.[29]

Dispersal and regrouping in the Zhoushan islands   55

Notes

1 Chen Bo, "Lanxiu shan zhi luan yu Mingchu haiyun de zhankai – jiyu Chaoxian shiliao de Ming chu haiyun 'yunjun' xumiao" (The uprising at Lanxiu *shan* and the beginning of the sea transport of grain in the early Ming, a description of the "transport troops" in early Ming sea transport of grain as gleaned from Korean historical sources) in Guo Wanping and Zhang Jie (eds.), *Zhoushan Putuo yu Dong Ya haiyu wenhua jiaoliu* (Putuo of Zhoushan and East Asian maritime cultural exchanges), Hangzhou: Zhejiang daxue chubanshe, 2009, pp 44–58; Chen Bo, "Haiyun chuanhu yu Yuanmo haikou de shengcheng" (Boat households for the sea transport of grain and the origins of pirates at the end of the Yuan), *Qinghua Yuan shi*, 2011, 1, pp. 105–111.

2 Zheng Xiao, *Wu Xuebian* (A record of what I have learnt), no publisher, 1567, reprinted in *Xuxiu siku quanshu*, Shanghai: Shanghai guji, 1995, 67/36b.

3 The story is given in numerous Ming sources, including Hu Zongxian, "Zhejiang shiyi" (Affairs of Zhejiang), in Zheng Ruozeng, *Chouhai tubian* (A collection of maps for dealing with maritime affairs), published under his direction in 1562. Hu's description may be found in *Zhongguo bingshu jicheng bianwei hui* (History of Chinese military texts), Beijing and Shenyang: Jiefangjun chubanshe and Liaoshen shushe, 1990, Vol. 15, pp. 474–475. Hu was responsible for the Ming government's defence against the pirates in the mid-sixteenth century, and his description of Zhoushan was frequently cited by other sources, including Zhejiang gazetteers.

4 *Dinghai xianzhi* (Gazetteer of Dinghai county), 1715, reprinted Zhoushan: Zhoushan dang'an guan, 2006, p. 326.

5 *Zhoushan zhi* (Gazetteer of Zhoushan), 1625, 1/19a.

6 Sheng-Si haiyang yu yuye zhi bianzuan weiyuanhui (eds.), *Sheng-Si haiyang yu yuye zhi* (History of the Sheng-Si sea and fishery), Beijing: Fangzhi chubanshe, 2011, pp. 155–157 and 230–231. The Sheng-Si islands are a group located towards the north of the Zhoushan archipelago.

7 Chen Zilong et al., *Ming jingshi wenbian* (Essays on state craft in the Ming dynasty), Beijing: Zhonghua, 1962 (first published c. 1638), pp. 2993–2998. On Wang Shu's memorial, see also Chapter 1 in this volume.

8 *Dinghai xianzhi* 1715, pp 40–42; *Ming Shenzong shilu* (Veritable records of the Ming dynasty, Shenzong reign), Nangang: Zhongyang yanjiu yuan, Lishi yuyan yanjiusuo, 1962–1968, pp. 3444–3445; *Ming Xizong shilu* (Veritable records of the Ming dynasty, Xizong reign), Nangang: Zhongyang yanjiu yuan, Lishi yuyan yanjiusuo, 1962–1968, pp. 3859–3860.

9 *Ming Xizong shilu*, pp. 2661–2663; on the early appearance of Portuguese ships in the area, see C.R. Boxer (ed.), *South China in the Sixteenth Century: Being the Narratives of Galeote Pereira, Fr. Gaspar da Cruz, OP and Fr. Martin de Rada, OESA (1550–1575)*, London: Hakluyt Society, 1953, pp. xxii–xxiii.

10 Lynn Struve, *The Southern Ming, 1644–1662*, New Haven: Yale University Press, 1984, pp. 96–97, 114–115; Huang Zongxi, *Huang Zongxi quanji* (Collected works of Huang Zongxi), ed. Shen Shanhong, Hangzhou: Hangzhou guji, 1986, pp. 175–178.

11 Xie Taijiao, "Xie Taijiao zouyi" (The memorials of Xie Taijiao), in Jiang Yasha (ed.), *Qingdai (weikan) shangyu, zoushu, gongdu, dianwen huibian* (A collection of Qing period (unpublished) edicts, memorials, official correspondence and telegraph messages), Beijing: Quanguo tushuguan wenxian suwei fuzhi zhongxin, 2005, Vol. 1, pp. 357–412.

12 *Dinghai xianzhi* 1715, pp. 91–92.

13 Wei Qingyuan, "Youguan Qingchu jinhai he qianjie de ruogan wenti," (On some questions related to the maritime ban and coastal evacuation in the early Qing), *Ming-Qing luncong*, Vol. 3, Beijing: Zijincheng, 2002, pp. 189–214; Zhu

56 *Xie Shi*

Delan, "Qingchu qianjie ling shi Zhongguo chuan haishang maoyi zhi yanjiu" (Chinese boats and their maritime trade at the time of the coastal evacuation in the early Qing), in Zhongguo haiyang fazhanshi lunwenji bianji weiyuanhui, eds. *Zhongguo haiyang fazhanshi lunwenji* (Essays in Chinese maritime history), Vol. 2, Taipei: Zhongyang yanjiuyuan sanmin zhuyi yanjiusuo, 1986, pp. 105–159.

14 *Dinghai xianzhi*, 1715, pp.398–399.

15 *Dinghai xianzhi*, 1715, pp.186–187.

16 *Dinghai xianzhi*, 1715, pp. 245–246; *Dinghai tingzhi* (Gazetteer of Dinghai sub-prefecture), 1885, 10/3b.

17 *Dinghai xianzhi*, 1715, p. 245.

18 *Dinghai xianzhi*, 1715, pp. 187–188; *Dinghai tingzhi*, 1885, 8/14b.

19 *Dinghai xianzhi*, 1715, pp. 346–347; Huang Hao, *Dinghai xian heyi shimin liuzang shilu* (A true record of the burial in Dinghai undertaken by the scholars and people of the entire county), in Liu Jiaping and Su Xiaojun (comp.), *Zhonghua Lishi Renwu Biezhuanji* (Collections of biographies of historical personages of China), Beijing: Xianzhuang Shuju Press, 2003, Vol. 34, pp. 449–455; *Dinghai tingzhi*, 1885, 10/3a.

20 *Dinghai xianzhi*, 1715, pp. 123–124

21 *Dinghai xianzhi*, 1715, pp. 116, 122.

22 *Dinghai xianzhi*, 1715, pp. 67–69.

23 *Dinghai xianzhi*, 1715, p. 139.

24 *Dinghai xianzhi*, 1715, p. 99.

25 James Cunningham, "Part of two letters to the publisher from Mr James Cunningham, FRS and physician to the English at Zhoushan in China, giving an account of his voyage thither, of the island of Zhoushan, the several sorts of tea, of the fishing, agriculture of the Chinese, etc., with several observations not hitherto taken notice of", *Philosophical Transactions*, 1753, pp. 1201–1209.

26 Cunningham, "Part of two letters to the publisher", p. 1207.

27 J.F. Davis, "Chusan, with a survey map of the island", *Journal of the Royal Geographical Society of London*, 23, 1853, pp. 242–264.

28 *Dinghai tingzhi*, 1885, 15/7b.

29 Huang, *Dinghai xian heyi shimin*.

3 The right to fish on Poyang lake as seen in a local record

Liang Hongsheng

This chapter draws on documents donated recently to the Regional Society Research Centre at Jiangxi Normal University that relate to fishing grounds in Xingzi county in Jiangxi province. They originated from the affairs of a group of people of the Zhang surname who refer to themselves as the Three Zhangs, and the fishing rights concerned relate to a small lake known as Knotweed pond (Liaohua *chi*) and the Long river (Chang *he*) that leads from there into the Wucheng city. First-hand documents on fishing rights are extremely rare, and this collection throws light not only on the legal aspects of the history of fishing but also the status of the people who were engaged in it as seen from the eyes of a local family.

The collection has been preserved by Mr Zhang, who was born in 1934 at Youshuzui Village at South Knotweed District, Xingzi county.[1] It includes various documents pertaining to tax collection and disputes over fishing rights, and some genealogies that relate to Mr Zhang's lineage. Most of the documents seem to have been written after 1950. However, they also include a manuscript of 87 pages entitled "Tax record of the river anchorages of Xingzi in the Ming and the Qing periods", which seems to have been written towards the last years of the Qing dynasty and that provides a valuable account of the late imperial situation. Together, the documents present an impression of how water rights were asserted from the Qing dynasty to the early years of the People's Republic.

Xingzi county lies to the north of Jiangxi province on the edge of Poyang lake, one of the great lakes linked to the Yangzi river. From my own visits to the area, I noticed that small lakes are found in many low-lying areas in the several counties there. In rainy seasons, when lake water overflows, it is common for the small lakes to be joined as one to Poyang. As the dry season approaches, the area in between the small lakes and Poyang lake would be drained, and land emerges that is overgrown with grass. Villages in the area both farm and fish. Mr Zhang's father made his living from fishing. In 1949, the family owned four *mu* of paddy land and 13 *mu* of dry land. During the Land Reform Movement in the 1950s, the family was classed as "upper middle peasant". Mr Zhang had attended school and knew how to do sums. With that background, he was recruited into the Land Reform Movement in 1950

58   *Liang Hongsheng*

as a land surveyor. In the following year, at the age of 17 *sui* (that is, 16 years of age), he became a village head. In 1953, he was in trouble with the work team that was sent to the village by the county government and was imprisoned for three years "for economic reasons". In 1956, he came out of prison and became village accountant. He also learnt such varied skills as repairing diesel tractors and playing music. During the Cultural Revolution, he suffered some criticism, but remained in the village propaganda team for three years. In 1975, Knotweed pond village built a 20-ton mechanized boat and he learnt to pilot it. In 1978, he became chairman of the village committee. In 1981, he retired from his post, built a 50-ton mechanized boat and went into the transport business. Six years later, he sold the boat, and moved back to his ancestral village, Youshuzui, where he subcontracted a part of the lake to raise fish. In 1988, he was responsible for clerical affairs when people of the Zhang surname in the county compiled its genealogy. He died in 2001.[2]

Knotweed pond and the rights of the Zhang surname

The edges of Knotweed pond fall under three district administrations: Liaonan *xiang* to the south, Liaohua *zhen* to the northeast and Hualin *xiang* to the northwest. For that reason, no single district administered it. Mr Zhang, collector of the documents, said in a report he wrote that the lake had always been the property of the "Three Zhangs". He said, "there were no deeds, but nobody disputed".[3] He also said that Knotweed pond provided for the sumptuous end-of-year meal known as *ma*. His son explained that to me – every year, when Poyang lake flooded, fish fry would be brought into Knotweed pond by flood water and, in order to allow the fish to grow to maturity, the Zhang surname had made it a rule that for 300 days of the year, no fishing was allowed in the lake. On the 24th day of the 12th lunar month, the ban on fishing was lifted for members of the Three Zhangs. Fishing, therefore, brought income for the New Year celebration, for which reason it was known as the provision for the New Year feast. For the same reason, Knotweed pond was also known as the Three Zhangs' *ma* lake (or sumptuous feast lake). Until 2005, only people from the Three Zhangs might subcontract fishing rights on the lake from the government.

There is a long record of water management at Knotweed pond. The first written reference to the lake may be found in the 1515 Nankang prefectural gazetteer, which records it as the Liao family pond, the surname "Liao" and the Chinese character for "knotweed" being homophonous.[4] By the 1673 edition of the gazetteer, the pond was named with the character for "knotweed".[5] Silting was possibly already a problem, for from 1719 there had been repeated reports of drainage works conducted under official supervision. A report of 1730 noted that 3,000 *mu* of land was flooded. The prefect of nearby Raozhou, who was sent by the provincial governor to investigate, reported that at Knotweed pond lived 2,100 households in 87 villages and they farmed 12,000 *mu*. When there was flooding, he said, their land would be submerged.

The right to fish on Poyang lake as seen in a local record 59

A channel was built to drain away flood water but, in addition, the officials planted the Chastetree fruit on the sandy embankments so that their vine-like roots might hold the sand in place. That did not prove a lasting measure, for the plants were cut by nearby villagers and the embankments did not hold. Repairs were so frequent that in 1816, the Nankang prefect funded land purchase to provide a rental income to pay for regular repairs. A collection of 200 cash per *mu* of land was collected from cultivators, while members of the gentry also donated land to add to their regular income. The initiative was managed by people who were referred to as "headmen" (*shoushi*). Frequent repairs continued and as late as 1872, the prefectural gazetteer made reference to their being managed by headmen. In 1865, however, as the Taiping Rebellion broke out and local militia were organized in defence, a new term appeared, "pond headmen" (*chishou*) who were responsible for drainage works. Not a great deal is known about these "headmen" or "pond headmen", except for occasional mention of their names in the gazetteers, so that we know their surnames were Zou, Wan, Liu, Li and Hu. There was no Zhang.[6]

The Zhang surname appears first in a map of Knotweed pond included in the 1871 Xingzi county gazetteer. Surnames appear on the map as an integral part of place names, such as the Zhangs of Banqiao, or the Lius of Banqiao. Interestingly, next to the name "Zhangs of Banqiao" is a line that says, "the Zhang surname has the fishing boat" (*Zhang xing qu yuzhou*).[7] The line would have implied that the Zhang surname at Banqiao had control of some fishing rights at the designated spot.

A ruling by a magistrate with the Liu surname recorded in the "Tax record of the river anchorages of Xingzi in the Ming and the Qing periods" in Mr Zhang's collection puts it beyond doubt that the Zhang surname held fishing rights.[8] The document is not dated but it is likely to have been written in the late nineteenth century or the first years of the twentieth, and in any case, within the Qing dynasty. Magistrate Liu noted that the dispute on fishing rights between people of the Zhang and the Li surnames had gone on for a very long time. He noted that one party had relied on deeds as evidence, and the other registration documents pertaining to tax payment. However, neither party had up-to-date records. He acknowledged that although the lakes and rivers all belonged to the emperor, fishing grounds could be privately held and that people of the Li surname had claims to certain tracts of the water. In this particular instance, he noted that the ebb and flow of the river had blurred boundaries. There were times when the water reached a high level, and when that happened, the Zhang surname should be allowed to go beyond the boundaries of the river even if that meant intruding into what might apparently be the grounds to which people of the Li surname held fishing rights. However, he noted specifically that when the water had subsided, the stretch of water to which the Li surname laid claims should be given exclusively to them.

The description raises a very interesting and important detail in the holding of land rights. The area in question included Knotweed pond and the Long

60 *Liang Hongsheng*

river. The Zhang surname, as the document makes clear (more below), held fishing rights on the pond and in some parts of the river. From the context of the document, it should be clear that the Li surname held rights in other parts of the river. Disputes arose easily when the water level was high, because what would have been a boundary of dry land separating fishing grounds would become flooded. For that reason, the magistrate suggested that boundaries had to be relaxed at times of flooding, even if they might be maintained in the dry seasons.

To resolve the dispute, the magistrate had both parties appear before him with their records. He sought to register their claims anew and provide a record that he would certify to be correct by applying to it his official seal. To do so, he would discard from their claims discrepancies in the record. As the record in question would pertain not only to fishing rights but also to tax, the magistrate obviously had a vested interest in the need for clarification. The registration record that is included in the magistrate's ruling throws considerable light on the nature of ownership on the lake and the river.

Magistrate Liu noted that prior to his ruling, the Zhang surname had held their rights in the name of one Zhang Shimou, who was a resident of the second precinct (*du*) in Banqiao village; that is to say, at exactly the location where the 1871 Xingzi county gazetteer had noted on a map the Zhang surname had "the fishing boat". Like registration in most parts of the Qing dynasty, the locality had obviously been demarcated by the *baojia* system, that is to say, groups of household would have been known as a *jia* and ten *jia* would have made up a *bao* (which did not necessarily fit neatly into the geographic precinct). Zhang Shimou was noted as the registered household of the first *jia*, and no other household in the *jia* was apparently registered. Zhang Shimou was not known as a landlord. Instead, the document refers to him as a tenant (*dian*). Nevertheless, tax was applied to his name, although it was clearly understood that it was paid by a number of households who together shared that tax registration. Together, they paid 60 piculs of rice and just under seven taels of silver.

The magistrate did not list the Zhang surname's holdings under the existing registration, but he applied to them a new registered household name. The Zhang surname properties were henceforth registered in the name of Zhang Menghai, who was said to have been a resident of the second precinct in Banqiao. He was no longer described as a tenant. Instead, he was referred to as a person who had "contracted to hold" (*chengguan*) properties. The properties were itemized, consisting of Knotweed pond and a stretch of the Long river. To make the point very clear, he used the term "taking care of the properties" (*guanye*) to describe the owner's rights, a term that may be translated as "taking possession of" and standardly appears on deeds of sale for land. The owner of fishing rights was also to be liable for tax. Zhang Menghai also "contracted to hold" the property formerly registered under Zhang Shimou in the sixth *jia*, and one Zhang Guochao, also of the second precinct in Banqiao, was included under the new registration for "contracting to hold"

The right to fish on Poyang lake as seen in a local record 61

lake properties that had come under one Zhang Feng at a place known as Li *jia* (literally "Li family").

Consultation of the Zhang surname genealogy compiled in 1946 included in Mr Zhang's collection shows that Zhang Shimou belonged to the 59th generation in the lineage. He was born in 1459, became a "stipendiary student" of the county, and was responsible for tax for the first *jia*. His name was the first listed in the genealogy for being responsible for tax at Knotweed pond and the Long river. Reference to the household under his name, and to responsibility over other households in the *jia* suggests that the ancestor's name was being used as the name for a tax account. The holdings of that account were, by order of the magistrate of Xingzi, reorganized under a new name, Zhang Menghai. Zhang Menghai is not found in the genealogy, which has an entry on Zhang Mengjun, who was born in c. 1724, and who died in 1786. He was a student of the county school and he "took over the contract" (*chengding*) of the tax of the first, sixth, fourth and tenth *jia* left by Zhang Shimou. The entry thus confirms that Zhang Menghai was none other Zhang Mengjun. Zhang Guochao can also be identified in the genealogy: he had lived from 1750 to 1815. Typically, therefore, tax had been registered under an ancestor's name, so that all rights accruing from him would have accrued to people who might claim to be his descendants.

Anyone familiar with Qing dynasty land law would recognize in this description that ownership of fishing rights was no different in law from ownership of land. Ownership had been registered first for vast undemarcated territories, and portions had been rented out to tenants in perpetuity. In this particular case, under the magistrate's guidance, the tenants had been given rights afresh so that they now owned the property and were directly responsible for tax payment. The question arises what might have happened to the party that was initially responsible for tax. The question was not raised, possibly because – with time – claims had already faded away.[9] The magistrate was dealing with the case not as a landlord–tenant dispute but as a boundary dispute between neighbours.

Of the neighbours, the "Tax record of the river anchorages of Xingzi in the Ming and the Qing periods" provides some additional information. Zhang Menghai registered not only for Knotweed pond, but also for three other *jia* that he shared with other surnames. Of the other surnames, the Lis possessed fishing rights over large stretches of the Long river, like the Zhangs. These were the Lis of Botou village (literally, "moorage village"), and when their holdings were re-registered by the magistrate, the record noted that in the second *jia* the Li surname had "contracted to hold" land that had formerly been tenanted by a household of the Zhu surname. From field interviews, it can be established that the Li surname of Botou village was a powerful lineage. The village was located exactly at the spot where the river drained away water from Knotweed pond. The village is now known for having excelled in martial arts and includes among its inhabitants some households registered as "fishing people" (*yumin*). In the first half of the nineteenth century, a martial

62 *Liang Hongsheng*

arts teacher from Botou, known as Old Third Li, was killed in inter-village feud with the Zhu surname.[10] It is possible to understand the magistrate's concern for relaxing boundaries in high water if the location of Botou is taken into account. In the flood season, flood water would have been channelled in the direction of Botou, and the Zhang surname people of Knotweed pond would have wanted to go beyond Botou to enter what they would have conceived of as the extension of their pond. In the dry season, however, the water having drained away, land would have been exposed near Botou, and there would have been shallow ponds where fish might be caught, which the magistrate said should be left to the Lis. The Zhang surname, owning rights on both the pond and the river, travelled back and forth past Botou.

By the twentieth century, one Zhang Heming referred to himself as Knotweed pond "manager" (*jingli*) in his petition to the magistrate in 1924. The petition concerns wilful destruction of the Chastetree fruit vines that were planted in 1730, the loss of which was causing the sand to slide off the embankment and silt the pond.[11] Another detail has been reported by a survey on fishing in 1937. The survey – not only of Knotweed pond, but of a much larger area covering seven counties – noted that in Xingzi county, only 500 households, numbering 1,000 people, were engaged principally in fishing, while 2,500 households, numbering 5,000 people, were engaged in fishing only as a side activity. It also recorded that Knotweed pond was particularly noted for the tapertail anchovy, and produced as much as 10,000 piculs of it in a good year. Its description of collaborative arrangements at the pond is particularly interesting. Twelve people made up a team that operated a large fishing net, paid for by one among them who was known as "net owner" (*wangzhu*). The "net owner" kept half the catch and the other 11 members of the team shared the rest. Nine such teams existed on the pond, operating nine large nets. According to elderly fishermen, those nets were hauled by two boats and the operation involved their making a fast turn in the water so that fish at the upper and middle level of the pond might be caught. They distinguished this mode of operation from "husband-and-wife" teams, which were much slower in motion. They also realized that they often drifted beyond their own territories as they fished and that boundary disputes were frequent.[12]

One last clue concludes the structure of the fishing people of Knotweed pond, and that comes from the genealogies. Obviously, if their rights were registered under the names of ancestors and claims were earmarked by positions of descent, the genealogies would have been important documents of ownership. It is interesting, therefore, that although Mr Zhang's collection includes a genealogy compiled in 1922, the Zhang surname of Knotweed pond are nowhere represented in it. The 1922 genealogy was compiled by a group of people of the Zhang surname who considered themselves as having been descended from four brothers, all of whom had the character "Lin" in their names, and hence referred to themselves collectively as the Four Lins. Mr Zhang had a copy of this genealogy, in all likelihood, because it was given to him or someone else in his own line when people of the Zhang surname

The right to fish on Poyang lake as seen in a local record   63

known as the Three Zhangs were entered into one written genealogy along with the Four Lin Zhangs in 1946. The genealogy compilers noted in prefaces they wrote for the 1946 edition that they had discovered more branches of the lineage, and that the Three Zhangs, in fact, were descendants of the first branch of descent. In ritual terms, that means that the Four Lins acknowledged the superiority of the Three Zhangs. The implications of that acknowledgement has to be considered in the light of the social statuses of the two groups: the Four Lins, having compiled genealogies from the nineteenth century, as is evident from entries in the 1922 compilation, had been more associated with scholarship than the Three Zhangs who had thrived on fishing in Knotweed pond and the Long river. Their acknowledgement of the lineage superiority of the fishing people must have amounted to a reversal in status, a feature that can be traced into the 1950s and beyond.[13]

Losing ownership of fishing rights

Land reform came to Xingzi county in late 1950 and was completed by the end of 1952. A total of 8,000 new land awards were made to 70,000 peasants. From February 1953, the county began the "democratic reform of the boat population". That was a movement that brought together land reform and the purging of local strong men (*ba*). A Xingzi County Fishing People's Association was set up at the same time.[14]

Only oral accounts can fill in the details. In 1950, for instance, half the population of Youcunzui village inhabited by Mr Zhang's family farmed and half of them fished. That is to say, many people among the Three Zhangs were principally peasants for whom fishing was a subsidiary occupation. Mr Zhang considered his own a fishing family, but they owned four *mu* of paddy and 13 *mu* of dry land and so he was classed as upper middle peasant. His son also recalled that because fishing was a seasonal activity, many fishing people also had land. However, because fishing was very profitable in the few years leading up to 1949, some people sold their land, and the father of Mr Zhang, the collector of the documents, bought some of it at the time. Nevertheless, land holding was not profitable, the area in which they lived being prone to floods. Moreover, as fishing people, the Zhangs were more used to looking upon floods as a boon to their income, because they provided greater opportunities for fishing. So, land was merely looked upon as a source for some vegetables or economic crops. Fishing people depended on fish for their livelihood.

In one area, the difference between the 1950s and earlier periods is quite definite. That is, since the establishment of the People's Republic in 1949, the Three Zhangs could no longer exercise exclusive rights to Knotweed pond or the Long river. After the Land Reform Movement, all such rights had been abolished. As early as 1950, the Land Reform Law had declared that all special-purpose land, including lakes, marshes, rivers and ports, and all reclaimed land owned by public institutions belonged to the state.[15] By

64 *Liang Hongsheng*

"public institutions", the law included lineages. The Three Zhangs could no longer exercise a claim in the name of their ancestors.

At the same time, status changes were also being introduced. The war situation from the late 1940s imposed strategic importance on means of transport. From 1949, a series of changes followed, leading from boats being requisitioned to their being licensed. By 1954, the first fishery cooperative was set up, and by 1960, the cooperatives had been subsumed under the State Mother-of-Pearl Lake Fish Farm. As a member of a state farm, the people on Knotweed pond were classed as "fishing population" (*yuye renkou*). Like fishing people elsewhere, the status allowed them allotment of ration of grain, a privilege that people classed as "peasant" did not enjoy. In 1972, the county government built "new fishing people's villages" (*yumin xincun*) in the suburb of Xingzi county city and encouraged people from the Three Zhangs to move in. Fishing was now regarded by the state as their principal occupation, and they were steered more and more in the direction of conducting their fishing in Poyang lake itself, rather than Knotweed pond.

By 1980, as private enterprise was revived, fishing became a profitable enterprise once again. As such, it drew into the occupation people who had never previously been engaged in it. Moreover, in 1979 and 1980, the Bureau of Fishery issued fishing licences to fishing people and fishing boats, and once again small groups, some of which consisted of people of the same surnames, established exclusive rights for operation in some areas. Massive traps were laid and explosives were used and in quite a number of his essays, Mr Zhang, the document compiler, was upset with the development. He wrote in 2000: "Many fishing people are pessimistic and disappointed. They are prepared to give up. So many fishing people from outside have invaded our fields. None of us has risen up to the occasion. Even the cadres are retreating." He also wrote: "New fishing people from outside are developing rapidly, but we have lost everything up river. We even have to rent from other people." His collection of documents constituted a reaction to the trend that he found so upsetting.[16]

Yet, in 1988, the Zhang surname compiled another genealogy, and the Three Zhangs were given central position. It is anomalous that they should have been, because the Four Lin branches were obviously better educated. The Four Lin branches together produced 97 persons who had graduated from high school or university since 1949, compared to eight from Banqiao or Youshuzui. Yet, it is quite credible that in genealogy compilation it was the Four Zhangs that took the leadership. Well-educated members of the lineage left for better opportunities in the city and so they became more removed from lineage affairs. In the 1980s, as more lineages were compiling their genealogies, the county governments became increasingly concerned with the likely advance of local power groups and warnings were issued that they might lead to "feudal superstition" or even inter-village feuds. Well-educated members of the lineage holding positions of responsibility outside the county were unlikely to want to appear closely involved with genealogy compilation,

The right to fish on Poyang lake as seen in a local record   65

even if they were active behind the scenes. The Zhang surname genealogy that resulted gave the impression that the fishing people were central to lineage organization. It even included a map showing the many spots on the Long river at which the lineage had held fishing rights, and that was at a time when those rights had already slipped from their control.

Obviously, Mr Zhang had compiled the documents donated to the Regional Society Research Centre at Jinagxi Normal University because he felt he needed to demonstrate that since the Ming and the Qing dynasties, some stretches of Knotweed pond and the Long river had, in some sense, belonged to the families known as the Three Zhangs of which he was a member. In that lies the greatest value of the collection. These were not isolated documents found in a library but had been accumulated over time because they had belonged to a group of people related by descent. This chapter has added to them by referring to the gazetteers and other sources, but has taken care to indicate very clearly when the discussion rests on outside evidence rather than Mr Zhang's collection. So, the question can now be asked, since when did Mr Zhang's family have a written document to prove their claim? Possibly no earlier than the adjudication by the magistrate that revoked their status as tenants and recognized them as households responsible for their own taxes for fishing rights. These tenants of fishing rights – and later, owners of fishing rights – lived not on boats but on shore, and they fished not all year round but only for a few months every year. They owned some land, but they saw landholding as secondary to fishing. They did not resemble a floating population. In the 1940s, they were upwardly mobile when they were incorporated into the written genealogy of an established lineage of their surname. By the Land Reform Movement of the 1950s, they were registered as fishing people, just as their exclusive rights to fishing were lost, and by the 1980s, they faced competition from people whom they considered to have never been trained in fishing. Set in this background, Mr Zhang's concern for establishing the family history becomes understandable. Fishing rights had never accrued by status until the 1980s and, when it did, a history was needed.

Notes

1 Mr Zhang's name and the names of other informants are withheld in this paper. The surnames are genuine.
2 Information provided through interview with Mr Zhang's grandson.
3 "Guanyu San Zhang zhengdun gonggong shiye qingkuang de huibao" (A report on the reform of public affairs by the Three Zhangs), manuscript included in Mr Zhang's collection.
4 Nankang fuzhi (Gazetteer of Nankang prefecture), 1515, 2/7b.
5 Nankang fuzhi, 1673, 1/22a.
6 Xingzi xianzhi (Gazetteer of Xingzi county), 1871, 2/69a–75a; Nankang fuzhi, 1872, 6/33a–37a.
7 Xingzi xianzhi, 1871, map appended to j. 1.
8 "Xingzi Ming Qing shidai hegang keshui fence" (Sub-volume of Xingzi Ming and Qing period river and port tax), manuscript, no date; Magistrate Liu who ruled on

66   *Liang Hongsheng*

this case noted that he was due for posting to Foliang and that description does not accord with any magistrate recorded in extant gazetteers of Xingzi, Nankang or Foliang. As the Xingzi gazetteer was compiled in 1871, it may be surmised that Magistrate Liu served in the county after that date.

9 Knotweed pond was the site of battle especially in 1863; *Xingzi xianzhi*, 1871, 14/72a–73a.
10 *Xingzi xianzhi*, 1990, p. 529.
11 *Xingzi xianzhi*, 1990, p. 559.
12 Du Haogeng, "Jiujiang Hukou deng qixian yuye diaocha baogao" (Report on the fishing industry of the seven counties at Jiujiang and Hukou), in Jiangxi sheng zhengfu mishuchu tongjishi (eds.), *Jingji xunkan*, 1937, 9(1), pp. 31–40 and 9(2), pp. 20–21.
13 Liang Hongsheng, "Cong 'Si-Lin wai' dao dafang: Boyang huqu Zhangshi puxi de jiangou jiqi 'yuminhua' jieju – jian lun Minguo difang shiliao de youxiaoxing ji 'duan shiduan' fenxi wenti" (From being "outside the four Lin branches" to being the main branch, the construction of the Zhang surname genealogy at Boyang lake and the result of its "becoming fisherman-like", and a side discussion on the effectiveness of Republican period historical sources and problems arising from "short-term" analysis), *Jindaishi yanjiu*, 2010, 2, pp. 76–92.
14 *Xingzi xianzhi*, 1990, pp. 20–21.
15 Jiangxi sheng renmin zhengfu bangongting (eds.), *Jiangxi sheng renmin zhengfu faling huibian* (A collection of law and commands of the Jiangxi province People's Government), Nanchang: Jiangxi sheng renmin zhengfu bangongting, 1952, pp. 155 and 175.
16 Tang Yanping, "Cong 'Xigang' dao 'Xinsheng': Ruihong yucun lishi bianqian de ge'an yanjiu" (From "Xigang" to "Xinsheng": the case study of the history of Ruihong Fishing Village), unpublished master's thesis, Jiangxi Normal University, 2008, provides interesting comparisons with Knotweed pond.

4 The complexities of property rights at Diaocha lake as seen from litigation[1]

Zhang Xiaoye

Diaocha lake is one of innumerable lakes located near Hanchuan city in the flood plain formed by the deposits of the Yangzi and the Han rivers in south central Hubei province. Its surface area has never been stable. During the rainy season, the lakes overflow and they merge one into the other. Over the ages, their scale has also been much reduced by reclamation. Dykes (known as *yuan* in this area) have been built that divide the lakes into ever smaller stretches separated by pockets of farm land, some of which bear the names of the lakes even after they have been drained. In 1769, as the Diaocha was filled in, so much pressure built up on the dykes that they burst. Flood water must have submerged much of the reclaimed land, for the government abandoned charging property owners the land tax and reverted to charging the fish tax (*yuke*). Changes in the land form and concomitant changes in tax charges made it all but impossible for any clear record to be kept of holdings.[2]

Nevertheless, the locals had clear ideas of their rights over the lake, such being expressed in the term *hufen*, which can broadly be translated as "lake shares". "Lake shares" covered not only benefits deriving from the water, but also sedimentary formations, fuel-gathering and even land. "Lake shares" might include absolute ownership over the lake and entitlement to annual rotations for exploiting the resources of the lakes, or entitlement to exploitation without absolute ownership, or even a share to some distributed dividend. The actual workings of the "lake shares" could take many forms. Very interesting details of such entitlements are found in a chapter entitled "Lake records" in the Diaocha Huang surname genealogy.[3] The Huang surname had been settled in the area for most of the Ming and Qing dynasties and some of their lineage branches are still living there. They were owners of "lake shares", and so the chapter includes documents that were produced in litigation with other surnames over "lake shares", such as land deeds and contracts that were signed within the lineage or with those surnames. The other surnames involved in litigation with them are still extant, and so it has been possible to track down some of their genealogies and compare their versions of the same events. This chapter draws very largely on those documents for an impression of how ownership at the lake might have worked.

68 *Zhang Xiaoye*

The origin of "lake shares"

According to Terada Hiroaki, in the Ming and the Qing dynasties, ownership was expressed by the character *"ye"*, which may be loosely translated as "property". To exercise entitlement to ownership was said to "hold the *ye*" (*guanye*).[4] Terada made the very poignant observation that *"ye"* was accounted for by its "origin" (*laili*). In the genealogies and land deeds of the area around Hanchuan city, such "origin" is described as "receiving shares" (*shoufen*). The "origin" of the Huang surname's "lakes shares" is described in terms of its history.

From their genealogical records, the Huang surname, like their neighbours and contestants, people of the Xiang, Sun and Wang surnames moved to Hanchuan at the end of the Yuan dynasty or the early Ming (say the fourteenth century). The Huang surname genealogy says that the first ancestor to settle was the venerable Jipu. It says:

> He went with his younger brother, the venerable Jitai, from Ji'an in Jiangxi province to Zhijiang in Hubei province, and went from there to Hanchuan in the second year of the Hongwu reign [1369], settling near Diaocha. He was married into the Xiang family. The venerable Jitai settled at Zaogang river.[5]

The Xiang surname's genealogy records that its founding ancestor moved from Shuangliu county in Sichuan province to Yingcheng county in Hubei in the Zhizheng period of the Yuan dynasty (1279–1368) before he moved on to Hanchuan. Careful reading of the prefaces to the genealogies – which were often contemporary documents drawn up at the time genealogies were revised – shows that these accounts were all later-day rationalizations. The Xiang surname, for example, was made up of people who had not all come from a single wave of migration.[6] The Sun and Wang surnames, likewise, had come from afar and settled and built up their properties. Only the Zhang surname's contrarian account might have contained the added sense of reality, for their genealogy notes that when their founding ancestor came, they put down straw as markers on their land (*chacao wei biao*) and took over the corvee service of an existing household so that they might register.[7] Lineage histories are not to be taken at face value, but they reflect claims to status and justification for entitlements.

Making a claim on "lake shares" by staking straw markers on the ground agrees with what I was told by people of the Huang surname. They said that when their founding ancestors arrived, "the lake was in a wild state, and all one had to do was to claim it". However, the Xiang surname, as incumbent settlers, already held rights to the lake. The story was told, therefore, that when ancestor Jipu married into the Xiang family, his wife demanded that her dowry should include properties from the lake, as a result the lake was

The complexities of property rights at Diaocha lake   69

divided into ten shares, four being offered as dowry. There is no documentary record of the story, but in one of the statements drawn up in the "Lake records" in the Ming dynasty, it was said that the Xiang surname ancestor had given Dasai lake to his grandson (daughter's son). In an interview, my informant of the Xiang surname accepted their relation to the Huang surname by marriage, but added that the Huang surname were originally fishing people on the lake and they had made up the dowry story to claim the lake as their property.[8]

Aside from dowry, the Huang surname genealogy also says that the Huang lineage had purchased some of their properties. The genealogical account associates the opportunity for doing so with floods: when farmland was flooded, many people sold their holdings and moved away. However, their fourth-generation ancestor, the venerable Shixi, did what he could to buy up land on the lake. It concludes: "For that reason, the islands in Diaocha lake belong to the Huang surname. Their holding (*guan*) of reeds, lotus flowers, water chestnuts and fish amounts to several hundred taels of silver."[9] Not to be missed in the sentence is the claim to the entirety of the Diaocha lake.

The lake seems to be known locally as the Huang Surname Lake, a name that suggests it was held collectively by people of the same surname. By the mid-nineteenth century, fourth-generation ancestor Huang Shixi divided the lake into ten shares to be held by himself and his siblings. The possibility that Shixi possibly lived two centuries before then does not seem to have mattered a great deal to the recipients of those shares. My informant of the Huang surname tells me that to this day, the ten shares still exist, but two lineage branches (the eldest and the third) have moved away. Deeds recorded in the "Lake record" show that the land around the lake was purchased in the name of the collective ancestral hall, but my informant tells me that if such land was assigned to a lineage, it becomes "private" lake property, different from holdings of the lake that provide offerings for ancestral sacrifice. When I press my informant on what "private" holding of lake rights might mean, he acknowledges that, as there can be no clear boundaries on the lake itself, the question of trespassing does not exist. He does not think wealth disparity between lineage branches would have contributed to lake shares being bought and sold, for the reason that as lake boundaries cannot be demarcated, any spare wealth would go into land rather than lake rights. My examination of the deeds included in the "Lake record" shows that they all pertain to land rather than water rights. I understand from what he says that the different branches are scattered on the edge of the lakes, and that territorial boundaries are recognized on land holdings but not over the lakes themselves. Records of litigation included in the genealogy from the Ming dynasty onwards provide some background to bear out this observation. They also provide an account of the evolution of the lake from multiple ownership into a single lineage's property.[10]

70　*Zhang Xiaoye*

Litigation in the Ming dynasty

Local administration in the Ming dynasty was very different from that in the Qing in many respects. Local officials in the Ming (magistrates and prefects) did not enjoy unity of command even within their own jurisdiction but were subject to pressure from princely households, military commands and, occasionally, even religious orders. Around Diaocha lake, in the fifteenth and early sixteenth centuries, the extra-administrative influence emanated from the family of the prince of Chu, who was allocated to Wuchang, the administrative capital of the provinces of Hunan and Hubei. The story begins in 1563, when a massive land grant was awarded to the newly instituted prince of Jing, the fourth son of the reigning Jiajing emperor. He was posted to De'an prefecture, on the border of Hanchuan, into which his holdings reached. He died within a few years of his investiture and left no heir, but his estate must have remained intact for, in 1589, it was awarded to another imperial prince, the prince of Lu. Dismayed contemporary local officials, who saw land taken out of their control and transferred to the princely households, wrote about the increase in tax burden on the local population aggravated by princely agents making surcharges as they pressed their claims locally.[11]

The intervention of the princes in local administration can be seen in various disputes noted in the "Lake record". According to a preface dated 1640, one Xiang Bocheng from the neighbouring Xiang surname lineage into which founding ancestor Huang Jipu had married, once saved the prince of Chu's son from drowning and was recognized as a guest of honour in the prince's household. When the story begins in the mid-fifteenth century, the Huang surname had gradually purchased the properties that had belonged to other surnames, and only a corner was left at Dao Bend that belonged to one Li Sizu in a village by the name Xiaoli *tan*. In 1485, when people of the Huang surname put their nets down at Dao Bend, Li Sizu came and confiscated their nets on the claim that he owned fishing rights at the spot. The Li surname people brought suit at Hanyang prefecture against Huang Shisheng, Huang Zhuo and Huang Yi for wounding and drowning. The prefect held both Li Sizu and the Huang surname's advocate, Huang Shixi's son Huang Pao, in custody. Huang Shixi, it might be remembered, was the fourth-generation ancestor alleged in lineage memory for having divided the lake into ten lineage shares. Both were put under torture during the trial, and Li Sizu finally admitted that the Huang surname had shares at Dao Bend, that there had not actually been any drowning and that he had brought suit because, being a weak party, his people had been constantly put under threat by the Huang surname. The prefect settled the dispute with a bond between the two parties, demarcating different parts of the river and its ponds as their respective properties. Under pressure from the household of the prince of Chu, thanks to the intervention of the prince's benefactor Xiang Bocheng, he allowed the false report of drowning to go without punishment.

The complexities of property rights at Diaocha lake   71

In 1512, Xiang Bocheng himself brought suit against a member of his own lineage, Xiang Boji, for having sold 20 per cent of Diaocha lake to people of the Huang surname. He said Boji held no share in the land and, therefore, had no right to sell any. He also used the opportunity to press for return of properties that had been otherwise acquired by the Huang surname from his lineage. There was, for instance, the Dasai lake, which had been granted by his ancestor to Jipu's grandson in the main line of descent to subsidize his studies. Bocheng said now that the young man had obtained his "student" status, the land should be returned. Bocheng also claimed that 51 *shi* of "firewood land" (*chaidi*) that had been bought by the same "student" from the Ye surname at Xiaoli *tan* (where Li Sizu's village was located as was learnt from the earlier litigation) belonged 60 per cent to the Xiang surname and only 40 per cent to the Huang surname. Under pressure from the prince of Chu, Xiang Bocheng had his way at the prefect's court. Huang Pao, who had represented the Huang surname in the earlier case, felt aggrieved at the judgment, and took his anger out on people of the Xiang surname as they were gathering firewood. Xiang Bocheng, in return, burnt down the firewood and accused Huang Pao of homicide. The prefect arrested Huang Pao, Huang Zhuo and a dozen others of the Huang surname and put them under torture, and this time no one from the Huang surname dared represent them. Other members of the Huang surname, for fear of arrest, went into hiding. Surrounding surnames such as the Zhang, the Liu, the Xiang, the He, the Wang and the Yang, came forward with the charge that the Huang surname had in previous years taken their holdings by force, producing false documentation in support of their claims. In jail, Huang Pao accepted the prefect's rulings, and only then did the prefect release him and his relatives from jail.

The Huang family was in ruins, but Huang Pao convinced his relatives that they must appeal to the emperor in order to supersede the influence of the prince of Chu's household, which had been supporting Xiang Bocheng. According to a story that came to be very much dramatized, he succeeded in striking the big drum at the imperial palace to sound his appeal, and the emperor decreed that his appeal would be granted should he survive being thrown on the end of a piece of rope over the high walls of the palace. He survived and, with the aid of the imperial decree, obtained a ruling from the provincial governor that the family properties be returned, Xiang Bocheng be punished and the prefect also be punished for his earlier judgment. It was only then that the Huang surname's properties were retained.

Stories abound of tension between the Huang surname and their neighbours, not only of the Xiang surname, and the tension was aggravated by the prince's agents imposing taxes and fees. In 1531, the Huang surname fought the Ye surname who had sold them the "firewood land" adjacent to the Huang surname's lake foreshore. The dispute had arisen when someone of the Ye surname wanted to dig a channel leading from their properties into the lake, and the Huang surname sued him at the provincial court. Although the dispute was summarily settled, again, through the mediation of Xiang

72 Zhang Xiaoye

Bocheng, neither the Huangs nor the Yes seemed satisfied with the settlement. Fresh trouble brewed when the land grant was made to the prince of Jing, and then, upon his death, to the prince of Lu, for their agents set about demanding payment of tax and fee from holders of land. At Diaocha lake, charges were levied on Ye Jing, the Huang surname's enemy of a generation, one of the richest men in the area, who resisted the demand and was arrested on account of his having killed the prince's agent who was sent to collect his due. To settle his score with the Huang surname, Ye reported that the Huangs were accomplices in his resistance. Facing another round of arrest, Huang Pao, now more than 80 years of age, paid one of the prince's men 300 taels to spare his men. The Huangs were released from jail, but the Ye surname went bankrupt. Another round of false charges against the Huangs was made when, in 1627, the magistrate died of a stomach ailment while surveying land at Diaocha lake and people of the Zeng surname accused the Huang surname of having instigated his murder. There followed a very long, drawn-out investigation during which people of the Huang surname were jailed, but which ultimately cleared them of the accusation. The family estate remained intact.[12]

Litigation in the Qing dynasty

Into the Qing dynasty, the disputes reported in the Huang surname genealogy came to be more closely supported by documentation. Moreover, because the documents cited often refer to Ming dynasty claims, it becomes somewhat clearer why events in the Ming had come to be dramatized in the local memory.

In 1684, the Huang and Sun surnames litigated over their respective rights on the lakes. Sun Gongchen charged the Huang surname with having under-reported their tax holdings, and the provincial treasurer ordered the Hanchuan magistrate to survey the disputed territory. According the "Lake record", the magistrate counted the registered holdings of other surnames within the properties of the Huang surname and came to the conclusion that the Huang surname possessed "wheat land, reed swamp and lake water" that should be registered for tax. The Huang surname countersued, arguing that the Sun surname had under-reported their holdings as well, and that those holdings should likewise be measured and taxed. The provincial treasurer entrusted the prefect of Hanyang for a remeasurement, and the prefect came to the conclusion that "the land and lake water of the two surnames were conjoined within the same embankment, the properties of one party should be registered for tax as should the other, and at the same tax rates". The decision apparently satisfied neither party, so a third attempt to survey the land was arranged in 1687. The assistant prefect who conducted the measurement came to the conclusion that because the land and the lake were both within the embankment, unlike land reclaimed from the foreshore at river estuaries, they had always been contained in the record and that, therefore, there had not been under-reporting of tax holdings. The net result was an agreement between the Huang and the Sun surnames in 1690 demarcating the

The complexities of property rights at Diaocha lake   73

boundaries between their respective holdings and, significantly, the declaration of a moratorium on fishing in the lakes from the first day of the eighth month to the last day of the tenth month every year, and the allocation of the respective rights of each surname on the levying of charges on fishermen. This is the first statement in the Diaocha lake records on fishing rights. Their surreptitious mention at the end of what might seem to be a dispute over land rights begs the question as to what the disputes over land had all along been about.[13]

The word that was used for charges levied on the fishermen was *"ke"*, a word related to the fish tax. Whether or not the landholding families held such rights in the Ming, by the Qing dynasty they enjoyed the right of collecting the fish tax from fishing families. Yet, there obviously was also a dyke behind which land was being reclaimed for cultivation. From the Ming to the Qing, therefore, families such as the Huang surname, by amassing land on the edges of the lake and being held liable for the fish tax, were able also to collect dues from fishermen on the lake. The rights to the one were closely tied to the rights over the other, as two other cases of litigation were to make clear.[14]

The first case was recorded in a ruling by the Hanyang prefect on a stele in 1792 in response to litigation that went as far as the provincial governor. The case had been brought by the Huang surname against people of the Cao surname for collecting reed on the edges of the lake. The suit recalled that in 1705 or 1706, one Cao Changxian, whose surname does not appear to be prominent among the landowners on the edge of the lakes, had petitioned for a pronouncement to be recorded on a stele that while owners of the lake such as the Huang surname were entitled to collect fish and lotus in the lake, the poor had the right to forage reed, grass and water chestnut. Since that stele was set up, in 1714, someone charged that Cao Changxian was "gathering reed by force and citing the stele as authority for doing so", asking that Cao be arrested and punished and that other people than the Huang surname not be allowed to gather reed at the lake. Nevertheless, in 1783, the Huang surname brought suit again to charge that other people were gathering reed at their lake. After eight years, in 1791, the prefect ruled in their favour and ordered that the earlier stele recording common rights to water chestnut and reed in the lake be destroyed so that there might be no misunderstanding to the exclusive privileges of the Huang surname over their property. He recognized that the Huang surname had the right to charge reed collectors for collecting reed at the lake, and ruled out the counterclaim by the foragers that the Huangs were extorting. Significantly, he ended his pronouncement by declaring that his order be obeyed by people in military as well as civilian households. The reference to military households opens another angle on local society on the edges of the lakes.

Local officials had not always given attention to such land disputes. A pronouncement by the magistrate over another dispute in 1792, the same year that the Huang surname fought the Cao surname at his court, recounted that in 1674, the prefect of Hanyang, that is to say, his superior, had ordered the

74   *Zhang Xiaoye*

litigants to gather at the City God temple to come to an arrangement by arbitration.[15] The details now available of the eighteenth-century cases possibly indicate increasing sophistication at the magistrate's yamen on complex land disputes.

The military households at Hanyang prefecture in which Diaocha and nearby lakes were located were held responsible for delivering the annual grain transport to the imperial government in Beijing. They belonged to one of six garrisons in Hubei province. As in all garrisons, the military households provided hereditary service and were supported by land that was set aside for them. Military households were mentioned in 1512, when it was said that neighbouring people took advantage of homicide charges against people of the Huang surname and took over their holdings. In 1885, people of the Zhang surname who were registered as military households brought suit about the Huangs, citing documentation dating respectively from 1697 and 1716. The documents are complicated, as the wording of the Zhang surname's charges would indicate:

> Ancestor Dianyang in 1697 and 1716 had bought lake shares from the ancestor of Huang Shucong in three deeds so that they might be responsible for paying the fish tax in silver. The household was registered in the name of Zhang Guangshuang, and Zhang Shunlu even now is in possession of the document. The lake shares remained the property (*zhaoguan*) of the Huang surname, who paid a rent. When Huang Shucong took over the property, he did not pay any rent. Because they were relatives by marriage, it was not convenient to chase him for payment.[16]

According to Huang Shucong, one Zhang Xingqi had shown him three deeds from the Kangxi period (1662–1722) and offered to pay him money if he would acknowledge that the Zhang surname had a share in the lakes. According to another report from the Huang surname, the lakes had always belonged to the Huangs and had never been sold to other surnames, and that Zhang Xingqi had made his claim when a dyke collapsed and the lake flooded in 1885, the year the charges were made.

The magistrate's deliberations illustrate the complexities of litigation over lake rights. He accepted that the deeds produced were genuine, but he noted that old deeds were plentiful in his county and were often produced in support of claims, and so he believed that good evidence rested only on tax-payment records. He found it questionable that Zhang Xingqi could have lived on the shore of the lake and yet have rented his lake property to the Huang surname. Moreover, he thought it unreasonable that the property could have been rented to the same party for 200 years and not a single lease could be produced. He also discredited the tax receipts that were produced, because they did not agree with the county government's tax collection records. In favour of the Huang surname, he found that repeated litigation in previous years had upheld their rights to the lakes, and that in those litigations, the

The complexities of property rights at Diaocha lake 75

Zhang surname had not been named as any interested party. He ruled in the Huang surname's favour, but added that because the Zhang surname lived by the lake, they should have right of access for "drawing water from the lake for irrigation, for drinking purposes and for transport", and that the Huang surname should not obstruct such rights.[17]

The dispute might have rested there. However, the Zhang surname, being registered as a military household, brought suit to what would appear to be the provincial tax intendant, who set aside the county magistrate's ruling on technicalities of trial procedures. The magistrate reacted with an analysis of the military household's tax behaviour. It was common, he said, for military households to purchase land from civilian households. That was because, he said, the military garrisons that had charge of taxation from military households maintained strict records of their land holdings, and registering civilian properties on their registers was regarded as a potential tax break. It did not take long for his deliberations to be put to the test. In 1887, the Huangs and the Zhangs were once again at loggerheads at his court.

The dispute of 1887 was concerned with newly reclaimed land on the lake. The Zhang surname, military households, had registered 54 *shi* of land, paying 0.1 *shi* of grain in tax for each *shi* of land, making a total of 5.4 *shi* of grain per year. They produced a tattered volume said to have survived from the Qianlong era (1736–1795) that noted that tax rate. The magistrate, who had to assess the extent of the Zhang surname's holdings, found that those values implied that the Zhang surname's holdings reached right into the Huang surname's territory and, indeed, would have absorbed all the newly reclaimed land in the area. The amount that was paid in tax was not questioned; disagreement rested primarily on the tax rate that was charged by the garrison and the amount of land that the Zhang surname might hold. The garrison offered no help when asked, for they said land measures varied and so did the tax rate, and, in any case, the registration record had been destroyed during insurrection at the time of the Taiping Rebellion 30 years earlier and none was extant. The Huang surname, moreover, produced records to prove that the tax rate was not 0.1 *shi* of grain for each *shi* of land, but 0.5 *shi* of grain, and that the Zhang surname held considerably less land than they had claimed. The Zhang surname retorted that their holdings consisted of submerged land that was put to reed, that they had depended on gathering reed to provide for their military service and that the Huang surname had been motivated to take over their land when a dyke gave way and lake water drained out so that their reed land was left dry. The magistrate found that the deeds produced were insufficient to justify the claims of either party, and sought to bring about a compromise. He awarded the land within the dyke to the Huang surname, and land beyond the dyke to the Zhang surname, charging tax according to the rate imposed on other garrison land at 0.22 *shi* of grain per *shi* of land, with the provision that civilian land be divided according to land deeds that were produced. Moreover, he ruled that should the Zhang surname remain

76 *Zhang Xiaoye*

dissatisfied with the decision, they needed to produce clear tax records from either the grain tribute, land tax or garrison offices to make another plea. The Zhang surname were dissatisfied and sought justice from other government offices, including the tax intendant, the provincial judge and the circuit intendant, but the magistrate maintained his ruling. He threatened to conduct a land survey over civilian land and retain for the county schools all land that could not be supported by documentation. With that threat he had his way, for the case was then closed.[18]

Conclusions: what can be learnt from the litigation about lake society?

A peculiar feature of the records of Diaocha lake is that fishing people and fishing come into the picture only in passing. Reading the litigation records, one would not have thought that fishing and foraging on the water's edge could have been a major occupation, but the 1992 Hanchuan gazetteer easily puts paid to that view. In 1948, of the population of 402,531 people registered in Hanchuan county, 158,330 or 39.3 per cent were fishing people. Their most important fishing grounds were in the Diaocha lake. The gazetteer acknowledges the edges of the lake were occupied by different surname groups, of which the Huang surname occupied the largest territory. They had drawn up regulations that were employed on the fishing people and that gave themselves the better fishing grounds and ferry points. They demanded payment of three to five yuan for each boat from people of other surnames (the payment was known as *huke*, i.e., lake tax) for the right of fishing in the lake. Moreover, outside surnames were bound to the fish markets that the Huang surname had established: one Huang Nangui, for instance, ran eight fish agents and 20 measuring scales, each scale having control over 20 or more fishing boats. Harvesting of water lily seeds and tubers, and water chestnuts was also strictly controlled, each boat engaged in harvesting having to pay for a ticket for the privilege. Violation of these regulations was punishable at the Huang surname ancestral hall by imprisonment or beating, payment of a fine or even confiscation of the boat. By 1950, after the establishment of the People's Republic of China, the fishing people were mobilized by the Diaocha Lake Management Office to set up six sub-offices, and they turned against the protection networks run by strong men such as Huang Nangui. In that year, 5,910 households, or 27,876 people, were registered as fishing households, of which 558 households, or 2,610 people, were specialist fishing people. At the beginning of the commune movement in 1956, there were 12,408 fishing households, consisting of 55,835 people. An impression might also be had of the conditions in which the different sectors of the population lived in the gazetteer's description of housing in the county: in the towns, mostly houses of brick or wood; in the lake area, mostly sheds made of reed or sorghum, and fishing people might also live on broken boats; on the plains, mostly brick and tile, and some sheds; in the hills, mostly houses of mud walls, either tiled or thatched.[19]

The complexities of property rights at Diaocha lake 77

After a flood in 1866, the Huang surname genealogy notes that the Sun surname took away 96 large nets and four fishing boats that had belonged to the Huang surname and fishing households Hu, Li and Xiang. The Sun surname in the following year went with arms to the mudbanks at Dao Bend to claim them for cultivation and physically fought with the Huang surname. The dispute led to another round of litigation that, according to the Huang surname genealogy, the Huang surname won.[20] Moreover, a 1902 record of a bond that the county magistrate required of different parties in litigation confirms that the holders of tax responsibilities to the lake made charges on fishing people. In this instance, the Huang surname reported that they had charged 1,400 cash for each fishing boat that fished on their lake, and that they had guards to patrol the area. When the patrol intercepted some fishing people who had not paid, the fishing people claimed that they too had rights to the lake because in 1884 they had purchased a lake share from the Xiang surname for 36,000 cash. The magistrate distrusted the evidence produced by the fishing people and the bond he required reiterated the need for them to pay the Huang surname for the right of fishing on Diaocha.[21]

In the background, it is also useful to note that in the 276 years of the Ming, the gazetteer reported 12 famine years, in some of which cannibalism was practised. In the 220 years of the Qing up to 1873 when the gazetteer was compiled, it reported only eight years of famine. Hubei came under much economic development between the Ming and the Qing, bringing much land into cultivation. Reclaiming land from the lakes for rice cultivation as fishing continued to be practised was very much a part of that history.[22]

What the records of Hanchuan and the Huang surname document is that the Huang surname made increasing claims on the foreshore of Diaocha lake from the Ming into the Qing. Moreover, the more they held, the more the Huang surname claimed exclusive rights to the lake. The process by which the claims were made involved litigation at different levels of government, be they the county, the prefecture, the province or in one instance, so it was claimed, at the imperial court. It is unlikely that fishing families living in sheds and subject to periodic starvation would be willing litigants and so, not surprisingly, parties engaged in litigation were settlers on land who already derived an income from their holdings at the lake, and the magistrates' concern at times to ensure that access to foraging on the lake be kept open indicates that the presence of a lower stratum whose livelihood was closely related to the claims but who themselves were not party to court battles. The readiness by which disputes to claims might be settled at court fuelled the predominance of written documentation in support of them. Hence, even though it was time and again acknowledged that boundaries could not be demarcated on the lake, and time and again demonstrated in practice that they could barely be maintained on land, documentation produced – including the record of previous litigation – was designed to demonstrate the acquisition of rights at earlier times. Nineteenth-century disputants produced documents from the seventeenth century, late seventeenth-century disputes produced documents

78 *Zhang Xiaoye*

from the early years of that century, and so on. This chapter has by no means represented all the documentation that was included in the Huang surname genealogy and many more documents would have been held by the Huang as well as other surnames than were ever produced in court. Somewhere along the way to fishing people establishing claims on the land near the lakes where they lived – possibly beginning in the Ming dynasty at Diaocha lake because we have no earlier reference to documents – was the introduction of legal documents into this area and of their acceptance as evidence for claims to rights. The use of legal documents would have given an edge to those who had been schooled to read and write, and who might produce the personnel who could operate in the legal process at the government offices, namely the people who had settled on shore.

Exactly how the princely families made a difference to the local politics in the Ming remains somewhat an open question. If the Diaocha lake had come under the patronage of the prince of Chu in the fifteenth century, why did his family accept quietly the inroad made by the prince of Jing in the next? If the prince of Jing died within a few years of his investiture, how was the estate maintained until it was granted to the prince of Lu 20 years later? Who empowered the tax collectors who irritated the locals and their magistrates by their demands as soon as imperial land grants were awarded? Who were they? Were they total outsiders or were they related to some locals, such as the Xiang family that ingratiated itself to the prince of Chu in the earlier century? One has to wonder, in the days when princely patronage weighed more heavily than magisterial decisions, what purpose was served by the lake proprietors' holding of land deeds. According the Huang surname's "Lake record", they did, but many were produced as evidence not in the Ming, but in the Qing.

This chapter has been careful not to assume that a common surname necessarily implied a lineage structure among people of that surname. Yet, over time, it is clear that a lineage structure was adopted among some surname groups, of which the Huang surname would be an appropriate example. The "Lake record" includes 12 deeds, of which six are drawn up in the name of the Huang surname ancestral hall (Huang *gong ci*), four in the name of "the fourth ancestor" (Huang *sigong*) and two in personal names. The two deeds in personal names were dated respectively 1637 and 1808. The other deeds were dated in the second half of the nineteenth century.[23] There is the tendency, therefore, for the later deeds to be made in the name of the corporate trust. Just for an example of the working of the corporate trust, an 1878 agreement drawn up among 12 parties in the Huang lineage provides for the redemption of land that had been mortgaged in three "large shares" (*dagu*) to be allocated by drawing lots in the names of branch ancestors, specifying that the land was deemed to belong to the ancestor and not to be sold to persons of other surnames.[24] A share-holding structure in which shares could be subdivided and sold was clearly implied by the deeds dating from 1808. In a deed of that year, vendors of the He surname sold to people of the Huang surname "Xu, Zheng, Luo and Wu [that

The complexities of property rights at Diaocha lake   79

is to say, four surnames] rights by four-year rotation, consisting of 1/28th of the rights to the lake in the Xu year, 1/18th of the rights in the Zheng year, 1/20th of the rights in the Luo year, and 1/24th of the rights in the Wu year".[25] This very detailed description of the lake shares suggests that at some time in the past, while four surnames had been held for tax and each (like the Huang and the Xiang at Diaocha) had collected tax for their respective year, as time went on, the right for collection had been parcelled out by subdivision. That arrangement in itself does not argue that a lineage structure had existed, but combined with the presence of genealogies and ancestral trusts, the impression is given that the lineage conformed to a corporate structure as defined by the literati. For most of its history, the leaders of the lineage would not merely have served ritual functions, but were marked out for their ability to defend estates owned by people of the Huang surname, as individuals or corporations.

Notes

1 The author is grateful to members of the Huang and other surnames and Mr Li Xianchang and others of the Hanchuan City Political Consultative Conference for their guidance in exploring such local research documents.
2 Hua Zhong, *Jiang-Han huqun* (Lakes of the Jiang-Han plain), Wuhan: Hubei renmin, 1974.
3 "Hu'an", in *Diaocha Huangshi zongpu* (Genealogy of the Huang surname at Diaocha), no date, j. 43, collected by the author in Manziying village, Taiping township, Zaoyang county, Hubei province. A preamble attached to the genealogy explains that people of the Huang surname who held the genealogy had branched off from Diaocha in 1697.
4 Sitian Haoming (Terada Hiroaki), *Quanli yu yuanyi* (Power and the suppression of injustice), Beijing: Qinghua daxue chubanshe, 2012, pp. 83–88, 218.
5 "Hu'an", p. 41a.
6 *Xiangshi zongpu* (Genealogy of the Xiang surname), 1990, pp. 2a–3a.
7 "Zhangshi zongpu xu" (Preface to the Zhang surname genealogy), in *Zhangshi jiashi* (A history of the Zhang family), no publisher, 2001, no pagination, held in the Hanchuan County Museum.
8 Interview conducted in July 2004.
9 "Hu'an", p. 41a.
10 Preamble to the *Diaocha Huangshi zongpu*, "Hu'an", pp. 38a–39a recording an agreement made in 1884 by people of the Huang surname to restructure "old shares" (*laofen*) into "new shares" (*xinfen*), and interviews conducted in July 2004.
11 Wang Yuquan, *Laiwu ji* (The writings of Wang Yuquan), Beijing: Zhonghua, 1983, pp. 136, 158 and 173–174; *Hanchuan xianzhi* (Gazetteer of Hanchuan county), 1873, 20/40a–42a, 46a–49a, 22/17b–18b, 22/23a–24a.
12 Preface dated 1640 in "Hu'an", pp. 1–2, is the principal source for these events. The disaster to the Huang surname brought by their dispute with Ye Jing is also recorded with much drama in the "Xueyuan lu" (An account of the revocation of false charges). A contemporary magistrate, Sun Guangzuo, also left an account of the events, stripped off the drama, in *Hanchuan xianzhi*, 1873, 22/23a–24a. The "Xueyuan lu" may be found at www.ihuang.org/a6-2-0059.htm (accessed 27 May 2013).
13 "Hu'an", pp. 4a–5a.

80 *Zhang Xiaoye*

14 The eulogy written by a contemporary to celebrate the contribution of magistrate Chang Yinghui, who served Hanchuan county in the Jiajing period (1522–1566) refers to fish tax being registered on the "crimson registers" (*chili*) at the land under demand for tax by Prince Jing. This is clear evidence that the fish tax accrued in the area from at least the sixteenth century. For the eulogy, see *Hanchuan xianzhi*, 1873, 20/46b.
15 "Hu'an", pp. 2b–3a.
16 "Hu'an", p. 16a.
17 "Hu'an", pp. 16a–17a.
18 "Hu'an", pp. 17b–27a.
19 *Hanchuan xianzhi*, Beijing: Zhongguo chengshi chubanshe, 1992, pp. 176 and 662–663.
20 "Hu'an", p. 11a.
21 "Hu'an", pp. 36b–46b.
22 *Hanchuan xianzhi*, 1873, 14/4a–18a; Evelyn Sakakida Rawski, *Agricultural Change and the Peasant Economy of South China*, Cambridge, MA: Harvard University Press, 1972.
23 "Hu'an", pp. 28b–40b.
24 "Hu'an", p. 28b.
25 "Hu'an", p. 35a.

Part II

As encountered in field research

5 Gods adrift: religious ritual and local society on Naozhou island[1]

He Xi

Naozhou is a small island off the coast of Zhanjiang city in Guangdong province. It is not known for any importance in the broad sweep of Chinese history, except for a likely mention as a stop-off point for the ill-fated Song imperial court in exile as it sought escape from the Mongols in the thirteenth century. It is occupied by a handful of villages and a community – it is not clear if "village" is the appropriate word as will be explained below – of boat people referred to as "*danjia*". The villagers, that is to say, the people who live on land and who are not "*danjia*", also take to the sea. I came across the island as I became interested in the fishing communities in the southwestern parts of Guangdong, and Naozhou seemed an appropriate designation for a study of the interaction between settlers on land and settlers on boats. I started thinking that there must have been a drawn-out process whereby the boat people steadily moved ashore. No doubt, such a process marks Naozhou's history, but it was more difficult to pin down than I had originally thought, and the difficulty, as I found out, had to do with the use of labels.

The recorded history

There simply is not a great deal about Naozhou in the standard histories. Administratively, in the Qing dynasty, it came under Wuchuan county in Gaozhu prefecture. It came in for a mention in 1684 in a report by the minister of works, Du Zhen, in the aftermath of the coastal evacuation; that is to say, the evacuation of the entire Guangdong coast that was mounted as a measure to blockade Zheng Chenggong's operations on Taiwan.[2] The 1822 Guangdong provincial gazetteer says that the island could house more than 1,000 families, and that, being rocky, most of its coastline did not provide anchorages for boats. The only anchorage, it says, lay somewhere between the rocky west and northwest, and villages coagulated there. Linked to military outposts in their surroundings, that corner was like a "city" (*cheng*), meaning more that it was fortified by the existence of a wall than its being characterized by very much trade.[3]

Naozhou was fortified because it was known as a haven for pirates. Troops were posted there from 1704. By 1716, there were five batteries on the island.

84   *He Xi*

By 1730, a police office was set up. That might not have been for the first time, for the records refer to an earlier police office from the sixteenth century that left no trace by the eighteenth.[4]

The Northern Anchorage and the Southern Anchorage

The anchorage that the 1822 Guangdong provincial gazetteer refers to is the Southern Anchorage (Nangang). That was where the military and police offices were located, at a place that today is known as Song Emperor's Village. In the 1850s, a school was built there adjacent to the military office.

Today, the Southern Anchorage has become the town of Danshui, where the Jinqian (literally, "in front of the ferry crossing") Tianhou temple still faces the sea. Local people claim that the temple was built in 1506. A present-day display board on the wall there claims that the temple holds a signboard dated 1575 but that was nowhere in view on my visits. In a corner, however, may be found an iron bell bearing a 1764 date, and an iron incense burner of 1825. Also on display is an honorific board dated 1880. The inscription on the bell reads:

> Fishing boat headman [*guzhang*] Wu and fishing-boat men [*guding*] recruited under him: Huang Fushang, Guo Jianxian, Huang Guozhen, He Qishang, Lin Huanju, Shi Guangfu, together donate this bell of 120 catties to be deposited at the Temple of the Heavenly Goddess [that is, Tianhou] at Naozhou. In this year Qianlong 29 [1764] on a certain day. Made in the Wenming Furnace.[5]

The inscription provides the clearest statement yet on the organization of fishing people on Naozhou in the eighteenth century: the fishing men were regarded administratively as having been recruited under headmen. The Wenming Furnace was located in Foshan, well-known for its iron bells that are found all over Guangdong and even beyond. The 1825 incense burner bears the name Jinqian Tianhou temple, by which the temple is still known. The 1880 board was donated by the police chief of Naozhou. The three objects show that both the fishing people and their officials worshipped at the temple.

The Southern Anchorage is still the more important anchorage on Naozhou today, but from the end of the Qing dynasty until 1970, it was rivalled by the Northern Anchorage (Beigang). People on Naozhou still remember that the fishing boats moored at the Northern Anchorage and the Zhentian temple there still holds a stele of 1828 entitled "Donations for the opening of the Northern Anchorage" that records its history. It says:

> Naozhou is an isolated island. The seas surround all four sides. In order to suppress bandits and to protect the peace, the force of military boats

Gods adrift: religious ritual and local society on Naozhou island 85

is needed. Moreover, the waterway here goes up to Chaozhou and Fujian in the north, and to Leizhou and Qiongzhou (Hainan) to the south. Fishermen going after their catches often have to anchor here.

However, there is no suitable port in Naozhou for boat anchorages. For that reason, military, commercial and fishing boats suffer annually from the typhoon. I have been appointed commander here for more than ten years. I know about this terrain. I consider that boats may find shelter only at the Northern Anchorage. However, there are sharp rocks at the entrance to the shelter, and boats may only enter when the tide is high. So I consulted my colleagues and we donated money to clear the rocks. The work took a month, and now boats can enter and leave conveniently and moor there. When the weather is not favourable, they now have shelter. Moreover, military boats in operation can also retreat into the anchorage when there is typhoon, and continue to protect commercial and fishing boats in accordance with imperial regulations. The project, therefore, serves two purposes. It serves the state and the people.[6]

The stele records that the donors included the commander of the Naozhou naval battalion, a company commander, three squad leaders, two county students and the headman of the fishing people, known as the manager of the fishing sheds (*gupeng zongli*). Interestingly, under the name of the manager of the fishing sheds are recorded names written in small-size characters that are now blurred but still partly visible, so that it may be seen that the manager actually had under his charge various fishing people (indicated by the word "*gu*" attached to their names). Aside from this stele bearing an account of the establishment of the anchorage, there is also another stele that is now quite blurred but on which the characters "*gaoshi bei*" (notice stele) and titles of various military officials are still quite visible. The two steles show that there was around the area a community made up of military men manning war junks and fishing people.

Gangtou (Port Head) village adjacent to the Northern Anchorage became a prosperous market. As late as the 1950s, located there were a ration station (food was rationed by then), a post office, a cooperative store, a clinic and a credit cooperative. However, the opening of the Northern Anchorage did not alter the strategic importance of the Southern Anchorage.[7]

Reference to the 1892 Wuchuan county gazetteer shows that in 1704 the Naozhou garrison was stationed in both the Northern Anchorage and the Southern Anchorage.[8] Those became the locations at which temples were built. The local people – that is to say, fishing people, including their headmen – collaborated in donating to them. The Northern Anchorage became the typhoon shelter, but because it was opened late, the government offices and the school had been located in the south. Although the fishing people's headman donated to the Northern Anchorage, all oral reports were adamant that the fishing people's sheds were always located in the south. From about

86 *He Xi*

1973, the Southern Anchorage was expanded to allow motorized boats to anchor, and the Northern Anchorage declined after that. As an anchorage, it is now largely defunct, but local people remember very clearly its replacement by the Southern Anchorage in the 1970s.

The land people

Nowadays, 53,000 people live on the 21 square miles of Naozhou island, and only in Hongwei district (*shequ*) are there boat people (*shuishang ren*). Hongwei is the only community known as a district, the other communities, aside from Danshui, are known as villages (*cun*). Hongwei is said to be inhabited by people from the outside, mostly from Wuchuan. Those people speak the Wuchuan dialect, and the place was, at one time, known as Wuchuan street.

In 1683, when the coast was inspected after the coastal evacuation by Du Zhen, minister of works, he noted that the villages on Naozhou, known as Upper and Lower North Village, Middle Village and South Village had not yet recovered from the evacuation. Today, those villages are still extant, and local people know them as the oldest villages on the island.[9] In 1810, Governor General Bailing reported that 2,700 households inhabited the island.[10] The 1892 Wuchuan gazetteer includes a map that shows that names such as Upper and Lower North Village really stood for village clusters, and villages were found not only at those locations but also scattered along the coast.[11]

Governor Bailing's population estimate was possibly derived from *baojia* registration; that is to say, registration of households with the purpose of establishing collective responsibility for criminal offences and local policing. A stele dated 1869 bearing an inscription celebrating the rebuilding of the Xianglong Academy on the island was signed off by people who referred to themselves as the headmen of the ten *jia* (*jia* was a *baojia* unit consisting of ten households).[12] An undated stele on the site where the school had been located refers to "holders of office of the ten *jia*" who were in charge of land belonging to the school, and includes the rather ominous line, "if [income] was inadequate, the *jia* would make up the shortfall by donation".[13] The two stele inscriptions make it quite clear that from the second half of the nineteenth century, at least, *baojia* had been organized among the villagers.

Where *baojia* had been organized, the *baojia* headmen served as intermediaries between county government and the villages, and this feature of the headmen's duties is borne out in the 1869 inscription. Documentation is so threadbare on this wayward island that it is worth translating the text in full:

> At the end of [the Song dynasty], pursued by Yuan troops, ministers Lu and Zhang came to Guangdong by sea, and the venerable Wen Xin stationed his troops at Jiangpu for defence. Ministers Lu and Zhang eventually moved to Duanzhou (Zhaoqing) and they died. Barely a year later, emperor Bing ascended the throne and made Naozhou a county … All institutions were set up by Ministers Lu and Zhang. Minister Lu

Gods adrift: religious ritual and local society on Naozhou island 87

recited daily from the books and, to provide for lecturing here, built the academy to teach the [unsettled] people. Minister Lu put his mind on the literary tradition, because he believed ... In the early years of the Xianfeng reign [1851–1861], Dou Xi, gentryman of Naozhou, appealed for donations, and moved [the school] to the vicinity of the government office ... [The building eventually collapsed] and so the elders petitioned the police chief, the venerable Wang. The magistrate, His Excellency Mo, ordered its rebuilding. The scholars and the common people all enthusiastically donated. The building complex included a vegetarian room, to its left, the Hall of the Three Loyal Ministers, and to its right, the Hall for the Support of Examination Candidates. The layout of the complex was similar to that of the Jiajing period [of the Ming dynasty, that is 1522–1566]. It became possible to teach students and to hire teachers of ability, and to remember that the school had started from the loyalty of Minister Lu from the Song dynasty. For the minister's scholarship and purity of mind, the school deserves to be known for having originated from a distinguished scholar. In its promotion of scholarship, our imperial state has not forsaken this distant corner to advance local people to officialdom ... Among the people in charge of the appeal for donations for this project were Chen Kuiyuan, etc.[14]

The preamble refers to the last years of the Song dynasty, when the boy emperor Bing, escorted by his trusted ministers, escaped to south China, hotly pursued by the Mongols. It is well-documented that he reached Guangdong and died at sea with his ministers but, although historians have made the claim that he might have reached Naozhou, or even set up court there, the records of his exact whereabouts are less than certain. Nevertheless, legends about the brief presence of the Song emperor abound in villages on the coast in this part of Guangdong and, obviously, they were known on Naozhou in the nineteenth century as this 1869 inscription makes clear.

The stele highlights three sets of events. First, the local people were interested in tracing a historical origin that linked the school to the loyalty expressed by officials to the dying Song dynasty. Second, they established the school with the approval of the Naozhou police chief and the county magistrate and, third, a selected few among the island's population were involved in the effort, among whom was Dou Xi, gentryman, who had led the previous donation campaign just a decade earlier. Nothing is known about Dou Xi, but the Dou surname is the most prominent on the island to this day (more on that below). He was no longer represented in the 1869 rebuilding effort, but three of the ten headmen of the *baojia* who were listed on the stele bore his surname. The names of the *baojia* headmen are preceded by three other names on the stele, and they possibly stood for holders of junior degrees.

Yet another stele, dated in the 1880s, shows an everyday occurrence that involved the government. Someone had complained to the county

88 *He Xi*

magistrate that visitors to Naozhou were not allowed to bring their own sedan-chairs (and carriers) but were required to hire the service from a sedan-chair headman on the island. The magistrate ordered that the practice be banned. Holders of junior degree and the headmen of the ten *jia*, including one of the Dou surname, reported that, indeed, sedan-chair service on the island had been controlled by a sedan-chair headman and that his charges had been steadily increasing. The magistrate, thereupon, informed the officer of the Naozhou garrison that a notice should be issued to ban the extortion exercised by the sedan-chair headman so that porterage might be maintained at a fair rate. What he did not say, but might have been implied in the record, was that the sedan-chair monopoly was exercised by none other than the island military, hence the villagers' support for his ruling.[15]

Nobody on the island seems to remember the ten *jia* anymore. When interviewed, the villagers refer frequently to "one Tan, two Liangs and three Dous" as the major surnames on the island, the same surnames that appear on the steles under the headmen of the ten *jia*. Of the three surnames, only the Dou surname possesses a written genealogy. When asked, the villagers indicated that it had never been the custom on the island to maintain written genealogies.

Mr Dou, whom I met on the island, is in charge of the management of the Tianhou temple at Jinqian. He is highly respected on the island, and has kept a Dou surname genealogy that is divided into two parts. One part records the origin of the surname and famous people bearing it in historical times. It traces the origin of the lineage to the Yellow Emperor of the earliest historical times, and records descent down to the 115th generation. All names in this section are linked by a single line of descent and there are many gaps, as, for example, the names from the third to the 68th generations. In this broken record, Naozhou is noted only in a few words:

> Following [a previous line of descent] are the descendants of ancestor Zhengzong of the first branch, who also escaped to settle on Naozhou [at the time of the Ming-Qing transition]. That was more than three hundred years ago. They include about 5,000 people. Because, at that place, ideas of the lineage are weak, up to today, genealogies are not compiled and there is no historical record. It is only known that historical records are extant recording that in 1840, 15th-generation ancestor General Zhenbiao was born there.[16]

Obviously, the Dou surname of Naozhou were unable to produce a written genealogy to support the more comprehensive effort of their namesakes elsewhere.

Dou Zhenbiao, mentioned in that passage, was a native of Nagan village on the island. He became admiral of the Guangdong provincial navy in 1840 and later served in Fujian. He fought in the Opium War. He died in 1850 while in post. In 1851, his body was returned to Naozhou and was buried at Tangfang village near the Northern Anchorage. His grave is still extant. There is also a commemorative archway that can be seen on the Old Street in front of the government offices at Songwang village that records an award given to him by the Xianfeng emperor in 1851.

The genealogy records that in 1927, people of the Dou surname at a place known as Dazhai in Wuchuan county added to General Zhenbiao's memorial hall and turned it into the Dou surname collective ancestral hall (*da zongci*). The genealogy that we were shown was compiled by the Dou surname people of Wuchuan. The genealogy would have allowed the Wuchuan people to consider that the general was one of them, and only for that reason was a mention made of the Dou surname on Naozhou.

Mr Dou recalled that settlement at Naozhou had begun much before the Qing dynasty. According to him, people of the Dou surname had come to Naozhou to protect the young Song dynasty emperor, Bing, when he was exiled to the island and pursued by the Mongols. The Dou surname would have settled from the twelfth century, according to this legend.[17]

Plate 5.1 A domestic altar on Naozhou (credit: He Xi).

90   *He Xi*

Although there are no ancestral halls on the island, there is an altar in every home. Tablets are placed on the altars to house two types of spirits: family gods (*jiashen*) and other gods (referred to simply as "gods", *shen*). As the villagers put it, when people "depart", they become family gods. They say that for the first three years after death, the name of the deceased is recorded on a tablet bearing only that name. After three years, the name is included on the board that records the names of all ancestors. It is also a rule that the names of married people are entered into the family tablet only as couples, and so it is necessary to wait until the deceased's spouse has also died before the names of husband and wife can be entered. Ancestors whose names have been forgotten can be entered collectively as "all the family gods of this household, old and young". Names have to be entered in the correct format. In the Tan surname's house in South Village, the family tablet includes four male and two female ancestors of unknown generations. Most families would seem to have eight to ten names on the tablet and their exact relations to the family (that is to say, who might be whose father or son) is often not known to the living. Gods other than family gods are also represented on tablets, but their names vary from family to family.

On my visits to Naozhou, I checked Mr Dou's description with the daoist priest, Mr Tan, who services 80 per cent of the temple sacrifices on the island. He was certain that family gods were represented on wooden tablets and not as human figurines, as would be found in some fishing families elsewhere.

The circulation of gods

A very peculiar custom in Naozhou is the circulation of the gods. In villages on the mainland, temple gods stay most of the time in their temples, even though at the festivals they may be housed temporarily in a matshed outside and occasionally are paraded in the villages. In contrast to temple gods, households would have their own domestic altars on which are deposited gods to whom the households pay regular sacrifice. On Naozhou island, many deities to which the villagers offer sacrifices are not housed in temples but are taken home. There are also deities that are not associated with any temple but are circulated by rota among groups of people. The person who knows most about the locations of the deities is Mr Tan, the daoist, who keeps a note of the names of all of them and who denotes each as military lord (*junzhu*), territorial lord (*jingzhu*), association lord (*huizhu*), lord of the port (*buzhu*) or lords of fortune (*fuzhu*). There are 47 such deities, 19 of which are associated with temples and 28 are not. The term "military lord" is reserved for the Tianhou. The other titles suggest that the figures of some deities circulate among villages, while others among people who have formed themselves into an association. Whether the "military" reference had anything to do with the garrisons is anybody's guess, neither Mr Tan nor the villagers can provide any explanation.

Gods adrift: religious ritual and local society on Naozhou island 91

Plate 5.2 Praying to a circulated god's statue at a domestic altar (credit: He Xi).

On my visits to Naozhou, I have seen domestic altars in private houses on which temple gods are placed, altars in temples from where they have been taken (or, as the villagers say, "invited") and even come across villagers in the act of taking the gods out or returning them. The point that needs be made is that the practice of taking gods out and returning them is very common, so common indeed that there are trolley-cars specially fitted out for transporting their statues. The movable statuettes are about two-foot tall, and they are housed in ornate movable altars.

Some examples from my visits to Naozhou will fill out the picture of gods in circulation.[18] The Northern Anchorage now comes under a district committee and is made up of 13 villages. The villagers sacrifice to Great Marshal Wu Three-Seven and the Great King, who are housed in two separate temples in Gangtou and the nearby village Huangwu. The Great King is also known as the Propitious Diaomeng Lord, a term that suggests the god might be engaged in exorcistic activities. The two villages are separated by the inlet at the anchorage at which ships used to moor. Both temples face the inlet. According to local people, Wu Three-Seven's statue was carved from a piece

Plate 5.3 Ferrying the god's statue on motorbike on Naozhou island (credit: He Xi).

of wood that was washed up to the spot where the temple is now located. The villagers discovered the log on the seventh day of the third month, hence his name "Three-Seven" and his festival is now held on that day every year. The Great King, according to villagers, may be identified with the Song dynasty minister Lu Xiufu (that is, Minister Lu on the 1869 inscription cited above), who met his end in this area along with the child emperor Bing. His true identity had been intentionally kept secret, they believe, for reasons that seem equally mysterious.

At Huangwu, not only did I meet a villager who was returning the god to the temple, but I also saw on the wall at the temple door many slips of red paper indicating the dates when villagers intended to take him home. On some of those slips it was written his presence was needed because a new house had been built, and on others simply because his blessing was needed. There were also villagers who promised an opera performance in return for his largesse. His birthday is celebrated for eight days starting from the fifth day of the fifth month, the day on which dragon boat races are held in many parts of south China. Villagers also recalled that in the days when boats moored regularly at the Northern Anchorage, the boat people of Hongwei held dragon boat races there every year. With the departure of the Hongwei people, the races had stopped.

Gods adrift: religious ritual and local society on Naozhou island 93

At another village, Menggang, I also came across people returning the gods to the temple. The Shuixian temple there housed General White Horse, the old and new statues of Tan Number Five and the Tianhou goddess. When I arrived at the temple, only Tianhou remained on the altar, the others having been invited out. However, while I was still at the temple, some women brought them back. When asked why they had invited the gods out, they said they had had a new boat built and because these were gods who were "in charge" of their district, they invited them so that they might join in the celebration (literally, they said, "*chijiu*", meaning "eating and drinking wine"). They did not know who Tan Number Five was, but they knew that the gods at this temple were "in charge" of their village for the "great god" (*dashen*) resided at Nakun village. Gods were obviously graded. As the daoist Mr Tan explained to me later, when the villagers said "in charge", they meant that their village was a "territory" (*jing*), that is to say, an area that came under the protection of the gods of a temple.[19]

The gods at Gangtou, Huangwu and Menggang were normally housed in temples but were invited out when needed, but there were other gods who normally resided in the families of their worshippers and were only brought to temples during festivals. Also in Menggang is the Pingtian temple, which houses a god known by the title of "the territorial Lord Shangguo Pingtian", whom villagers said was really the loyal Song minister Wen Tianxiang (that is, the venerable Wen Xin cited in the 1869 inscription). Lord Shangguo Pingtian normally sits on an altar in the house of a villager who enjoys the privilege of housing him by rotation. Therefore, in his temple is found only his wooden spirit tablet wrapped in red cloth. He returns to the temple only during his festival. At the doorway of the temple are pasted many red slips of paper booking dates for inviting him out. The day I visited, the statue of the god was deposited in the house of one of the four managers of the temple (*yuanshou*) for the year. The family was now living in a new house, but the altar for the god was set up in the old house, outside which were found also many red slips inviting the god's presence.

Gods who were not associated with any temple could be taken care of by their worshippers through a rota. In the Southern Anchorage, the Association Lord Guangzhao Taishan Kanghuang great emperor was rotated every month on the 16th day of the month to one of his 12 managers' house. In a leap year, the rota would consist of 13 people. Receiving him into the house was a ritual affair and a ceremony was conducted by a daoist for the purpose. Again, his altar was set up in the old house. From that altar, he was invited by nearby villagers to their houses. Another popular deity at the Southern Anchorage is the Association Lord Old Minister Zhengyi Spiritual Officer of Great Magnitude Ma. On the day I visited, he was resident in a villager's house in Xianbao village but had been invited by another villager from Dedou village. The Dedou villager had invited not only him, but also two Mazu (Tianhou) figures, Guangzhao, Huaguang, the earth god and his

94 *He Xi*

wife. The statuettes of many gods circulate in any one area. In the Southern Anchorage, there are some 30 of them. There is no permanent temple in the area. When there is a celebration, villagers set up a matshed as the gods' temporary abode.

Many temples that one now sees on Naozhou have been built very recently. Set in the historical context, there were few temples on the island in the past. In the words of Mr Dou, the manager of the Jinqian temple, the three statues of the Mazu at the temple there "sit permanently and cannot be moved, while other gods move around". In other words, only the three statues of the Mazu at Jinqian are permanently housed in the temple, all other gods on the island circulate. Every year in the third month, on the occasion of the Mazu festival, the Jinqian Tianhou temple holds the festival known as the Embankment in the Third Month (*sanyue po*) in which some circulatory gods are also brought to the temple to partake in sacrifice. Again, no one knows why the festival is called what it is, but *prima facie*, the name suggests an occasion when boat people might come onto the embankment from their boats and take part in a celebration at a temple on shore. The land people consider their biggest festivals to be the annual celebrations of Marshal Kang (Kang *yuanshuai*) and Marshal Che (Che *yuanshuai*) in the third and seventh months, and the parade of all gods in the first month, and the difference in emphasis between them and the Jinqian Tianhou temple adds to the impression that the annual celebrations catered to different clienteles.

Marshal Kang and Marshal Che are represented by four circulating statuettes, two of each, and are all known as "association lords". They are not housed in any temple. The villages on the entire island are divided into six equal teams to cater to their sacrifice. Each team is responsible for housing them for one year. During the parade of the first month, which starts from the spot where the government office used to be located, Marshal Kang and Marshal Che lead the way, while the other gods draw lots to gain their respective positions in the parade. For four days starting on the 25th day of the third month, the two gods have to "perform their filial duty to their parents" (*huan fumu xiao*), in a ceremony dedicated to the Eastern Peak Equal-to-Heaven Benevolent Sage the Great Emperor of Longevity. The Great Emperor of the Eastern Peak is not a god on the island, and Mr Tan, the daoist, is the only person on the island now who knows how to perform the ceremony, although he also fails to provide a story that explains why Kang and Che's relationship to Eastern Peak might be described in terms of filial piety. He sang me a few lines from his prayer for the occasion:

> This morning I pay respect to the Lord of the Eastern Peak, to honour the pledge that was made many years ago. My mother suffered for the ten months she bore me, and worked hard for the three years she raised me. The debt I owe them is beyond what I can repay, and I pray and thank heaven's blessing. [I ask that] surviving parents may add to their fortune and longevity, and parents deceased may enter reincarnation early.[20]

Gods adrift: religious ritual and local society on Naozhou island 95

Mr Tan's books had been passed on to him by his uncle, most of them hand-copied during the Republican period. He said the ceremony must be conducted within a camp surrounded by 14 flags. All the people who "enter the camp" must eat only vegetarian food. The ceremony must be held in the open, rain or shine. He emphasizes that the gods are not to be brought into the camp. The ceremony is meant to indicate sorrow, and so the four godly statuettes carry with them a pot of paper flowers on the parade. No villager takes the flowers home, they are burnt when the ceremony is over. The content of the lines he sang me, the strict enforcement of vegetarian food and the castigation of the gods from the ceremony suggest that it might have had a Buddhist origin. At the conclusion of the ceremony, the incoming team takes over from the incumbent team to serve the gods for the coming year.

On the third day of the seventh month, the ceremony is conducted in a totally different way. This is the occasion of the two gods' festival. A matshed temple is set up in Yanlou village in which the four statuettes sit on an altar. There is also a pot of paper flowers, now divided into red and white colours. Villages pluck these paper flowers to take home as they pray for offspring. A white flower denotes the birth of a son and a red one, a daughter. The flower is taken home and put on the domestic altar. If a child is born to the family during the year, the family repays the gods by the presentation of a pot of paper flowers in the coming year.

A very special part of the ceremony in the festival of the seventh month is that at the conclusion of the celebration at Yanlou village, the gods are taken by boat to the mainland at Xuwen county. Villagers say that is because people from Naozhou who have a part in the ceremony have migrated to the mainland, and so the gods go with them. This aspect of the festival is the strongest indication yet that the circulation of the gods on Naozhou has been a part of the regular custom. They are not necessarily housed at a temple, but they are tied to the communities of their worshippers, even if the worshippers move around.

Many villagers on Naozhou have boats and fish. Fishnets are everywhere. Yet, when asked, aside from the people of Hongwei, no one would accept that they had lived on boats. It should perhaps be left an anomaly that, on Naozhou, except for Danshui, local religion has focused on gods who are not pegged to a marker on the ground, such as a temple or a shrine, but are moved from house to house within a community. One might have thought that would have been a feature that would suit a floating population. That, however, can be better understood after the history of Hongwei has been described.

From stilt sheds to production brigade[21]

The houses of Hongwei now lie along a road by the coast within easy walking distance from Jinqian and the crossroad where there used to be a fishery cooperative. They are houses of several floors, complete with shops on the ground floor. They now have even two temples in their midst. The Hongwei

96   *He Xi*

people agree that until the 1990s, there were still sheds along what is now the street, and that for a long time, they lived in those sheds. The sheds are referred to as "*gupeng*", "*gu*" being the name given to the very small rowing boats they used. Characteristic of the *gupeng* is that they were built on stilts over the foreshore, so that for most of the time, water came all the way up to the stilts. They recall:

> People who lived around here worked at sea. They came from the "upper four counties" [a term commonly used to denote the several counties near Guangzhou] and that is why the people here speak *baihua* [Cantonese]. They drifted and lived in sheds. They were known as Danjia. Hongwei used to be a barren hillside and that was why they settled there.

The reference to the "upper four counties" is interesting. The term is often used in contrast to the "lower four counties", which would have included Leizhou and Zhanjiang, just across the bay from Naozhou. Cantonese-speaking Guangzhou has always been the homeland for the Danjia people coming out of the Pearl river delta.

They also remember that living in sheds was closely related to their status. They were known as "people of little sheds" (*pengzailao*) or, even more rudely, "pigs of the little sheds" (*pengzaizhu*).

Another difference between the land and boat people had to do with their fishing. The land people consider themselves "half peasant and half fishing people" (*bannong banyu*) and were classed as "peasant" during the land reform in the 1950s. The boat people were "pure fishing people" (*chun yumin*) and were classed as "fishing people" in the land reform. A land villager explained to me: "They work on big boats, we have only small boats." The Hongwei party secretary, whose father had also been Hongwei party secretary, said to me emphatically: "Hongwei is made up of pure deep-sea fishing people. People in other villages, including Jinqian, are not engaged in deep-sea fish-ing." The catches from deep sea were salted before they were sold. Only fish caught near the foreshore would have been sold fresh. By the 1950s, all the catches were sold to the fishery stations.

In interviews with local people, "big boats" were associated with "deep-sea fishing". The two modes of operation also related to ownership and employ-ment. The land people owned their small boats. They were operated by the family, who often also had some land on shore, which is why they were also "half peasant". People who worked on "big boats" were hired hands. Some of the boats might be owned by local people, but many by people outside Naozhou.

At Hongwei, Mr Wu, 72 *sui* (71 years of age), spoke to me at length about his experience working on a "big boat". His father had owned a boat, but it was destroyed in a typhoon. That was in Dianbai county on the mainland, where he was born. When he was three *sui* of age (two years old), he was sold to Naozhou. He went to school on Naozhou. In 1952, at age 12 *sui*, he took

Gods adrift: religious ritual and local society on Naozhou island 97

to sea. He learnt to handle a sailing boat, which was owned by somebody else. He fished off the Guangdong coast, from Shanwei beyond Guangzhou to Sanya on Hainan. Their boat went to the fishing grounds in the fishing season and stayed out for eight to ten days at a stretch. It had a crew of about 13 to 14 people, including four women who were the owner's relatives. He remembered that land reform came in 1953 or 1954, and fishery reform came at the same time. They were assigned their class status at the time separately as fishing people who owned boats, fishing people who did not own boats, fish dealers (*yulan*) and fishing workers. He was given the status of fishing worker. That, according to Mr Wu, was a good class status.

Mr Wu married in the 1960s. He lived in the sheds at the time. A shed-house included a sitting room and two bedrooms. There was electricity by then, but each family was allowed only a single lightbulb, which had to be switched off by 11.30pm. There was no running water and so they took water from the well. His wife stayed in the shed-house while he went out to work, and he spent much of his time on the boat. When their children were born, they were born in the shed-house. He was nostalgic about shed living. He lived in a shed with his family whenever he came back from sea. They hired someone to build the shed, but no rent had to be paid. It was clean and comfortable and the air was always fresh. The toilet was only a floorboard away and everything was easily washed away by the sea. In those days, people called the area the "fishing sheds"; the name Hongwei came later.

The changeover to deep-sea fishing came largely in the 1970s. Mr Wu recalled that wooden boats used to be built in Yangjiang and Beihai on the mainland. After the fishing brigade was established, the brigade started machine shops and dockyards. When ships were built, people had to sacrifice to Wu Three-Seven "at the Great King Temple in the Northern Anchorage".[22] Mr Wu said the Northern Anchorage used to be the largest fishing port in the whole of the Leizhou peninsular. The sailing boats and Danjia boats were all moored there. There were thousands of them, including boats that had come from other fishing ports such as Caotan and Jianghong in Guangxi province. At the time, the Southern Anchorage was very shallow. But all that changed in 1973, when under the provincial government's directive, the Southern Anchorage was dredged and turned into a port. It then took over from the Northern Anchorage.

Asked about gods, he said ship-owners had figures of gods on their ships, in the form of little statuettes. The Shuixian (water fairy) temple at Hongwei had been there for a long time. Some people said the god was Qu Yuan.[23] In the old days, when people died, they were buried on shore. No money was paid for that, they were just buried wherever it was convenient. At home, people sacrificed to ancestors. The ancestors' names were recorded on a tablet, at the back of which was a record of when they were born or died. Mr Wu could name his forebear up to his great grandfather. He kept no genealogy, but he knew the word ordering used for given names in their lineage. He had relatives all over the place, in Shanwei, Wushi, Beihai and other places. In Hongwei,

98 *He Xi*

the Wu, Zhou and Liang surnames were the most common. Their ancestors had come from Dianbai, Wuchuan and Shanwei, as well as nearby places.

Conclusion

Confronted nowadays by the prevalence of brick village houses on Naozhou, it is easy for the visitor to forget that such houses are a relatively recent phenomenon and that until the 1970s, most houses were really wooden sheds. Permanence as expressed in buildings until then was expressed only as a manner of speaking. The boat people's sheds on stilts over the foreshore were not necessarily less permanent, they simply signified a continuation with boat-living to a greater degree than the settlements in sheds on land. When landowning villagers who also regularly fished and foraged on the foreshore were recognized on Naozhou as "peasant" in the 1950s, the Land Reform Movement was doing no more than carrying on a classification that had been in place for centuries. However, setting them apart from "fishing people", who did not own land, who worked on deep-sea fishing boats (and possibly also transporters), and lived in sheds on stilts over the foreshore ossified the labels in a way that had not been known earlier. Boat people did move on shore, acquire land, adopt the ritual symbols of land villagers by building ancestral halls and, thereby, become land villagers, even if collective memory sometimes retain stories of their origins as boat people. In Naozhou, the difference in language as we find it now between the land villagers and Hongwei suggests that the two populations were being kept apart.

We can presume that the land villages on Naozhou were settled from the early seventeenth century when the coastal evacuation was lifted and troops were stationed on the island. Some of the villagers would have come from Leizhou peninsular, as indicated by the dialect they speak. It is not surprising also that the major family produced a naval officer in the nineteenth century, for some of the villagers would have maintained close connections with the garrisons, by descent or marriage. The villages were probably quite poor and so the only houses built of brick or stone would have been the government offices and the major temples, of which there were very few. In fact, we can be certain only of one temple that was built before the nineteenth century – the Tianhou temple at Jinqian. On the mainland, it would be common even in poor villages to maintain earth god shrines, and common sacrifice at the shrines denoted territorial connections. On Naozhou, earth god shrines were not prominent and in their place and that of temples was the practice of circulating figures of deities among associations made up of households. The fact that the iron bell was donated to the Jinqian Tianhou temple by the boat people makes it quite definite that they were a substantial portion of the clientele served by the temple. Add to that the practice of their keeping statuettes of ancestors and gods on their boats, and the occasional deposition of the statuettes at the temple, for example, during temple festivals, the rudiments may be surmised for the practice whereby

Gods adrift: religious ritual and local society on Naozhou island 99

some of them would have contributed towards carving a statue to circulate among themselves, which might also be centrally located for collective worship at times. The practice of circulating the gods found among the land villages, therefore, would have had its origin among the practices of the boat population.

Whether or not some of the land villages had had an origin from boat-living, therefore, it might be argued that in the past the religious practices of the boat people and the land people formed a continuum. They worshipped essentially the same types of deities, they practised ancestral sacrifice in much the same way, and while they regularly sacrificed at some temples, they also participated in circulating statuettes of gods among family groups. Some gods, therefore, were associated with particular temples, some with villages, and many circulated with no fixed abode. When gods circulated among families that were housed on boats, they denoted connections that were not necessarily territorial but that were, nevertheless, communal. Communities settled ashore absorbed land-based labels and practices, passing on the label of *"danjia"* to newcomers living on boats and stilt sheds, who, in time, might also move ashore. Hongwei came at the end of that process, and household registration ensured that no one followed for it to pass the *"danjia"* label onto. It became the odd-one-out, the token *"danjia"* in an island community of land villages.

Notes

1 The author acknowledges with thanks the help of Chen Zhijian, Dou Guangdong, Tan Haoran, Tan Fazhan, Chen Cunhua, Chen Hongming and the many villages of Naozhou island who provided hospitality and information on her visits. Funding for the research on this paper has been provided by Hong Kong SAR University Grants Committee Areas of Excellence (Fifth Round): The Historical Anthropology of Chinese Society.
2 Du Zhen, *Min-Yue xunshi jilue* (Brief account of reconnaissance in Fujian and Guangdong), c. 1684, *Siku quanshu*, 2/4a.
3 *Guangdong tongzhi* (Gazetteer of Guangdong province), 1822, reprinted Shanghai: Shangwu, 1934, pp. 2383, 2488.
4 *Gaozhou fuzhi* (Gazetteer of Gaozhou prefecture), 8/19b, 17/5b–6a, 21a–22a, 28b, 23/1a.
5 Seen by author in Jinqian Tianhou temple on 21 November 2007.
6 "Juan kai Beigang beiji" (Stele inscription on donations for the opening of the Northern Anchorage), 1828, seen at the Wu Sanqi temple at Gangtou village at Beigang.
7 Interviews by the author on 5 July 2012 at Naozhou.
8 *Wuchuan xianzhi* (Gazetteer of Wuchuan county), 1892, 4/92b.
9 Du Zhen, *Min-Yue xunshi jilue*, 2/4b.
10 Lu Kun and Deng Tingzhen (eds.) *Guangdong haifang huilan* (An overview of naval defense in Guangdong), 1838, reprinted Shijiazhuang: Hebei renmin, 2009, pp. 856–857.
11 *Wuchuan xianzhi*, 1892, "Wuchuan xianzhi tu" (map of Wuchuan county), 29a.
12 The stele is held in the Zhanjiang Municipal Museum.
13 Stele seen by author on 4 July 2012 at Songhuang village on Naozhou island.

100　*He Xi*

14 Some lines are blurred and the translation has taken the liberty of summarizing from readable text.
15 "Gaoshi" (Notice) stele seen by author on 4 July 2012 at Songhuang village on Naozhou island.
16 "Doushi zupu" (Dou surname genealogy), unpublished manuscript, seen on Naozhou, p. 10.
17 Interview by author at Naozhou on 21 November 2007. See also, He Xi, *Yishen yizu: Yue xinan xinyang jiangou de shehuishi* (Ancestor and deity: a social history of the construction of local religion in southwestern Guangdong), Beijing: Sanlian shudian, 2011, pp. 238–239.
18 I attended the Tianhou festival at Naozhou on 26–28 April 2008, and returned on 4–7 July 2012 to visit the villages that participated in it.
19 The term is also used in Fujian, see Kenneth Dean, "Transformations of the she (altars of the soil) in Fujian", *Cahiers d'Extrme-Asie*, 1998, 10, pp. 18–75.
20 "Dongyue chan hao, Yuhuangao yiben" (Confessions to the Eastern Peak, admonitions of the Jade Emperor, one copy), unpublished manuscript, seen on Naozhou on 6 July 2012.
21 This section comes mainly from a meeting with members of Hongwei village on Naozhou on 5 July 2012.
22 Mr Wu might have misremembered that Wu Three-Seven was housed in the Great King Temple, or his reference to the temple might simply be an indication of location and not the building itself.
23 The water fairy temples on the foreshore in many parts of south China sacrificed to the dead at sea whose bodies were washed up on the coast. It is not uncommon that they come to be ascribed to Qu Yuan, who drowned himself in political protest in the Spring and Autumn period. The ascription of recorded history to local deities is common practice.

6 Incense associations among small-boat fishermen on Tai lake

Xia Yihong

Tai lake is shaped like a crescent stretching from east to west. The northeast shore is taken up by marshes, its many inlets are referred to by local people as "ports" (*gang*). Before Liberation, fishing boats of two to three tons moored on the east. On the west, however, lived a different population. They were made up of fishing people who did not man large ships. They referred to themselves as "boat people", and land dwellers nearby called them "net-boat ghosts" (*wangchuan gui*).

The fishing people have their own religious organizations, known as incense associations (*xiangshe*). Before the establishment of the People's Republic in 1949, they took part in different incense associations according to where they fished, the type of equipment they used for fishing and the size of their boats. After 1949, these organizations were banned along with their religious practices. Moreover, the fishing people were registered like the rest of China's population and subjected to collectivization. By the 1960s, while they were organized as a commune, the government had made arrangements for many to move ashore. Many were housed at Temple Anchorage (Miao *gang*) on the edge of Tai lake in Wujiang city. Nevertheless, although the fishing people had houses on shore, they continued to live on their boats. Most of the fish they caught were sold to Suzhou city and nearby towns. The winding rivers that flowed into Tai lake connect them with the waterways of the mouth of the Yangzi river all the way to the suburbs of Shanghai. Since the end of collectivization and the beginning of market reforms in the 1980s, many fishing households have become independent operators and revived their religious practices. In the 1990s, many began to farm crabs for sale. Because crab culture does not require living on boats, many more have moved ashore from that time. When asked, the fishing people say their ancestors moved to this area in the Qing dynasty.

Since 2005, the present writer has been studying an incense association that is organized among these fishing people, the Xu Family's Hall (Xujia *gongmen*) at Temple Anchorage, who were small-boat fishermen moved ashore. No previous study of this group has ever been conducted, the closest published research on the subject being Chen Juncai's various publications since the 1980s, which deal more with the big-boat fishermen.[1] This chapter gives a

102   *Xia Yihong*

brief report of its organization and activities. Much of what is reported here is obtained from interview reports and participant observation in their religious celebrations.

Historical background

Before 1949, small-boat fishing people lived on their boats. That is to say, they lived as families, consisting of husband, wife and young children. When the children reached 16 *sui* (15 years of age) or so, parents would try to buy them a boat. The family fished as a single unit. They sold their catches to dealers, although the division between dealers and fishing families was not always exclusive. Some fish-dealers might also have served as headmen for *baojia* household registration. Opportunities for cooperation abound in the fishing process. The husband-and-wife team could fish on its own, but successful fishing often required a few boats working together. The richer small-boat fishing people fished with stake traps. These consisted of funnel-shaped channels marked out by bamboo mattings staked into the bed of the lake, along which fish might be driven to a close-ended encirclement. After Liberation, it was estimated that the 156 households of fishing people at Temple Anchorage operated 38 stake traps. It was common for fishing households related by family connections and working together to moor at the same port.

Small-boat fishing people tended to marry only small-boat fishing people. Like land people, they considered themselves to be patrilineal and patrilocal, but the practice was common for families to adopt children. Some adopted children were collected from charity orphanages on shore, while others might have been derived from exchanges arranged among families. They were commonly raised as their own children, and others, male or female, might be raised with the specific intention that they might become future spouses for their own children. Where the family had daughters but no sons, it was common for a man to marry in, and their descendants might accrue to one or both lines. It was considered important that harmony be maintained in the underworld as in the present world, and so it was important that the married-in man's patrilineal line was continued.[2]

From before Liberation, incense associations were common within the community of small-boat fishing people.[3] Such associations were found all over the Yangzi delta, from Huzhou to Shanghai. An indication of their existence would have been a house behind a temple on the waterway in which were hung portraits of deceased ancestors. Such portraits had been sent to the temples by families of means. There was much continuity in membership to these associations, for descendants continued to sacrifice within the associations in which their ancestors had taken part. An incense head (*xiangtou*) was responsible for ensuring that matters related to annual sacrifices were properly carried out. The incense head was usually male. He had to be acceptable to his members, who could vote with their feet if they were not satisfied with his performance, and he often gained his appointment through succession, as a

Incense associations among small-boat fishermen   103

relative or as a disciple. Master and disciple did not necessarily have the same surname. Deceased incense heads were known as "commanders" (*xianfeng*) or "old masters" (*laoye*). Commanders are remembered for their bravery, not for their being ritual leaders. The fishing people talk about the commanders' powers in protecting communal interests. They regard the commanders as their ancestors. Each incense association has its own ancestors and so members of the association see themselves as a family. The association might divide, and incense heads might change, but the gods and spirits they sacrifice to do not change.[4] Before Liberation, almost all fishing people were members of incense associations. In 1965, the Tai Lake Commune that had charge of the boat people conducted a survey and found that 95 per cent were members of religious organizations.[5]

The Prosperity Association (Xinglong *she*) is the largest incense association on Lake Tai. Its membership is made up of small-boat fishing people. The founding incense head, Xu Zhenglong and Xu Yangchun, were also well-known among even fishing people who were not members of the association. No one quite knows how they were related, aside from Zhenglong preceding Yangchun – some say they were father and son and some say they were brothers. The Wang family, whose history will be detailed below, is closely connected with the association.[6]

The history of the Wang family

People of the Wang surname who now live in Temple Anchorage use the surname Xu in their religious rituals. They are members of an incense association, the New Prosperity Association (Xinxing *she*), which is separate from the Prosperity Association. However, it shares many rituals in common with the Prosperity Association, although it holds the birthday of Xu Zhenglong a month earlier.

In 2009, when I came to the village, Mr Wang, who was aged 50 or so, explained to me:

> We are now in the sixth generation. In the *yang* world (world of the living), we have the Wang surname; in the *yin* world (world of the dead), our surname is Xu. When we write our names on offerings that we send our ancestors, we use the surname Xu, for otherwise they will not be able to receive them. About the two surnames, Xu and Wang, we are not the same Xu surname as the ones in the old Prosperity Association. Our old ancestor is ours. Among our senior generations, the first ancestor Wang Jinlong lived in the same generation as old incense head Ancestor Zhenglong. Zhenglong was the master, and Wang Jinlong was his disciple.[7]

As to the "two surnames, Xu and Wang", another Mr Wang who was close to 60 years old said to me:

104   Xia Yihong

> We started out as fishing people in the sea. Then [ancestor] had a wife from Yangzhou who had come to Suzhou. She had the Xu surname. He also had another wife who had the Wang surname but who didn't give birth. The Yangzhou woman gave birth to three children. All her children were given the Xu surname. In the old days when we went to sea, we had big boats. After we came to Suzhou, we changed and became like other people [that is, using small boats]. At first, the two brothers Jinlong and Shoulong took refuge here. We started out from Baiyang *wan* in Suzhou. We got to where we were by speaking good words. Wang Jinlong became master. There were only thirteen families at the time.[8]

By "speaking good words" he meant that their relationship with Xu Zhenglong was arrived at by seeking help from the elders in the underworld. After that, Xu Zhenglong's elders in the underworld became the Wang family's relatives, and the New Prosperity Association gained its recognized status. If we could assume that a generation lasts 20 years, we may reckon from Mr Wang's age that his ancestors came to this place at the end of the nineteenth century, possibly shortly after the Taiping Rebellion.

From the 1950s to the 1980s

In the socialist reforms of the 1950s, fishery cooperatives were set up under the guidance of the government. Along with those reforms, incense associations were banned. The changes that were introduced in this period cannot be exaggerated. In order to engage the fishing people in the reforms, the provincial party committee had sent work teams to hold many meetings with them. Fishing people who were for the most part illiterate were told to contrast the new society with the old, and to identify themselves with the reforms. The cadres found that the most effective method of popular education was to ask the fishing people to "speak of their bitterness" (*suku*) and to identify the capitalists and landlords who had brought them about. After "accounts had been settled" (*jiaodai*) with them, and anti-revolutionaries had been pointed out, elections were held among the fishing people to set up fishing people's associations (*yumin xiehui*). Under the guidance of the Chinese Communist Party, the fishing people were now told that they were now "in charge as masters" (*dangjia zuo zhuren*). Schools were built and they were taught to read. Until then, the fishing people of Tai lake had known of themselves as members of families associated with incense associations. Only as they took part in those meetings and learnt to read did they realize that they were "fishing people" (*yumin*), that they should identify with "fishing people" living in other parts of China, that they now had the new China behind them and that they were not to be despised any more.[9]

In 1958, the fishing people were grouped into a commune. That lasted for only two years, because in 1961, commune administration was broken up again into work teams. The fishing village of Temple Anchorage began from

Incense associations among small-boat fishermen 105

that time. They continued to live on their boats. They were distinct from peasants (*nongmin*), who had land. The fishing people had rights over stretches of water. However, in the frenzy to become self-sufficient in the 1960s, some fishing people also began to reclaim land by the lake for the purpose of cultivation and, for a while, they did become self-sufficient. Collectivization came to an end only in the 1980s and private enterprise emerged again.[10] However, from the 1960s, family planning was also more stringently enforced. In the 1970s, each family was allowed three children but by the 1980s they were allowed only one child. Propaganda for birth control also discouraged adoption. The shrinking population created the roots for the predominance of uxorilocal marriages and for young couples to have to succeed to both the patriline and the matriline.

Private enterprise coming to life in the 1980s brought many changes to the fishing people but one of the most important developments was the farming of crabs, which were sought after in increasingly prosperous cities such as Shanghai. Crabs had to be farmed in enclosures. By 1995, the Tai Lake Fishery Management Committee (Taihu *yuye guanli weiyuanhui*), which had charge over the industry, restricted the setting up of crab enclosures to families that possessed fishing permits. The fishing people long settled in the area benefited from that ruling. They could either farm crabs themselves, or they could rent out their allotment to outsiders. Many became sufficiently wealthy to build houses on shore. A village on land soon became the main venue where they interacted.

Because the permits were issued to nuclear families and might be inherited but not sold, they became family treasures that could only be kept if the family could propagate. Many families, therefore, were reluctant to allow their daughters to marry out. They were also unwilling to share their business. Every family ran its own business, even though in farming crab for the market, it was necessary to share information or even capital. However, they understood it was their duty as brothers to help one another and they enjoyed social life together. They entertained frequently and the mahjong houses in the village were always full.[11]

In the 1980s, after the commune disbanded, religious activities revived. For example, marriage was not only an affair of this world; it had to be accounted for to the masters of the underworld and so an essential part of the wedding ceremony was to notify the ancestors. Ancestral sacrifice also revived and, along with that, many of the features of the incense hall. The ceremonies for sacrificing to the ancestors is known as "paying back" (*dan*), and consists of inviting their presence, offerings of wine and food, and the singing of songs by the officiant, who is sometimes, but not always, the incense head. The songs tell stories from history, not necessarily relating to the ancestors or the gods.[12]

The generation that had been in charge of religious activities from before Liberation had either passed away or become too old. Younger people were needed to succeed into their positions. Interestingly, the reason usually given for taking up such positions was that "they did not volunteer to do so, but the

106 *Xia Yihong*

masters came to them". The fishing people believe that modern hospitals were good for *yang* illnesses, but there were also *yin* illnesses that had to be treated by "people who could speak" (*kaikou ren*), that is to say, people who could allow the spirits to speak through them. They would find out if the ancestors' displeasure had brought about misfortune. The fishing people believe that speaking for the ancestors carries rewards and punishments. When I first came to Temple Anchorage in 2009, the villagers told me that the former incense head died all of a sudden as he was working and they believed that his death had come about because he had fought to gain his position as incense head. Being incense head also carried risks of a different sort: in 1985 and 1991, the local public security office came down on the incense heads in the name of "smashing the class structure within religious organizations". After purging several reputable incense heads, the local government tacitly accepted the continuation of religious activities as "family sacrifice" (*jiating jisi*). Calm has been maintained since that time and, as the fishing people say, "even village cadres join incense associations".[13]

The fishing people believe that their fortune depends on the ancestors being looked after. Because crab farming is highly risky, they believe that success depends on influence being exerted in the underworld. They think that an enclosed stretch of water, crossroads or the bamboo enclosures are all guarded by their own gods. There is even a guardian god for farming crab in an enclosure (*weiyang lutou*) who has to be sacrificed to at the new year and before the crab-eating season. Under such beliefs, the incense halls came to life again.

By 2000, there were major incense halls under local leadership at Temple Anchorage. Three of them were named Prosperity Association, after the historic association of that name. These were Xu Guanming's Old Prosperity Association of the Xu Family's Hall (*Xujia gongmen lao Xinglong she*), Li Jinguei's Prosperity Hall (*Xinglong she*) and Yang Changgen's Prosperity Hall (*Xinglong she*). Of the three, Xu Guanming's hall became the most representative of the now defunct old Prosperity Hall.

The Xu family's Prosperity Association

Neighbours said of Xu Guanming: "When he first started performing rituals, he was too embarrassed even to sing." He was born in 1931. In 1965, he was reprimanded for having joined some of his Temple Anchorage neighbours for going out to burn incense. Before that, there were signs that he might be a potential recruit for the Chinese Communist Youth League, but joining an incense association destroyed his chances. So, when local religion revived in the early 1980s, he did not take part. However, towards the end of the 1980s, his wife was ill, and many "people who could speak" said that "the ancestors had come up to his door". Only then did he agree to become an incense head. His wife said to me: "When he took up the responsibility, I recovered."

Before local sacrifices were banned in the 1950s, the last incense head was Xu Tujin. The incense heads of two of the Prosperity Associations were

Incense associations among small-boat fishermen 107

associated with him: Lin Jingui was his son-in-law and Yang Changgen was married to his niece. They both came from a fishing area in Wujiang county but had lived in Temple Anchorage for many years and his household was registered there. Li was an incense head from the end of the 1970s, and he had a larger following than Xu Guanming. When Xu started, he learnt the rituals from Li, and quite a few of Li and Yang's followers came over to him. Asked why they defected to Xu, the followers said: "Our ancestors burnt incense with Xu Zhenglong and Xu Chunyang." Xu Guanming and his wife confirmed that. They said to me: "The Xu surname is the proper line of descent from ancestors Xu Zhenglong and Xu Chunyang. We have come down from the proper line of descent, and that is why we are the Old Prosperity Association."[14]

When I asked him about the origin of the name Xu Family's Hall, Xu Guanming told me:

> The association was known as the Tai Lake Prosperity Hall. There are six or seven prosperity halls, but only my family has the Xu Family's Hall. Formerly, the Xu Family's Hall was not well-known. It has been around from my grandfather's days, but, in those days, it wasn't well-known. Why do we call it a "public hall"? That is because people can come here to burn incense. Incense is not burnt in a "private hall" (*tangmen*).[15]

The "public hall", in effect, was the little temple right by his house. Many people come to burn incense. On the first and 15th days of every lunar month, an unceasing stream of followers come to burn incense. They come from within his incense association, from other villagers, from fishing communities elsewhere and even from the farming villages.

The little temple is made up of two rooms. In the inner room are three altars, now encased within glass panes. On the altars are three types of statues: direct ancestors of the Xu family, ancestors of members of the current Old Prosperity Association and some important deities. Xu Guanming knows them like members of his family. In the altar to the right, the most prominent figures are Xu Zhenglong and Xu Chunyang. They are the objects to which much of the incense is offered. Near those two are Xu Mingyang, Xu Jinyang, Xu Fayang, Xu Shungao and Xu Shunfa, all ancestors. To their side are Xu Guanming's father, uncle and a deceased brother. Xu Guanming says he will also place the statues of Xu Jinyang's sons, Xu Shunfu and Xu Shunxing, up there. On the left-hand side altar are deceased women, including Xu Jinyang's wife and daughter, Xu Guanming's mother, Xu Shungao's daughter, Xu Yunxiong's wife, Xu Xingsheng's mother, Xu Shungao's wife and daughter, Xu Shunfa's wife, Xu Shunfu's wife, Xu Zhenglong's mother and Xu Chunyang's wife. There is also Xu Mingsheng's mother: "She is Mingyang's granddaughter," Xu Guanming says. "Mingyang was Mingsheng's great great grandfather, Mingsheng's mother's grandfather. He was an 'adopted son-in-law'" (that is to say, he had married into the Xu family).[16]

108 *Xia Yihong*

Plate 6.1 Entrance to Xu Family Hall (credit: He Xi).

The altar in the middle houses the statues of ancestors of members of the incense association and other people who had been associated with it, such as Xi Dacai, Master Wang, Mrs Chen, Mo Sanbao, Sun Ruiguan and Miss Princess. "Miss Princess came from Xu Fugen's family. He [Fugen] had come from northern Jiangsu, and was her uncle. He died some time ago. They were descendants of Xu Guoxiang," Xu Guanming said. He also said Sun Ruiguan had come from Xishan Island also in Tai lake. He was a "commander" in the Sun family. Mo Sanbao was Xu Guanming's uncle (father's sister's husband), Master Wang was a "commander" for the Wang family, Xu Qibao had lived in Tangdian in Huzhou and was the ancestor of Qian Yunbiao who was incense head of the New Qian surname incense hall there. There were also several statues placed in the outer room of the temple. They belonged to Su Number Three, Su Number Four, Zhou Guanlin and Zhou Dexiang, who were reputable "commanders" in the area. Xu Guanming said Zhou Dexiang had been adopted by ancestor Xu Chunyang to be an incense head, and Zhou Guanlin was his son. Xu Chunyang had a lot of followers, and so he also gave some to the Su brothers, Three and Four. As for the deities, they included the God of the Eastern Peak at Tiger Mountain in Suzhou, the Guanyin of Hangzhou, Prince Liu of the Liansi marshes in Jiaxing of Zhejiang province, Uncle Xiaoqing and the Guanyin of Temple Anchorage. Prince Liu of Liansi

Plate 6.2 Altar at Xu Family Hall (credit: He Xi).

marshes commands respect over a very substantial part of the surroundings stretching from Tai lake to Shanghai. His annual festival is attended by people from many places, including the incense associations of Temple Anchorage. The other deities seem to be local.

Xu Guanming and his wife told me that when the fishing people heard that they were building a temple to house Xu Zhenglong and Xu Chunyang, people came from far and near to offer their congratulations. The decorations they presented adorn the temple. Mr Xu said: "They all came of their own accord."

When the fishing people were still living on boats, the incense head kept the portraits of their gods and spirits on a sheet of cloth that he brought out as he conducted sacrificial ceremonies. Li Jingui used individual portraits, single sheets of paper on which was drawn the portrait of a god or spirit, so that the incense head could arrange them in combinations preferred. He also had small figures at home to represent his masters. When Xu Guanming started as an incense head, he learnt to use individual portraits and figures from Li. But he made big figures, and many of them, so that his establishment began to look like a temple. He opened up the temple to his followers. They could deposit figures of their ancestors there, burn incense to them, and present them with adornments and presents. His temple is filled with plastic flowers,

110   *Xia Yihong*

daily necessities and toys (including motor cars and aeroplanes), "anything that the gods might be fond of". They could also come and ask the gods and spirits to answer their questions. In December 2007, I witnessed the installation of the statue of Xu Mingyang on the altar in the Xu Family's Hall. The statue was presented by Xu Minggen who was incense head at the Prosperity Association at Badu in Wujiang county and who traced his descent from Xu Mingyang. At the end of the ceremony, Xu Guangming said: "Now we can't say we have great-great-grandfather Xu Zhenglong and only three ancestors. We have to say four ancestors now."[17] From that time on, he added another ancestor's name to his regular prayers. As more statues are moved into the hall, there are more spirits that Xu Guangming sacrifices to. The biggest celebrations are reserved for Xu Zhenglong and Xu Chunyang, respectively on their birthdays on the third day of the eleventh month and the 17th day of the eighth month. Celebrations consist of prayers and the performance of singing, as in the "repayment" rituals. They might also include parades. Incense associations organize parades for their members to attend celebrations of their protective deities, not only in their own villages, but also to temples outside. The biggest one of those, the Liuwang (Prince Liu) temple at Liandang, draws very substantial followings.

Xu Guangming's comment on there being four ancestors after the inclusion of Xu Mingyang on the altar is very revealing. When asked, he is able to describe the family connections that might be ascribed to the statues on the altars and, thereby, the relationships among groups of living people, but those connections are enacted by the inclusion of statues on the altar. What I witnessed, therefore, was the consolidation of the relationships of incense heads through the tracing of lineage connections between their ancestors. Xu Guangming does not keep a written genealogy; the altar, in effect, *is* the genealogical record.

In 2009, the Old Prosperity Association had care of 82 fishing people's households, including people of the Li, Xi, Shi, Xu, Sun and Wu surnames. They were divided into eight groups, each of ten households. Each group had a group leader. Every year, each group leads a collective ceremony to pray to the gods. The Xu surname maintains a special connection to their two ancestors who hold positions of esteem in the temple. Only the two group leaders of the Xu surname might be in charge of preparing for sacrifice on their birthdays, although every household joins in.

Because the public security department takes the view that they do not intervene as long as incense-burning is kept as a family activity, there is a tendency for the incense heads to stress the family aspect of their activities. Yet, membership of the association remains multi-surname. In fact, anyone might join, provided the gods give their approval, through people who speak on their behalf. In recent years, therefore, land villagers who have been attracted by crab farming have also joined, and, by joining and providing the feast that goes along with sacrifice to the gods, have won recognition as members of the fishing people's community. Gone are the days when the incense head held a

Incense associations among small-boat fishermen 111

leadership position in the community. Current incense heads realize they hold essentially a ritual role, their previous administrative role having been taken over by the cadres. What is very clear is that the incense heads believe that they perpetuate a culture that ties in with a long tradition. "People say we are Buddhists, or Sectarians. I think we are daoists," Xu said to me. Contrasting their practices with the Christian churches that are now springing up, he says: "We conduct our own religion. We are Chinese."

Notes

1 Chen Juncai, *Taihu yuye shi* (A history of Tai lake fishery), Jiangsu: Jingsu sheng Taihu yuye shengchan guanli weiyuanhui, 1986; Chen Juncai, "Taihu yumin xinyang xisu diaocha", in Shanghai minjian wenyijia xiehui (eds.), *Zhongguo minjian wenhua* (China's folk culture), Shanghai: Shanghai xuelin chubanshe, Vol. 5, 1992, pp. 80–113.
2 Chen, *Taihu yuye shi*, and my interviews conducted in the second half of 2009.
3 I have heard the fishing people describe the incense association as the "big family" (*dajia*), contrasting that with the lineage, described as "family" (*jia*) and the domestic group as the "small family" (*xiaojia*).
4 Chen, "Taihu yumin xinyang xisu diaocha", pp. 88–90.
5 Chen, *Taihu yuye shi*, p. 47.
6 Chen, *Taihu yuye shi*, p. 90, citing apparently internal information, says this of the Prosperity Association: "It is the most extensive influential organisation among Tai lake small-boat fishing people. The incense head had used his religious position to collaborate with the enemy. He was active from 1932, and set up the association in 1937. Among the fishing people of Tai lake, he had 145 households among his clients. He also had followers among the fishing people on the rivers in the Suzhou suburb. He had under him five other incense heads and they had a grip on worshippers. In 1956 alone, they collected 3,949 yuan from them. His activities were banned in 1961, but the sub-incense heads continued sporadic activities until 1963." In Jiangsu, secret societies that might have collaborated with the Guomindang and, by implication, the incense associations, became a concern for the provincial government in the 1950s and 1960s. For an outline on that history, see Wang Haiyan and Wu Dongsheng, "Jianguo chuqi Jiangsu qudi huidaomen gongzuo shulun" (A discussion of the abolition of religious societies in Jiangsu in the early years of the People's Republic), *Nanjing yike daxue xuebao (shehui kexue ban)*, 2002, 2(7), pp 122–127.
7 Interview on 26 December 2009.
8 Interview 9 December 2009.
9 "Wujiang xian shuishang gongzuo baogao, 1953.1.21–2.5" held in the Wujiang County Archive, Chen Juncai, Taihu yuyeshi, pp. 59–62.
10 Chen Juncai, "Taihu xiangzhi gao xuanji" (Selections from the local history of Taihu), in *Suzhou shizhi ziliao xuanji*, Vol. 30, no date or publisher, www.dfzb. suzhou.gov.cn/zsbl/217827.htm (accessed 8 May 2013); "Wuxian Taihu gongshe lishi ziliao huibian, 1949–1979" (cyclostyle), Wujiang County Archive; interviews in second half of 2009.
11 Interview with personnel in the Tai Lake Fishery Management Committee on 6 January, 2009.
12 Chen, "Taihu yumin xinyang xisu diaocha", pp. 103–106.
13 This was widely known among the local people and I heard it reported many times in the field.

112 *Xia Yihong*

14 Interview on 10 December 2007.
15 Interview on 22 March 2006; compare also interview notes recorded in Ōta Izuru and Satō Yoshifumi, *Taiko ryūiki shakai no rekishigakuteki kenkyū: chihō bunken to genchi chōsa kara no apurōchi* (Tai lake society in late Qing and Republican China, researched through the study of local documents and fieldwork), Tokyo: Kyūko Shoin, 2007, pp. 277–290.
16 Interview on 12 December 2007.
17 From my field notes of 11 December 2007.

7 Some examples of the responsibilities and succession of "incense heads" (*xiangtou*) among the fishermen of Tai lake

Ota Izuru

On Tai lake, fishing people set up associations to facilitate their religious activities. Such associations are led by people known as "incense heads" (*xiangtou*).[1] They are often succeeded within the blood line, although the associations are built less on family or lineage connections and more on territorial and communal relationships. Not a great deal is known of the work of the incense heads within the associations. Recent reports on the subject have noted that, in a general sense, members of the associations pray to the gods for protection against career failures and illnesses, and the incense heads are instrumental in maintaining group solidarity. Yet, it has remained unclear what role they play in the periodic rituals conducted by the associations, of which there are many, including ceremonies held at the altars maintained domestically by the incense heads, and periodic pilgrimages made by members of the association to temples over a substantial stretch of the lower Yangzi delta, reaching from Tai lake to Shanghai. I was puzzled by exactly this problem until I realized that singing "songs of praise to the gods" (*zanshen ge*) is an integral part of those ceremonies and that commonly it is the incense head who sings these songs before the gods. An important ingredient of the incense associations is, therefore, the troupe of musicians who accompany the incense head in his performance. In this chapter, I report on some of my observations at ceremonies and interviews with several incense heads to discover what responsibilities they hold for religious ceremonies, including the singing of songs of praise to the gods.

I came to the conclusion that the incense head performs the "songs of praise to the gods" from observations I made during ceremonies I witnessed. The performance demands skills and so how those skills are acquired relates to how their positions are transmitted. In my interviews with incense heads, therefore, I try to find out how skills are passed on.

Shen Xiaolin of Haolang village in Tongli township is descended from ancestors who were fishing people. He is an incense head and so he leads worship at temples and shrines. The temples he leads pilgrimages to include Shangfang hill near Suzhou, the Liuwang (Prince Liu, also known as Liu Meng) temple at Liansi marshes, the Grandfather Yang temple at Jinze, the Taijun temple at Shizong and the City God temple at Beixuejing.[2] By his description, he

114 Ota Izuru

Plate 7.1 Singing the "song of praise to the gods" (credit: Ota Izuru).

attends these temples annually. It is not clear if the same disciples follow him on the various pilgrimages. Shen says his association is known by a different name at different temples, such as the Ancestor's Association (*taiqin hui*), the Baimao grass association (*Baimaoqiang she*), the Young Master's Association (*gongzi she*) or the Old Master's Association (*taiye she*).

I asked him to sing me the songs he sings at the altars. One day in December 2009, he performed for me. In his performance, I asked him to sing for me the Liuwang Confessions (Liuwang *chan*), sung for a god who is widely worshipped in the Yangzi delta. It would have taken well over ten hours to sing the entire song, and so he sang only an excerpt. He did that with the musical accompaniment of three people who flanked him as he sang. Shen Xiaolin sang with a little gong in his hand, which he struck as he sang. There was not much of a tune to the singing; it was more like storytelling in a flat tone. His three companions kept the beat with a bronze drum, a big gong and a small gong. I have seen the same arrangement on other occasions and I am prepared to believe that this was standard for singing the "songs of praise to the gods".

In August 2010, when I ran into him by chance as he was performing in a temple, again, it was not another member of his team that sang the "songs of praise" but Shen Xiaolin himself.

Some examples of the responsibilities and succession of "incense heads" 115

Plate 7.2 Scroll showing pictures of gods and ancestors (credit: Ota Izuru).

The point that should be noticed is that the incense head was himself the key performer. The musicians who accompany him sometimes change, but the singer of the "songs of praise" is always the incense head. Singing the "songs of praise", therefore, may be regarded as the major responsibility of the incense head. Does he, therefore, hold a special relationship with the deities?

An answer to that question may be attempted from the manner of succession into the incense head's position. According to Shen Xiaolin, there was the Baimao Association from the time of ancestor Shen Fuxiang. Shen Fuxiang was incense head, and he maintained an altar at home for sacrifice to Old Master. He also took his members to the temples to burn incense to the gods. He never charged any money for his service. It was said that one year, when they took Old Master's statue out on parade, they ran into a dispute with a neighbouring association, but Shen Fuxiang was very good calming everybody down. He had no sons, only daughters, and so he recruited a son-in-law into the family. After that, the incense head was Shen Xuchun, Xiaolin's grandfather, who passed the position to Shen Huiying, his father. In Huiying's time, there were 70 to 80 households in the association. Xiaolin's father passed the position to his elder brother, Yongfu. During Yongfu's time, the People's Republic was established and Yongfu gave up serving as incense head for fear he would get into trouble. So the line was broken until Xiaolin

116 *Ota Izuru*

took it up when the economic reforms started in the 1980s. They now have 20 households in the association.

I asked him what he had to do as incense head. He said that the incense head collects donations ("incense money", *xiangyou qian*) for temple repair, but they demand no reward for curing illnesses. During festivals, they take their members on pilgrimages to burn incense at temples. If someone wants to join, the Old Master's view is sought. That takes place by his descending on the body of a Buddha-woman (the mediums are always women, according to Shen Xiaolin) and speaking through it. Ultimately, the incense head divines the Old Master's view by throwing divining blocks.[3]

I also spoke to Ni Chunbao of Fishing village, Pingwang township. Ni Chunbao's ancestors were fishermen. He is currently incense head of the Qisheng (seven lives) Association, and he also sings the "songs of praise to the deities". I saw him perform on two separate occasions, in April 2010 and March 2011. Again, as he sings in front of the altar, he is accompanied by three musicians playing percussion instruments, the bronze drum and small gongs.

According to Ni Chunbao, the Qisheng Association was set up by ancestor Ni Gaoming 400 years ago at the Liuwang temple at Liansi marshes. For that reason, that temple is particularly important to the association. Among the fishing people of the townships of Pingwang and Luxu, the ancestor was very well-known. He could help people settle disputes and cure illnesses. After Ni Gaoming, the position of incense head passed on to Ni Qiugou and Ni Fuxing. After that, the line was broken until the late 1970s. The ancestor revealed himself to Ni Chunbao and ordered him to take over, to lead members of the association to worship the gods, and so Chunbao became the incense head. The association has 116 households among its members, but only Ni Chunbao knows how to sing the "songs of praise".[4]

Shen Quandi of Wealthy Fishing village in Songling township is the youngest incense head I have met. When he was born in 1969, his parents were still living on a boat. I saw him perform in April 2010. He sang the "songs of praise" to the accompaniment of three woman disciples who played the big gong, the bronze drum and a small gong. He is now incense head of the Young Master's Association. As far as is known, in the first half of the nineteenth century, the association was led by Shen Yuxiang; it was passed onto his great grandfather Shen Honggao in the mid-nineteenth century, then his grandfather Shen Fucai in the late nineteenth century, then his father Shen Ada in the twentieth century. In other words, he knows the names of his forebear for four generations. Nevertheless, it should be made clear that the association was named "Young Master's" only recently. It used to be known as the Shen Family's Hall (*Shenjia tangmen*), and the name Young Master's Association was adopted because since 2004 Shen Quandi's followers have believed that he is the son (hence "young master") of the City God. At Shijiashe village in Tongli township, there is a temple devoted to the "Little" City God, who is known to be the son of the City God of Suzhou prefectural city.[5] When

Some examples of the responsibilities and succession of "incense heads" 117

people apply to become members, Shen Quandi asks the old City God – that is to say, the Suzhou prefectural city god – to descend on his body to seek his permission. I was told that the three women who accompanied Shen Quandi's singing had no previous connection with the Shen Family's Hall prior to their becoming members but had been summoned by the old City God to join. Members of the association have come primarily from the fishing villages, but membership has now expanded to nearby towns. There are now several hundred members.[6]

My fourth example of an incense head is Shen Ruisheng, of New Fishing village, Luxu township, who performed the first "song of praise to the gods" I heard. That was in September 2004 in the Great Fairy (*daxian*) temple at Luxu. Shen Ruisheng had learnt to sing from his father, Shen Xiaodi, along with his younger brothers Gensheng and Jinsheng. When they perform, only Shen Ruisheng sings. He is also accompanied by three musicians playing the gong and the bronze drum.

Shen Ruisheng still lives on a boat. He is incense head of the very well-known Banner Canopy Association (*qisan she*) in the Tai lake region. The ceremonial skill had been passed on in the family. As far as can be recalled, Shen Wanchang passed it on to Shen Yutang, who came to this area to escape from the Taiping Rebellion. Shen Yutang passed it on to Shen Wanzhen, then Shen Jingao and Shen Xiaodi. Shen Xiaodi was Ruisheng's father.[7]

In all the ceremonies I have attended for the singing of "songs of praise for the gods", the singer – invariably the incense head – does so standing in front of the altar. The deities on the altar are represented as small statues or portraits. The incense head succeeds not only into the singing, but also into the lines of relationships that, over generations, had developed with the deities or spirits represented by them. Over the past few years, there have been some changes. When I first visited Shen Xiaolin in December 2009, for example, the small statues and portraits were housed on his boat. When I visited him again in March 2010, he proudly took me to his newly built ancestral hall (*citang*) on land. The installation of the representations of deities and spirits in an ancestral hall was probably a practice he had learnt from the land population. Traditionally, their altars would have been set up on boats.

In 2009, Shen Xiaolin did have a house on shore, but he also had a sizable "family boat" (*jiachuan*) that he took me to. In a room on the boat were hung portraits of gods. He said they had been painted by someone from Suzhou city.

At the centre of the upper row sat Liuwang. To Liuwang's left and right were the Second Master of the Shen Household and the Third Master of the Zhu Household. The "Shen household" refers to Shen Xiaolin's father's line of descent, and the "Zhu household", his mother's line of descent. There were also other gods known as Second and Third Masters, who were presumably Liuwang's younger brothers. I noted in particular that on the last row were portraits of Shen Xuchun, Shen Huiying, Shen Yongfu, Zhu Yugao and Zhu Liangfa. These were Xiaolin's immediate family, being, respectively, his

118   *Ota Izuru*

paternal grandfather, his father, his elder brother, his father-in-law and his grandfather-in-law. Of those five persons, Xuchun, Huiying and Yongfu were incense heads prior to Xiaolin. The collective portraits indicated the lines of descent of the incense head. Xiaolin had another elder brother, who had not served as incense head, and his portrait was not included.

When I saw Ni Chunbao sing the praise of the gods on 1 April 2010, he also did so in front of the portraits of the gods. Like Shen Xiaolin's portraits, they were included in a picture divided into an upper, middle and lower section. The upper section presented the portrait of Liuwang and other gods, the middle section the "five sages" and the "five masters" and their wives, and the lowest section, his own master, Ni Gaoming, and two incense heads who preceded Chunbao himself. When I asked Shen Ruisheng on 11 August 2011 who the people were portrayed in the picture he posted on his boat, he said curtly that aside from Liu Meng and Old Master Yang, "everyone was an incense head".[8] That summed up the content of the portraits.

In the context of the presentation of the incense head's legitimate descent, I should refer also to Xu Guixiang's hall, which is described in Xia Yihong's contribution to this book (Chapter 6). In my opinion, the choice of statues at Xu's hall for presentation on the altars is not different from the presentation of the incense head's line of descent through portraits. The descent being traced is not a genealogy by birth, but the line of succession of the incense head and the source their authority in the gods. To take this argument further, it may be observed that upon death, the incense head takes his place among the gods to whom he makes offerings over his lifetime. This seems to be a practice peculiar to the incense heads, not of the majority of fishing people in the Tai lake area.

Elsewhere, I have written about the religious associations attended by fishing people of the Tai lake area that were managed by incense heads.[9] The associations had a role in the settlement of disputes among members and they also provided the means whereby the powers of the gods might be sought in fighting illness or bad fortune. The incense heads have portraits of the gods in front of which they sing songs of praise to them. It is also known that spirits descend on the persons during the ceremonies. In this chapter, I have concentrated on that narrative to identify the incense heads themselves as officiators of the ceremonies. They themselves sing the songs of praise in communication with the gods. In the settlement of disputes or the curing of illnesses, they seek the intervention of the gods who can speak through them. Moreover, they have the legitimacy provided by history: the history of succession of incense heads from before 1949 is publicly known, and the manner by which that is known has much to do with the portraits exhibited at places of worship. Those portraits would have been placed on their boats in the old days, but in recent years, they have been installed in worship halls that are managed by the incense heads. The descent line of authority, being exhibited on altars along with portraits of

Some examples of the responsibilities and succession of "incense heads" 119

the gods, signifies powers held by the incense heads. By those powers, they retain the loyalty of their followers.

Notes

1 For background see Ota Izuru, "Taiko ryuiki gyomin to Ryumoushou sinkou – senkan, sansinka wo jirei toshite" (The fishing people of the Tai lake region and belief in General Liu Meng – examples of public scrolls and songs to the gods), in Sato Yoshifumi and Ota Izuru (eds.), *Chugoku nouson no minkan geinou – Taiko ryuiki shakaishi koujutsu- kirokushu 2* (Popular crafts in Chinese villages – oral history from Tai lake area social history 2), Tokyo: Kyuko shoin, 2011, pp. 75–88.
2 Liuwang and Grandfather Yang are among the most important gods to the fishing people at Tai lake. See Zhang Fanglan, "Ryumoushou densetsu to Gokou Soukau Moushoukai Chosa" (An introduction to the survey report on belief in General Liu Meng) in Sato Yoshifumi and Ota Izuru (eds.), *Chugoku nouson no sinkou to seikatsu – Taiko ryuiki shakaishi koujutsu kirokushu 1* (Beliefs and livelihoods in Chinese villages – oral history from Tai lake area social history 1), Tokyo: Kyukoshoin, 2008, pp. 71–90, and Ota Izuru "Taiko ryuiki gyomin sinkou zakkou – Youseisin, Johozan dairouya, Daikunsin wo chusin ni" (Miscellaneous notes on the beliefs of fishing people in the Tai lake region – a god with the Yang surname, the Great Master of Shangfang hill, and the god Grand Master), *Kyushu rekishi kagaku*, 2011, 39, pp. 1–20.
3 Interview with Shen Xiaolin on 11 August 2011, in in Sato and Ota (eds.), *Chugoku nouson no minkan geinou*, pp. 276–279.
4 Interview with Ni Chunbao on 8 March and 11 August 2011.
5 I visited the temple located at Shijiashe village, Tongli township, Wujiang county on 4 September 2006. The Little City God is also discussed in Hamashima Atsutoshi, "Sekkousho Shozanken Shoujokobyo chosa houkoku: jokobyo oboegaki (1)" (A report of the survey on the Little City Temple in Xiaoshan county, Zhejiang province – a note on city god temples), *Osaka daigaku bungakubu kiyou*, 1999, 39, pp. 47–74.
6 Interview with Shen Quandi on 20 August 2010. Shen Quandi indicated he was the 11th generation after the founder of the association.
7 Interview with Shen Ruisheng on 27 December 2011. The Banner Canopy Association is also referred to in "*Jiangnan wangchuan hui–Liutangzhe de Yunhe Minsu*" (Festival of the net-fishing boats of Jiangnan – remnants of the popular culture on the Grand Canal), *Wenhua jiaoliu*, 2013, 3, pp. 51–54, and Zhang Juemin, *Wangchuan hui yingxiang* (Portraits of the net-fishing associations), Shanghai: Shanghai meishu, 2003.
8 Interview with Shen Ruisheng on 27 December 2011.
9 Ota Izuru, "Taiko ryuiki gyomin no koutou to "sha" "kai" – Kahoku nouson chosa to no hikaku shiron" (The incense heads of the fishing people of the Tai lake area and their territorial shrines and associations – comparison with surveys from North China villages), *Chika kiniarite*, 2009, 55, pp. 45–56.

8 From respect for the gods to sacrifice to the ancestors, creating lineage culture among the fishermen of Weishan lake

Diao Tongju and She Kanglue

In recent years, it has come increasingly to the attention of ethnographers and historians that the boat people on the edge of Weishan Lake in Shandong conduct a ceremony known as "continuing the genealogy" (*xu jiapu*). The ceremony has been of interest because it is thought it might incorporate elements of lineage practices, in the sense that some representations of the ancestors are permanently established and sacrificed to by descendants, and that geographically scattered groups of descendants establish linkages among themselves through tracing common descent lines. This chapter does not argue against the general conclusion that has been drawn on the basis of these observations, but sets it in historical context. It begins with doubts that were raised in our observations at "continuing the genealogy" and other celebrations. True enough, the local people refer to them as lineage (*zongzu*) practices. They recall that the sacrifice at New Year, now often described as an ancestral sacrifice (*jizu*), as sacrifice to the "old ancestors" (*laozu*). When asked, they say that every year, the ceremonies have been conducted by tradition. Researchers do wonder if such practices have been continued from the time when boat people actually lived on boats, or if they have evolved along with their settlement on land. As boat people do not leave written records, an understanding of the historical situation is fraught with difficulties. For lack of a written record, this chapter will not settle the issue definitively. Nevertheless, from circumstantial evidence that will be presented, it argues that the tradition among boat people had, for a long time, been closer to sacrifice to gods, and only in recent years have they celebrated the same ceremonies in the name of their ancestors.

Weishan lake and Wei village

Historically, the land people looked down upon the boat people of Weishan lake, calling them the "lake cats" (*humaozi*). Nevertheless, from the 1960s, like boat people in other parts of China, the Weishan lake boat people have been gradually moving ashore. Even then, because, they continue to be engaged in fishing and water transport, their livelihood has not departed from the lake.

Plate 8.1 Incense for the ancestors on board a house boat at Weishan lake (credit: He Xi).

Weishan lake is located in the south of Shandong province. It is now the largest lake in north China and provides livelihood for 140,000 fishermen. Wei village is a small village on its northern shore. In 2011, it had a population of 2,100 people. It is multi-surnamed, the surnames Hu, Shen, Ding and Wang being in the larger numbers, together making up 80 per cent of the village population. Through familial, marriage and ritual adoption, the villagers are connected to one another. They do not have land; in the past many lived on small boats, fishing in the lake. Today they have religious practices similar to the land people's, even though it is quite impossible to judge from how far back such practices originated. For example, at funerals, they report the death to the local earth god, just like the land people would. They also celebrate festivals such as the Mid-Autumn like the land people do, with the clear understanding that the full moon signifies family unity. Like many people living on the lake, they have settled on shore but continue to depend on the lake for their livelihood.

The villagers settled on land in the 1960s and 1970s, as government water control projects channelled more water into the lake. The government thought that the changing ecology threatened their livelihood and because, in any case, it was in line with policy to persuade boat-living people to diversify, it moved many of them to shore. As the fishing people moved ashore, their fishing equipment and boats were now collectivized. All those changes came about quite smoothly. In 1975, the government divided the lake into fishing districts, and made it mandatory for all persons and fishing boats to be licensed in order to fish at a specific district on the lake. According to villagers interviewed, Wei village cadres did not realize the importance of that division of fishing rights until after other villages had taken their shares. As one villager said: "After we came ashore, we sold our boats, we had no farm land and no fish ponds, and so we started the shipping company." From that time on, Wei village came to be well-known for its shipping business on the lake. By the end of the 1970s, as collectivization gave way to private enterprise, many fishing families went back to their old trade of fishing. Economic revival in the 1980s brought wealth and now signs of prosperity are apparent to any visitor of Weishan lake.

People who are settled on land near Weishan lake, whether or not they had moved up from the lake, now practice two ceremonies that strongly indicate beliefs in ancestors: the ancestral sacrifice at New Year and the ceremony known as the "continuing the genealogy" held every few years among people of the same surname but living in different places. Those ceremonies have to be looked at along with other ceremonies that the boat people conduct for they all have to do with the "old ancestors".

The old ancestors

By the term the "old ancestors", Wei villagers do not refer only to ancestral procreators, but also to gods. That is very clear from their terminology and the collection of drawings that many families possess that are brought out in periodic ceremonies. The "old ancestors" is a term that Wei villagers use for all the spirits (and deities or ancestors) represented on those drawings.

The portraits vary in length from 90cm to 200cm, and are approximately 90cm in width. They are usually individually rolled up, and so are often referred to as "scrolls" (*zhou*). In different ceremonies, different scrolls are hung up in central places as the principal targets of sacrifice. For example, for ancestral sacrifice at New Year, villagers hang the scroll known as the Bright Hall (*mingtang*) as the focus of sacrifice; for the "gathering for god Tang" (Tang *shen hui*),[1] they hang up god Tang's scroll; for the Great King's gathering, the Great King's scroll; and so on. Whichever scroll is hung in central position, the other scrolls are also displayed so that other gods, ancestors, or spirits, might also partake in sacrifice.

It can reasonably be accepted that the Bright Hall drawing depicts the lineage. The foreground of the drawing is occupied by an altar, on which is drawn an ancestral tablet bearing the characters, "lineage ancestors of three generations of ... surname" (*moushi sandai zongqin*). Below that is the drawing of an elderly couple, captioned, "deceased grandfather" and "deceased grandmother", that is to say, the progenitors of the lineage. Below the couple are several ancestral tablets, recording the names of their sons. They are the

From respect for the gods to sacrifice to the ancestors 123

ancestors of the different branches stemming from the progenitors. Following from the branch ancestors are lines of descent, on which are written the names of ancestors of each and every generation, leading up to the present. Empty space is left below the current generation for names of their sons and grandsons. The ancestors of every generation appear on this drawing, the aim of which is to denote the prosperity of the lineage and its generational order. It serves both as a genealogical record and as a focus of sacrifice. The drawing is kept on a scroll so that it can be hung up on occasions when ancestral sacrifice is needed, akin to the "family scrolls" (*jiatang zhouzi*) commonly found elsewhere in Shandong. Even when fishermen move ashore or have grown rich, they continue to represent the ancestors they sacrifice to with such a scroll. The use of the scroll in ancestral sacrifice is a feature of the fishing people's customs, not a result of their lack of communal property.

Gods are also represented in scroll drawings. One of these is the goddess Tang. The fishing people say that this young woman represented on the scroll is "the ninth sister of the southern heavenly gate" (*nan tianmen jiujie*) and she stands perpetually at the household entrance. Below her on the drawing are imperial commissioners holding military titles, general Nine Dragon, earth-god Zhao Gongming, the four venerable gentlemen of the Shen and Liu surnames, Commander Zhu, General Zhang and the gods of wealth of the five directions. They are all represented on two rows beneath the goddess Tang, the figures in the first row being dressed in the military style and riding big horses, and those in the next row in the style of civil officials. Towards the lower end of the drawing are the altar of heaven and the five peaks, in front of which is placed an altar bearing a tablet that reads, "the three realms of heaven and earth" (*tiandi sanjie*).

Three more drawings round up the many gods and goddesses sacrificed to. One of them is devoted to the "great kings" (*dawang*). In the middle of the drawing sits the bodhisattva of the old hall, who is flanked on both sides by the Venerable Guan and the Buddha of the Western Heaven. On the following row are represented the god of fire, the Erlang god (a common god in north China), the star god in charge of life, General Guan, the gate of heaven and the gate of earth, and then the various great kings, including the four great kings of the golden dragon, and the lesser venerables, including Yan, Xiao, Di, the third lady of the fish king, and the scholar of the altar. There is also a drawing referred to as the "venerable masters", representing the protector gods and goddesses, including the six imperial commissioners who grant peace and wealth, and the seven fairy ladies who have charge of child-rearing. There are other drawings for gods and goddesses of all sorts, many of whom the worshippers know little about. A picturesque one denotes a fairy carrying a feather fan flanked by four serving boys, below whom stand various fairy women, including two named respectively as the fairy mother and the fairy ancestor of the boat.

Essentially, families related by descent have in their keeping some seven or eight similar scrolls, even though not every family holds them. According

124 *Diao Tongju and She Kanglue*

to custom, elderly people beyond the age of 60 *sui* (59 years of age) are not required to sacrifice regularly to the "old ancestors" and so they pass the scrolls they own to their eldest son. Other sons and their descendants participate in sacrifice in the eldest son's house. However, there are occasions when the younger sons or their descendants might wish to have their own copies of the drawings to sacrifice to in their own houses, for example, when they meet with ill fortune. Should that happen, new drawings have to be initiated (*kai-guang*) through a special set of ceremonies. This process is known as "setting up the old ancestors" (*chu laozhu*), and carries the implication that the line carrying out the activity is now independent of the eldest line. A man whose younger sons have "set up the old ancestors" sacrifices in the house of the eldest son he lives with. However, he continues to lead the sacrifice, which is attended by all his sons and their descendants who have not set up their own old ancestors.

The "old ancestors" include the ancestors of the Bright Hall, the goddess Tang and the many gods, goddesses and fairies represented on scrolls. It is important to grasp the ambiguity in the word "ancestors" as used by the fishing people in order to understand what might appear to the outside observers as "ancestral" sacrificial ceremonies. "Ancestors" is an ambiguous concept embodying forebear of previous generations as well as the gods, goddesses and fairies. Moreover, because the forebear, gods, goddesses and fairies are represented on scrolls that are passed down within the line of descent, the possession of the scrolls, referred to as a "hall" of "old ancestors" (*yitang laozu*), indicates the presence of a descent line. Because family division involves "setting up the old ancestors", when the fishing people think of lines of descent, they think of the "halls of old ancestors" held by different family groups. When asked about family segments, they are often unable to provide precise descriptions. Instead, they describe such "halls of old ancestors". Likewise, when they participate in "continuing the family genealogy" (of which more will be said in the next section), they participate as a "hall of old ancestors". When the genealogy is printed, it is similarly distributed to each such "hall". Ideas of the family and the lineage are also, therefore, built into practice. During the New Year, junior members of the lineage attend sacrifice exclusively at the "hall" of the senior member of the lineage who possesses the scrolls. The practice seems to highlight the continuing of sacrifice along a family stem, and what becomes the lineage as represented in a genealogy is the collection of groups of such stem families.

We can assume that the fishing people of Weishan Lake have persisted for some time around the scrolls known as the "old ancestors". We can also assume that prior to their settlement on land, each group participating at a "hall" consisted only of the immediate descendants of two to three generations, and that they split into independent "halls" when the numbers increase. From what we know of the scrolls, the objects of sacrifice are not exclusive to lineage forebear. In recent years, the division between lineage

From respect for the gods to sacrifice to the ancestors 125

forebear and the gods, goddesses and fairies has become marked. A result of this tendency can be seen in the periodic ceremony known as "continuing the family genealogy".

On four separate occasions in 2009 and 2010, the authors and their students took part in sacrifice to the ancestors at Weishan lake. On those occasions, we saw that the names recorded on the scrolls were read aloud as prayers were offered to invite or bid farewell to the "old ancestors". The New Year celebration, for example, involved bidding farewell to them a week before New Year's Day, as they made their annual attendance at the court of the Jade Emperor, welcoming them back two or three days before New Year, and celebrating with them on New Year's Eve and New Year's Day. In prayers offered for the farewell and the invitation, all the names on the scrolls, not only ancestors' but also gods' and fairies', were read out. On New Year's Day, the scrolls were hung on the walls of the house and offered the first meal of the year. Prayers were also offered outside the house to Heaven and Earth, and for that ceremony, the scroll bearing the characters "the three realms of heaven and earth" was placed on the altar. Those ceremonies show that the family's religious life is centred around the scrolls.[2]

Continuing the family genealogy

The ceremony known as "continuing the family genealogy" is now very common in the area bordering Weishan lake. It is carried out once every five to ten years, and it brings together many family groups to the same place to sacrifice to the ancestors and the gods. The family group brings its own scrolls to partake in the collective celebration. The term suggests that the ceremony builds on the idea of a common lineage for all participants. It includes feasting, religious celebration and participation by young and old, men and women. Nowadays, it is often taken care of by a "lineage management committee" (*zongzu lishihui*). Guests are also invited from among friends and relatives.

The person in charge of the ceremony is known as the altar head (*tantou*). He is regarded as a religious specialist, known as the *duangong*. He carries out the entire ceremony in consultation with the host families, and he provides all the material needed in the ceremony as well as the initiation for new scrolls. The position is usually occupied by a highly respected person, and his work is paid for like the work conducted by any *duangong*.

At the location where the celebration takes place, a temporary shed is built. To avoid the rainy or the cold season, it usually takes place in spring or autumn, in the third to fourth lunar months, or the ninth and tenth lunar months. Depending on the financial strength of participating family groups, the ceremony may last from two to four days, a four-day ceremony being regarded as a magnificent demonstration of wealth. In the shed, offerings are made to the ancestors and gods, and the *duangong* performs the drum song. There is an inner chamber that allows the *duangong* to change his clothes and rest, but it is also a place where the scrolls are displayed. It

126 *Diao Tongju and She Kanglue*

is regarded as a religious space from which women are barred. The rest of the shed makes up the outer chamber. A straw mat is thrown on the ground there on which the *duangong* performs the drum song. The audience sits on stools on its two sides. On the walls of both inner and outer chambers are hung representations of silver ingots made with tin foil. At the entrance to the outer chamber are displayed banners bearing the lines, "Thanks-giving ceremony to the gods," and "Here opens the door of wealth", and on the walls of the inner chamber are hung paper-cut portraits of gods in two colours: black for the "lower", or worldly, gods (*xiajie shen*), including Tang goddess and the local (or lesser) gods and fairies, and blue for the "upper", or heavenly, gods (*shangjie shen*), including Guanyin, the Jade Emperor, that is to say, bodhisattvas and gods that are well-known across most parts of China and that in imperial times had been given imperial recognition. The "upper" gods are also referred to as "vegetarian" (*su*), indicating that they are offered only vegetarian food, while the "lower" gods are offered also meat. Behind the shed is a 10m-high flag post that is set up after the shed has been built.

On the altar in the inner chamber, the most significant display consists of containers known as "bushels" (*dou*). It is conceivable that in the past, when wooden bushels were used for measuring grain, wooden bushels were indeed used in the display. Nowadays, wooden bushels are hard to come by, and so miscellaneous containers are used instead, wrapped in red paper bearing on it the name of the family that has deposited the specific bushel on the altar. The bushels are sometimes referred to as the wealth-god bushel (*caishen dou*), and are used to provide a temporary abode for the spirits of the ancestors. The name on the bushel indicates the name of the most senior ancestor, while other ancestors are represented on slips of red paper that are inserted on the bushel, along with little colour banners indicating the five directions, and a weighing scale, a sword, a mirror and a comb all of which objects offer protection against evil spirits. The location of the bushel in relation to the altar indicates proximity to the ancestor. For that reason, the senior line (descendants of the ancestor's eldest son) is entitled to the central position facing the altar, and other lines place theirs on the two sides. Disputes on the location accorded a family group are common.

The celebration is conducted over three to four days, of which four components are essential. They include singing the history of the ancestors (*chang jiaqian*), inviting the gods into the shed (*shen jinpeng*), thanking the gods (*choushen*) and making offerings (*shangli*).[3] The *duangong* plays an important part in all these ceremonies.

The celebration begins when the altar head strikes the gong and another *duangong* begins to sing the ancestors' history. From that moment until the end of the ceremony, incense must continuously be burnt at the burner in the inner chamber. The song recounts the ancestors escaping from famine, begging for food and, eventually, emerging from poverty. As part of the song,

Plate 8.2 Scrolls displayed in "continuing the genealogy" ceremony (credit: Diao Tongju).

the *duangong* also informs the ancestors, represented by a scroll that had been kept by the host family, the reason for the current ceremony of "continuing the genealogy" and the order of events to follow in the next few days. A part of the ceremony consists of the *duangong* "going around the lanterns" (*zoudeng*). Holding his drum, he sings as he traces what would seem like the numeral 8 to gather the ancestral spirits from all directions to join the celebration and to partake in the offerings. This part of the ceremony concludes with members of the lineage kneeling down to pray to the ancestors, and divining if the ancestors are satisfied with the arrangements to follow.

On the next day, the spirits enter the shed in a ceremony. During this ceremony, family members take their scrolls into the inner chamber so that they may be hung up to partake in the offerings. The eldest son or grandson is responsible for taking the scrolls and praying in the five directions as he approaches the shed. Praying to the five directions is an indication that the gods and fairies of all five directions are invited to the celebration. Because of the solemnity of the occasion, a pig's head has already been placed on the altar in the inner chamber. At the same time, in the outer chamber, some tables have been arranged so that family bushels may be put on them. Again, the ordering of the bushels is observed: the senior line's bushel is kept at the front and the others are placed behind it in the order of seniority. At midnight, every family holding its scrolls of the "old ancestors" approaches the inner chamber. Again led by representatives of the senior line, members of the families take their scrolls, wrapped up in red cloth, into the shed, stepping over a burning fire at the entrance as they do so – both red cloth and fire protect the scrolls from evil spirits. Once in, they hang the scroll with the figure of Guanyin at the top of the bushel, and place the other scrolls either in the bushel or on the sides. As they withdraw from the chamber after having done that, the *duangong* walks among the bushels holding his drum and sings. After the singing, the families in the order of seniority take the bushels into the inner chamber along with all their scrolls. Some families come with more scrolls than can be hung up, not uncommonly several dozen scrolls or more, in which case only one scroll is hung up and the others are laid on the side of the bushels so that the ancestral spirits represented may also partake in the offerings.

The offerings consist of live animals such as pigs, sheep and chickens, which are slaughtered in the inner chamber one day before the ceremony closes. The offering must also include the drawing of human blood. The slaughtered animals are offered in front of the altar, and a mutton soup is made of the sheep offering to be drunk in the evening. When this ceremony of thanking the gods has been concluded, on the last day of the celebration, friends and relatives – primarily women who have married out of the lineage – make their offerings. These offerings consist of paper money, firecrackers, cakes, fruit, wine and cigarettes. The women are not allowed into the inner chamber but, as the women pray outside, the offerings are taken inside for presentation to the ancestors by the men. The offerings are retrieved by evening and either taken away by participants or consumed. The boisterous atmosphere resulting from those activities contributes to the spirit of celebration of the occasion.

When the ceremonies are completed, participating families take their scrolls home. However, one necessary step has yet to be carried out for that to be possible. That is because when the scrolls are taken into the inner chamber, a long-legged god has been invited to keep watch over them so that they may not disappear. Before they now leave the inner chamber, the altar head has to cut out a paper figurine to represent the long-legged god and, using a knife, cut that figurine into two on a bench placed at the entrance of the shed. Only when the watch-keeper has been dismembered can the spirits of the ancestors and the gods depart. When the scrolls are once again brought back home, members of the family let off firecrackers in welcome. All incense, candle, ritual paper offering, banners, portraits of "upper" and "lower" gods have to be burnt. The red cloth that married-out daughters provide in gift will be divided by members of the family.

It needs to be pointed out that the ceremonies of "continuing the genealogy" as described does not include an element of genealogy compilation. Elderly people refer to the ceremony as "making offerings to the gods" (*jingshen*) among themselves, and only as "continuing the genealogy" when they describe the ceremony to outside people (including academic investigators).[4]

From respect for the gods to sacrifice to the ancestors   129

They may even add that "continuing the genealogy is sacrifice to the ancestors" and say that inclusion in the genealogy is the objective of the celebration. The observer who attends the ceremony can see in it an element of ancestral sacrifice, but it should be equally obvious that, not only ancestors, but gods and fairies are sacrificed to. Why, then, has the ceremony been described as "continuing the genealogy"?

It should be understood that the fishing people of Weishan lake are among the poorest of fishing people. In the indigenous classification of the fishing people by their livelihood, the Weishan lake fishing people are known for fishing in shallow water using nets tied to short pieces of bamboo (known as *lan*-fishing). They are, for the most part, illiterate, but they know that escaping from famine, their ancestors had come to this area from Shanxi, Henan, Hebei and elsewhere. Commonly, they refer to themselves as people of other provinces, such as Xinhua county in Yangzhou prefecture or Yancheng county in Huai'an prefecture. It is possible that the ceremony now known as "continuing the genealogy" had arisen at a time when, in recognition of the scattering family groups over many places, some people had thought of a common periodic festival to provide for some sense of unity.

But in those early days, there would have been no written genealogy. The only activity remotely resembling the extension of a genealogy in those days would have been the very occasional affirmation of a set of characters to be adopted in personal names. In those days, organizers of the festival would have provided a big boat or two on which ceremonies would have been conducted, while members of family groups would have come from all directions in their own boats and, for the duration of the celebration, deposited their scrolls in the holds of the big boats.

However, until the 1980s, "respect for the gods", like much of popular religion, was classed as superstition by the government. During the Cultural Revolution, the activity was banned. It is likely that while the government was cautious about popular religion, and because the communal celebrations in the Weishan lake area had always included both gods and ancestors, local people increasingly narrated them as ancestral celebrations. The emphasis on ancestors may also be taken in connection with an interest in compiling genealogies that was current in the 1980s, beginning with villages on land before it was adopted by the fishing people. In that context, "continuing the genealogy" became a reasonable practice in association with such celebrations. The "lineage committee" that oversees the celebration may call for publishing another compilation of the lineage genealogy, and the "Bright Hall" scroll that the family possesses can readily supply the information needed for continuing the genealogical lines. One of the earliest genealogies compiled among the fishing people, the *Genealogy of the Shen Surname of Wuxing Hall* (*Wuxing tang Shenshi zupu*) compiled in 2001 makes a strong statement in its preface for the need to sacrifice to a common ancestor, but it is obvious that for more than a century, there was no common genealogy. Just as obvious is that the current mood has now quite

130 *Diao Tongju and She Kanglue*

accepted the need for a common genealogical compilation, as a conversation with a participant at a "continuing the genealogy" ceremony in 2010 quite brought home to us researchers:

> Answer: It is worth my spending time and money to join this continuing of the genealogy. I have to account to future generations as to who my forebear are. I am not used to life here in the north ... but I have come to continue the genealogy ... because after that, I take the genealogy home and I can see which branch is closest to mine. That is the meaning of continuing the genealogy.
>
> Interviewer: Are there people who don't want to pay money to continue the genealogy?
>
> Answer: That would be foolish and short-sighted. You are not thinking of your descendants if you don't want to spend that sort of money.[5]

The man had come to Weishan Lake in Shandong from Changzhou city in Jiangsu province to attend the ceremony. His description made it clear he found the participation worthwhile.

Conclusion

In stressing the importance of the scrolls depicting gods and fairies in the ceremonies that the fishing people of Weishan lake refer to as "sacrifice to the ancestors" or "continuing the family genealogies", this chapter does not argue that a sense of lineage is necessarily weaker or stronger than that exhibited among people living on land. Rather, this paper makes the point that when the fishing people of Weishan lake refer to figures on their scrolls and periodically sacrificed to as "ancestors" (*zu*), they have by tradition not restricted the usage of the term to their forebear. The impression that is given by the use of the term and the representation of the scrolls is that they have knowledge of the names of the deceased of their immediate family. Beyond the immediate family, they come under the protection of gods, fairies and named or unnamed procreators of entire lines. Yet, unlike land people who have possessed written genealogies for long periods of time, they are unable to provide the names of ancestors within the line beyond their father's or grandfather's generation.

There is no way of knowing since when the fishing families of Weishan lake had developed the practice of meeting periodically to sacrifice collectively to the gods and ancestors represented on their scrolls. What is fairly clear is that the practice was revived in the 1980s and gradually took on the character of an ancestral ritual in which continuing the genealogy came to play a part. Converging their practices on those of the land people might have been one reason of this trend, but another reason would be the perceived need to label the occasion as something other than popular religion. Despite the label,

From respect for the gods to sacrifice to the ancestors   131

sacrifice to the gods, in addition to ancestors, has remained an inherent part of the ceremony.

Notes

1 Note from the editors: It is not clear from the ethnography if Tang *shen* was the name of a god or a generic term to refer to the gods of the Bright Hall.
2 We published our report on those visits in She Kanle and Liu Xing, "Yumin chunjie zizu yu zongzu juhe – yi Lunan Weishan hu qu wei zhongxin" (The fishing people's new year ancestral sacrifice and lineage solidarity – with a focus on the Weishan lake area in southern Shangdong), *Minsu yanjiu*, 2011, pp 187–202.
3 Note from translator: The Chinese word used is "shen", which may be translated as either "god" or "spirit". The term is used for gods as well ancestors.
4 The five-yearly celebration is sometimes referred to as the "little occasion for respecting the gods" (*xiao jingshen*), and the ten-yearly celebration the "big occasion for respecting the gods" (*da jingshen*).
5 Interview by She Kangle on 19 April, 2010 outside the shed in which ceremonies were conducted at a "continuing the genealogy" celebration.

Part III
As contemporary stereotypes

9   Land supports fishing people

The fishermen of Dongting lake from the 1930s to the 1950s

Wong Wing-ho

Dongting lake lies astride the provinces of Hubei and Hunan. The flow of the Yangzi river enters the lake from the north and drains out of it towards the south and southwest. As the flow slows in the lake, sediments are deposited, forming mudbanks. Such land has been embanked and cultivated. Embankment reduces the surface area of the lake: between 1542 and 1860, the lake covered 2,300 square miles in its peak season, but by 1949 that had been reduced to 1,680 square miles. Because the mudbanks formed by the sediments remain low-lying, embankments create enclosures, in many of which are small lakes surrounded by farmland.[1] The farmland attracts immigrants and so the communities formed on them are relatively recent. Temples, ancestral halls and powerful lineages are uncommon, houses are scattered rather than clustered. Compared to other parts of Hubei and Hunan, the banks of Dongting lake represent recent developments and the villages lying on them are culturally and politically peripheral to urban centres such as Xiangtan and Hankou.

The fishing people of peripheral communities

The most detailed reports on the fishing people of Dongting lake were written by Zhou Di in 1940.[2] Zhou was the director of the Hunan Fishery Company Preparatory Office, and his two essays on the fishing people became the locus of future discussions. According to Zhou, there were three types of fishing people in Dongting lake in the Republican period. The first type was made up of people who were settled. Most of them lived on the edges of the lake and they fished in shallow water. The second type practised net-fishing, and they lived on their boats. The third type was described as "half-fishing and half-farming", and included settled as well mobile populations. The classification blurs the distinction that he went on to make in his articles: around the edges of the lake, there were big landlords who controlled the shallows and who set up permanent seine nets with which they fished, and they were different from the poor who skimmed the surface for what they could find. The poor made up what he called settled or half-fishing and half-farming inhabitants on the edges of the lake, living primarily on the mudbanks beyond the embankments. In addition, there were the fishing

136 *Wong Wing-ho*

people who sailed into Dongting lake during the high fishing season and who either lived on their boats or set up temporary sheds on the mudbanks. During the fishing season, Zhou said, the Dongting lake came to life. With the outside fishing boats gathering there, the merchants followed, as did the teahouses and the sing-song girls. The markets sprang into existence. When the fishing season passed, life receded back into quietness.

Boat-living fishing people

Zhou Di reports that the boat-living fishing people conducted the larger fishing operations on Dongting lake. They were also the richer, as their catches tended to be more valuable. They operated large fishing boats, using wind-net and small-mesh nets. Wind-net boats were among the largest boats that sailed on Dongting lake and could withstand strong winds and rough currents.

The boat-living fishing people operated primarily on the eastern side of the lake. The *Hunan Economic Enterprises*, a government record published in 1935, noted that all around the Dongting lake were 18,130 fishing households and 13,630 fishing boats. Of those, several thousands were noted as fishing boats operating nets and 500 were noted as sailing boats.[3] They were found entirely in the counties of Xiangyin, Yueyang and Hanshou, located respectively on the southeast and southwest corners of the lake. Only in the north and northwest were net-operating boats not noted. The north and northwest parts of the lake had been filled in by reclaimed land, and only on the southern sides of the lake might be found large expanses of waters. The *Hunan Economic Enterprises* also reported that sailing boats were found on the lake, and rowing boats in the rivers that flowed into and out of the lake. That description agrees with the reports of the distribution of the different types of boats around the lake.[4]

The net-fishing people fished for shad and whitebait. The bony shad was considered a delicacy in many parts of coastal China. For most of the year, the fish might be found in coastal waters, but at the end of spring and beginning of summer, they swam up the Yangzi to spawn their eggs. After that, they returned to the sea, leaving their fry to grow in the tributaries and lakes of the Yangzi, until by autumn they too would return to the sea. The Shanghai newspaper *Shenbao* left a report of the annual cycle of shad fishing in 1893. It said:

> The shad is found in Dongting lake. Every year, at the end of spring and beginning of summer, as it goes into the Yangzi, fishing people along the river cast their nets to catch them. At the beginning of the season, it fetches twice its usual price. From the beginning to the end, the season lasts only a month. After that, it is impossible to find a single fish on the market. So, the fishing people make a profit from every fish, and when the season is over, they stage the opera to thank the gods. From the 27th and 28th days of last month [fifth lunar month], opera had been staged on

Land supports fishing people: the fishermen of Dongting lake   137

the bank of the river. Three to four hundred boats gathered, practically forming a village.[5]

Despite this very positive description in the newspaper, the shad is not frequently mentioned in the gazetteers of the counties around Dongting.[6] It is likely to have been a very localized fishing activity, unlike the whitebait.

Like the shad, the whitebait swims up the river from the sea in early summer to spawn. A small fish, it lays its eggs among the rushes and reeds. The adult fish stays near the lake surface and can be caught by net. Whitebait fishing appears, from reports by Zhou and others, to be located towards the west of Dongting lake and the description of net-fishing accords with Zhou's report that this manner of fishing was conducted by boat-living fishing people. It is possible to conclude, therefore, that an annual seasonal flow of fishing boats arrived in Dongting lake. In terms of quantity, however, the amount of whitebait caught appears quite tiny compared to reports of overall annual production, and so the seasonal inflow of fishing boats probably amounted to no more than a portion of what Zhou called the settled fishing people and the half-fishing and half-farming population.[7]

Fishing people settled on land

According to the *Hunan Economic Enterprise*, the most common fish caught in the counties around Dongting lake were common carp, silver carp, grass carp, bream, Chinese perch and gold fish.[8] The annual catch of all fish amounted to 370,000 piculs, of which whitebait made up only 1,500 piculs.[9] According to Zhou Di, fishing began annually from the third lunar month. The early season lasted from the third month to the fifth month, but fish was not plentiful then. From the sixth month to the seventh month, the lake would overflow, covering all the vegetation that had grown in the marshes during the early season, and during this time, nets might be used to catch fish that gathered near the surface. A fish ban was imposed in the eighth and ninth months so that fish might propagate. The tenth month was the season of plenty, for as the lake water receded, it would become possible to reach the fish that stayed nearer the vegetation. The seasonal nature of fishing on the lake meant that either fishing had to be combined with other activities or, especially in the case of boat dwellers, seasonal migration up-river in search of fish would have been necessary as the fishing seasons closed on the lake.

In the plentiful season, lines, traps and seine nets were commonly used in shallow waters. Seine nets were operated by wealthy fishing households. Considerable preparation was needed to attract the fish by planting reeds, and bamboo matting was used for three rows of netting surrounding the area. Fish were driven from the outer enclosure to the inner enclosure through trap-doors. As the reed was removed, it would be exposed and caught. The netted area was reported by Zhou to have consisted of 20 to 30 *mu*, and planting the reed alone took 30 people working together. Compared to the operation

138 *Wong Wing-ho*

of a fishing boat, which often took only three people, running a seine net was a capital-intensive operation. Seine-net operators were, therefore, landlords on the edges of the lake, unlike most land-settled fishing people. Many settled fishing people were quite poor. Except for some who owned their own boats, others hired out their labour. Zhou described a village known as Foot-and-Hand Gully (Jiaoshou *keng*) where fishermen went into the water naked, even when the weather had turned cold. They would emerge after only half an hour in the water to warm themselves by a fire on their boats, before entering the water again. He said the sheds they lived in were shabby. Writing in the tradition that characterized much of social reporting in the 1930s and 1940s, he thought that the small fishing families were being bankrupted by the exploitation of landlords.[10]

There certainly were charges to be paid for fishing in the lake. It is far from clear who made the charges, for aside from referring to those people as "masters of the lake" (*huzhu*), the writers of the 1930s and 1940s have left little description of who they were. They reported that the masters of the lake had their own armed men, who could torture fishing people for violating their rights or even burn their fishing tools. Li Zhenyi, a reporter who visited the Dongting lake in 1946, cited a land deed he collected that showed that the rotation system of controlling land and water rights applied there as it did elsewhere. The buyer might collect dues by rotation, set up barriers and shelters, recruit fishing people to operated nets and share in the profit made from selling the fish as well as reeds and firewood.[11] Zhou collected information on the charges made by masters of the lake: they were made according to the manner of fishing and the size of the nets. In addition, fishing people paid for the right to enter the lake, a charge that was paid not only by land-settled fishing people but also the boat-living migrants. He reported that many fishing people were unable to pay the charges and opted instead to give up 50 per cent of the catches to the masters of the lake. Because charges were also levied for the sale of the catch, he estimated that a fishing family might retain only 20 per cent of the value of their catch after all charges were made.[12]

An example: Wanzi lake

Actual examples are hard to come by. Nevertheless, a 1942 survey report of the southern portion of Dongting, known also as Wanzi lake, shows that fishing was conducted by both boat-living fishing people and settled villagers.[13] The report states that 60 per cent of the annual total catch came from net fishing. The fishing boats carried nets described as floating nets, sinking nets, shrimp nets and whitebait nets. Floating and sinking nets required the cooperation of two boats, suggesting that trawling was the desired operation. That was the manner of fishing from the tenth lunar month of each year to the fourth lunar month of the following year. From the fourth month to the eighth month, the boats worked separately to catch the whitebait, shrimps and the "pointed-mouth fish" (*jianzui yu*, Luciobrama macrocephalus), the largest

Land supports fishing people: the fishermen of Dongting lake 139

catches consisting of whitebait. At the time of the survey, ten pairs of boats operated in the lake, of which nine and a half had come from Hubei and only one boat belonged to local people. From the tenth to the fourth month, line fishing by these boats also accounted for 20 per cent of the annual catch. The natives operating lines and nets, traps and seine nets accounted for the rest.

Catches from the fishing boats, the seine nets and the traps were collected by fish merchants who gathered at moorages to buy from them. The purchases were sent elsewhere by specialized junks equipped with tanks for transporting live fish. The poorer fishing people themselves took their catches to the county city to sell to fish merchants. The scales used for deliveries at moorages were reckoned at 20 taels to the catty, and the ones at the county city at the standard 16 taels to the catty, implying a discount by weight when merchants purchased at moorages. The difference might explain why the poorer people went direct to the city: the fishing boats paid the premium for the convenience of selling in bulk.

The masters of the lake were on good terms with the fishing people. They charged a fishing tax (*shuike fei* – a term reminiscent of the fish tax demanded from imperial times rather than a Republican tax) from the fishing boats but not from the smaller fishermen. The tax was commuted to a fixed rate depending on the going price of fish. Net-fishing boats paid 50 per cent of their catches, settled by a weighing scale that the lake masters produced for the purpose on the fishing boats. The practice determined the annual cycle of charges levied by the masters of the lake. Net-fishing boats paid fish tax for the early season from the fifth month to the eighth month, a fishing ban was imposed from the eighth month to the tenth month then when the fishing season opened in the tenth month, the lake masters set up temporary sheds on the shore of the moorages and dispatched their patrol boats to spot violators, who could be detained, fined or beaten, and whose boats and fishing tools might be destroyed.

Fishermen or peasants?

Li Zhenyi was a newspaper reporter for the *Central Daily*. In 1946 and 1947, he wrote two articles about the Dongting Lake in which he said:

> Reclaimed land on this lake has been brought fully into cultivation by the sweat and blood of two million peasants. It has created luxury for a minority of landlords. The soil of newly reclaimed land whets the appetite of all local gangsters, whether they have had experience in reclamations. This is the land of brute force. "By force one controls land and water," so it is said. "The lake water is made lean to fatten the land reclaimed." Lean and fat characterize the peasants and their landlords.[14]

Li's articles gave the impression that in the continuous reclamation of Dongting lake, the lake surface area kept declining while land on its edges had been increasing. He had visited the lake along with an official delegation

140 *Wong Wing-ho*

dispatched by the newly established Yangzi River Water Conservation Bureau to report on the conditions of the peasants living on its edges. There had been reports of disputes over land rights and the suffering of the peasants. The delegation, in its report, argued that unwieldy embankments on the edges of the lake had brought problems to water control and the peasants were indeed being exploited. It did not say that, therefore, the surrounding land should not be reclaimed, merely that there should be order in the development of reclamation. Li Zhenyi's newspaper articles presented very much the same line of argument.

What needs to be noticed in these reports is that the people being exploited were said to be peasants. Li's article, "Walking around Dongting Lake" said of them:

> Near the fields by a collapsed embankment at Liuhe on the south bank of West Port, I saw several peasant families who remained loyal to their land ... Of two hundred peasants who used to live here, only about a dozen had remained on this desolate shore ... The old farmer was rowing a boat, coming home with fish.[15]

Fields near collapsed embankments were exposed to flood water and could not be put to crops. From his description, it is clear that Li had visited a village that had been abandoned after the embankment had collapsed. The old farmer he saw was no longer farming; he was engaged in fishing. If confirmation is needed of the central position of fishing to the farmer's way of life, it might be found from the petition of a group of people who were dispossessed of their land:

> We holders of the property [*yemin*] had lived here for generations. We follow the water, making a living from fish, shrimps, firewood and grass. We do not want to give up the land we have occupied for generations. But we can neither move nor make a living ... Even then, every year we have paid our land tax, as can be certified from our tax receipts.[16]

The people that Li Zhenyi saw as "peasants" were, by their own description, making a living from fish, shrimps, firewood and grass. They were held responsible for land tax, but they fished for a living.

Zhou Di wrote in 1942 during the Sino–Japanese War but before the Japanese gained control of Dongting lake and its surroundings. For a short time, while the area remained under the nationalist government's control, it became an important food-exporter, and its salted fish could be sold as far as Chongqing, the wartime nationalist capital. Zhou was responsible for setting up the Hunan Fishery Company (Hunan *yuye gongsi*), which was to manage the fishing grounds, provide capital for fishing people and alleviate the hardship imposed by the masters of the lake. By 1943, the area had fallen to the Japanese and that brought an end to the company. The war brought

Land supports fishing people: the fishermen of Dongting lake 141

much destruction to shipping on Dongting lake, including fishing vessels, and hence, after the war, there was considerable interest again in the hardship faced by the local people. By then, the language in which social issues were discussed had come to be strongly dominated by social class analysis. The term "peasant", therefore, came easily to be used by Li Zhenyi. Somehow, in the new language of social science, the fishing people dropped out of the discourse.

Notes

1 Zhang Shijun and Liang Nianzhi, "Hefeng yuan fangwen ji" (A visit to the Hefeng embankment), Xin Hunan bao (ed.), *Hunan nongcun qingkuang diaocha*, Changsha: Xinhua shudian, 1950, pp. 47–57.
2 Zhou Di, "Hunan zhi yuye" (Hunan fishery), *Hunan sheng yinhang jingji jikan*, 1942, 1(1), pp. 177–184; Zhou Di, "Dongting hu zhi yumin" (The fishing people of Dongting lake) *Hunan sheng yinhang jingji jikan*, 1943, 1(4), pp. 187–193.
3 Xiangyin county had 930 boats using nets, and Hanshou county had 4,300 boats, including an unspecified number of line fishers, which would have been smaller boats.
4 Zhu Xinong and Zhu Baoxun (eds.), *Hunan shiye zhi* (Hunan economic enterprises), Changsha: Hunan renmin, 2008, first published as *Zhongguo shiye zhi: quanguo shiye diaocha baogao zhi si: Hunan sheng* (China's economic enterprises, report of a national survey of enterprises, Vol. 4, Hunan province), Shanghai: Shiye bu guoji maoyiju, 1935, pp. 681–683.
5 *Shenbao*, 18 July 1893.
6 *Yuanjiang xian zhi* (Gazetteer of Yuanjiang county), 1810, 1/22b notes the shad as a local product; *Yiyang xian zhi* (Gazetteer of Yiyang county), 1874, 2/16a states that the shad was not found any more.
7 Zhou, "Hunan zhi yuye", pp. 179–180.
8 The names of fish are identified in Li Shanghao, "Dongting hu shixi baogao zhi yi – shiyong yulei" (Dongting lake practice report no. 1 – edible fish), *Zhongshan xuebao*, 1941, 1(6), pp. 33–36. Various types of carp have remained the most common edible fish of the Dongting; Li Hongbing and Xu Deping, "Dongting hu 'sida jiayu' ziyuan bianhua tezheng ji yuanyin fenxi" (The "four family fishes" of the Dongting lake, special features and analysis of the changes to a resource), *Neilu shuichan*, 2008, 6, pp. 34–36.
9 Zhu and Zhu, *Hunan shiye zhi*, pp. 688–691.
10 Zhou, "Hunan zhi yuye", pp. 179–180; Zhou, "Dongting hu zhi yumin", p. 187.
11 Li Zhenyi, *Hunan de Xibei jiao* (The northwestern corner of Hunan), Changsha: Yuzhou shuju, 1947, p. 109.
12 Zhou, "Dongtinghu zhi yumin", pp. 190–191.
13 Jingji yanjiu shi (Research office), "Yuanjiang xian Wanzi hu yuye diaocha," (A survey of fishery at Wanzi lake in Yuanjiang county), *Hunan sheng yinhang jingji jikan*, 1942, 1(1), pp. 291–294. The essay acknowledges the help of Zhou Di and others for providing information. It was probably compiled by the research office of the Hunan provincial bank, which published the journal in which it appeared.
14 Li, *Hunan de xibeijiao*, p. 111.
15 Li, *Hunan de xibeijiao*, p. 109.
16 Li, *Hunan de xibeijiao*, p. 109.

10 Going beyond pariah status

The boat people of Fuzhou in the Chinese People's Republic

Huang Xiangchun

Fuzhou city was opened as a treaty port by the Treaty of Nanjing in 1842 after the Opium War. Thereafter, it grew along with other treaty ports on the China coast through the rest of the nineteenth century. As trade boomed and merchants grew wealthy, as an urban elite appeared and material life came to be intertwined with symbols of modernization, economic and social changes seeped into the livelihood and social structure of the city and its surrounding neighbourhood boat population. The population was numerous, but a number would not be meaningful, for what counted as a boat person (or household) was subject to precisely the changes that were afoot. Popular perception associated menial occupations with the boat people; the government wanted to regulate them through household registration in the *baojia* system of collective responsibility; the boat people saw themselves eking out a living in between tradition and modernity or, more precisely, between continued sacrifice to local gods or the Virgin Mary (known locally as Christian Mother Mary); and post-1949, the government of the People's Republic saw them as an oppressed people who had to be liberated. Yet, the 1950s saw the definitive transformation of the Fuzhou boat-dwellers' pariah status. A government decision settled once and for all their ethnicity: they were not to be classed as ethnic minorities and, in that sense, they were one with the rest of the Fuzhou city population.

Geography and background

The reclamation of sedimentary land at river estuaries had been going on in earnest at Fuzhou from the sixteenth century and, for that reason, it should be safe to assume that for many people, it had been a long process of being involved in land reclamation, settling ashore in communities that were coagulated around territorial shrines, and embracing ancestral sacrifice through the building of ancestral halls, very much in the process that has been traced by Zheng, Dean and Szonyi for the Fujian coast.[1] Szonyi's study of the lineages of Luozhou is particularly relevant in that Luozhou's location on the southern edge of Nantai island to the south of Fuzhou city places it

Going beyond pariah status: the boat people of Fuzhou   143

almost at the heart of the reclamation. Local histories written in the second half of the nineteenth century recall the "great surnames" (*daxing*) living in large villages of several hundred households at Cangshan district across the river, and that religious celebrations were focused on the temples of the religious district (*jing*) cutting across surname and lineage divisions.[2] Vestiges of modernization appeared with the growth of the city, so that by 1880, when the Shangshu temple of Longtan district was repaired, not only was the involvement of merchants quite apparent, but among the donors were also the Longtan Fire-Fighting Society, and the Charity Burial Association. The presence of such voluntary associations indicates the gradual evolution towards local self-management well before the onset of the Chinese Republic in 1912.[3]

Nevertheless, the movement to settle ashore as lineages was only one aspect of the changes that came over the fishing people on the outskirts of Fuzhou through the ages. The rapid urbanization of Fuzhou from the second half of the nineteenth century had been brought about by sea-borne trade, which meant that junks, and then steamers, plying the China coast, loaded from and offloaded at Fuzhou to teaming smaller craft that connected with the many towns and villages up and down the Min river and its tributaries. Therefore, as the landward settlement exhausted available sedimentary foreshores for reclamation, the riverine and coastal trade had been able to absorb a considerable portion of the surrounding population. Landing places were obviously valuable assets subject to considerable competition. The opening sentence from a document found in the Fuzhou archives dated to 1949 recording an appeal from ferry operators who were displaced by a steam-launch company gives the flavour of an acceptable argument in favour of territorial entitlement. It says,

> On the Butterfly Creek of Cangxia islet in Taijiang district, for many generations historic relics have remained. That creek has been, for generations, the mooring station of us eight families. We run ferries there and through our hard work make our living.[4]

The appeal to history was not all about a sense of identity. Occupational status was very much defined by government household registration, enforced in the Republican period along with the newly founded police force, and historical memory justified the claim to occupational status.

Again, in the background were the wider changes in local government experienced in many parts of China from the nineteenth century into the twentieth. The Qing government had practised *baojia* registration of households, but for most of China, the Qing dynasty county magistrate was not well-represented in the villages where *baojia* was to be implemented. From the last years of the Qing dynasty into the early Republic, government administration was largely taken over by gentry establishments, such as the chambers of commerce. When the police force was launched under that arrangement, it

144　*Huang Xiangchun*

came very much under local control, and so *baojia* registration was gradually merged into policing. By 1927, with the re-establishment of centralized government, the provincial Department of Civil Affairs took control of *baojia*, and the police office in every city and county had charge of a household registration office that assisted in *baojia* registration. The registration of people, households and land was to be the basis for social control, corvee service, taxation and, especially, the suppression of Communism. In 1932, in accordance with the Law on Household Registration and the Regulations on Village Pacification, Fujian province launched its own *baojia* regulations, enforcing collective responsibility for neighbourhoods of five households. In 1935, the province promulgated the Revised Regulations on *Baojia* Registration in Bandit [that is to say, Communist] Pacification Districts, which enlarged the neighbourhood of collective responsibility to ten households. It set up household registration teams and model counties, incorporated immigrants into the districts and provided rations of foodstuff and salt.[5]

Households were registered by neighbourhoods. For the land population, that meant registration according to their fixed abode. What constituted a neighbourhood for the waterborne population was more problematic and had to be specially defined. The regulations of 1935 referred to people who lived on the same boat as a "boat household" (*chuanhu*). In most circumstances, the household would consist of a family, as it was the practice for sons to set up their own families on a boat different from that of their parents. Boat households were registered according to the town or village at which they regularly moored: groups of six to 15 households were designated as a *jia* unit, and *jia* groups of six to 15 *jia* were designated a *bao* unit. Where fewer than six households were moored at a town or village, they were merged into land-dwelling *jia* units for registration purpose. Boat households that also had an abode on land were registered in land-dwelling *jia* units. The county government provided a certificate that included a registration number to be displayed on the boats. The *bao* office for boat-dwelling households was established on land, but the *jia* office was located among the boats. If the boats moved or if household membership changed, it was the responsibility of the household head to report to the *baojia* heads, who in turn reported to the town or village office, where a record of the report would be kept.[6]

The Republican government was right to regard the registration of water-dwelling households as a subject fraught with difficulties. Its archival records show that implementation departed considerably from the legislated ideal. The records spoke of the difficulties of registering a mobile population, but it must be understood that many boat people dodged registration because they did not see registration as falling within their interest. The Republican government had been imposing taxes on fishing boats, ferries, use of the rivers, policing and even for *baojia* registration itself. Registration with *baojia* meant a greater chance to be allotted taxes and corvee. As war set in during the last years of the 1930s, army press-gangs made use of the *baojia* records to conscript or to demand payment in lieu of conscription. The boat people

Going beyond pariah status: the boat people of Fuzhou 145

believed that they stood a greater chance than the land people to be press-ganged into the military, that the land population could manipulate the *bao-jia* offices to their advantage to the extent that they fought over the control of boat-dwelling *baojia*, so boat people dared not moor by the shore during times when press-gangs were about.[7]

The distinction between land- and boat-dwelling in household registration strengthened identity as land or boat people, but it did so only because within popular conception, the boat people had always been thought of a class apart from the rest of society. They were known by the demeaning term of *"keti"* or *"quti"*, much as boat people in the Pearl river were known as the "Dan".[8] The *"keti"* were said to be engaged in demeaning work, for not only did they work as transport coolies but boats were used for carrying firewood and human excreta, for prostitution and, above all, for smuggling. Despite the common impression, in specific instances the land- or boat-dwelling status was often quite ambiguous. When the new government of the People's Republic dealt with class conflict among the boat people in 1951, they commonly referred to the headmen of the *baojia* as "rascals and local bosses on land" (*lushang de liumang dipi*), even though it is clear from descriptions of their activities they had originated from the boat population. A certain Jiang Deyu, who sublet farmland to boat-people tenants, was known by his nickname *"Laoti"*. While *"lao"* would have been a descriptor for a man, the character *"ti"* obviously referred to his *"quti"* or *"keti"* status.[9] In the records of the Maritime Customs of 1941, among the many types of boats used by the smugglers were the Lujia *dang*, which the records noted as "fast boats specially built for smuggling at a little island known as Lujia *cun* which was unsuitable for agriculture, whose population had little choice not to follow other occupations".[10] Lujia, in reality, was an island that was gradually put under cultivation from the early years of the twentieth century. Interviews by the present author in 2002 revealed that the village was inhabited by people of the Liu and Jiang surnames who had moved ashore from boats only in the 1930s. They said they depended on fish and clams for a living, but they also occasionally went into trade. They had rented land from land people, including people of the Lin surname of Shanggan. Shanggan was the hometown of Lin Sen, Guomindang politician and chairman of the national government from 1931 to 1943, and because the landlords' families were engaged in smuggling, the villagers of Lujia, who as boat people knew the riverways well, had little choice but to help them.[11]

Despite household registration, which was never comprehensive in any case, there was no sharp social break between land and river. Yet, because territorial rights were closely contested even among different groups of boat people, trade associations appeared among them as contests for power that had evolved under the Republican state before 1949.

An origin for trade associations may be found in the Regulations for the Formation of Social Organizations promulgated by the provincial government in 1927, but they mushroomed in 1945 when, after the Second World War, much social life was revived. Among the many occupational, religious

146 *Huang Xiangchun*

and cultural associations registered were also seamen's and transport work-ers' groups. In such contests for government recognition, the idea of "we, the local boat people" came to be instrumental as a claim for rights and privileges. In a petition of 1946 for the registration of the Majiang Luggage Transport Labourers' Union, the petitioners wrote, in clear attack on people they described as outsiders who had come into their territory from nearby Changle county: "Livelihood on the water, especially at the stretch of the river at the Luoxing Pagoda, should be a privilege enjoyed by people who live on boats; how can it be taken over by people from Changle?"[12] Or, in 1947, a petition delivered by the Jiangbei village office on behalf of "poor boat people" read: "The boat people have no land to farm, and in their destitu-tion purchase their food supply from the markets in the city; for that reason, they have always benefited from charity and reduced-price rice purchases in Fuzhou."[13] From territorial rights to charity relief, the boat people claimed their special status.

Yet another claim for social difference sprang from religion. Roman Catholicism was introduced into Fuzhou in the seventeenth century. Into the Qing dynasty, for about 120 years prior to the Opium War (1840–1842) it was suppressed even though an underground Church was likely to have been in existence as it was in nearby Fuan, as Eugenio Menegon has now documented in detail.[14] After the Opium War, three Roman Catholic churches were built in Fuzhou, respectively in 1848, 1868 and 1899. By the twentieth century, more churches were built and many boat people were converted. According to a report in 1953, in the first, second, third and fourth marine districts (see below), Roman Catholics numbered 4,521 persons and 929 households, mak-ing up respectively 37 and 36 per cent of the total population and households of the four districts. The marine districts were a Roman Catholic stronghold in the city, making up 45 per cent of all the city's believers. Moreover, as the report noted:

> Believers among the boat people were deeply imbued with religion. They converted as families. Some families had been believers for seven or eight generations, and, for that reason, were particularly susceptible to the imperialist ideology. It was because of that influence that social reform had not been successfully carried out.[15]

It should be obvious from this statement that some boat families had been converted from the nineteenth century or even earlier.

Roman Catholic practices among some boat people were often noted by observers in Fuzhou. The church at Fanchuanbu that was built in 1868 was commonly regarded as having been built for the sake of the boat population.[16] Even as social surveys found that boat people's practices were similar to the majority of Chinese (Han) people's practices, the Japanese writer Nogami Eiichi, writing in 1937, noted that because many boat people (whom he referred to as "Dan people") practised Roman Catholicism, their ceremonies

Going beyond pariah status: the boat people of Fuzhou   147

were different.[17] Not only were their ceremonies different, but they had also, according to Roman Catholic practices, purchased land for a grave yard north of Fuzhou city (which to this day is locally known as the Keti Hill), and burying their dead there broke the custom of purchasing land from nearby local people for their graves.[18] Even among the boat people, the acceptance of Roman Catholicism stands out. As a boat person told the present author in 2003:

> We boat people had many god figures on the boat. Aside from the Venerable Shangshu, we had Guanyin, the Milk Ladies, Mount Tai, Taibao, and many fairies and great kings. We did not all worship the same gods. However, over in Fuzhou, many boat people believed in Roman Catholicism [*Tianzhu jiao*]. That was because they did not know how to worship, and so people despised them. For that reason, they became Roman Catholics. For those of us who followed our practices well, why would we have to become Roman Catholic?[19]

There was possibly more than a tint of criticism in those remarks. For the boat person who made them, worshipping the traditional gods was being true to tradition; converting to Roman Catholicism was its betrayal.

The many strands of social identification, being registered, being popularly labelled, having or not having converted to Christianity, all came together in the 1950s as the government of new China sought to revolutionize society.

The marine district, land reform and ethnicity

During the Republic, the Guomindang-controlled government had set up two district offices (*gongsuo*) within Lin Sen county that had purview over the stretch of the Min river that went by Fuzhou. Under those offices, there were 41 *bao* and 55 *jia*. There was also a Special Seamen's Party Office, under which there were party branches. There was a Marine Police Office, which ran a marine police. Affiliated to the government were also the secret societies, known as the 108 gangs, or the Flowers of the Twelfth Months. The boat people whom they had purview over were supported by the trade unions. As a government report in 1953 described it, the boat people were "politically oppressed, economically exploited, ideologically deceived and socially despised".[20]

In 1949, as soon as Fuzhou was liberated, the boat people of Fuzhou city came under a series of administrative changes, the first of which was household registration. As early as October that year, except for five *bao* where geographic mobility was considered too substantial for registration, the government divided the area occupied by the boat people into 15 sections, each to be supervised by a policeman dispatched from the Public Security Office (*gong'an ju*). By July 1950, a marine district (*shuishang qu*) was set up covering the stretch of the Min river between the Taijiang district (that is, the area south

148   Huang Xiangchun

of Nantai) on its northern bank and the Cangshan district on the southern bank. In January 1951, its boundaries were defined and the population under its purview were divided into 26 *bao* and 325 *jia*, including 3,312 households, 14,808 people and 8,664 boats.[21] By March, it was decided that because of their proximity to Fuzhou city, an urban designation would have been more appropriate to the population, and so they were divided into five residents' committees, having purview over 244 residents' groups (*jumin xiaozu*), each committee being supported by 500–1,000 households and each residents' group consisting of 40 to 80 households. Households and boats were registered, and their "port status" (*gangji*) was formally created.[22] In 1956, the marine district was abolished as an independent district, but a marine office was placed under Cangshan district having purview over five residents' associations. Over the next year, the number of marine offices and residents' associations changed, but that structure remained.

Government documents in the years to follow make it very clear they understood the complexities of registering a roving population. The report on the "construction of democratic government" of Fuzhou City Marine District in 1953 said:

> The entire district consists of 3,783 households and 16,932 persons. There are no towns or villages. The people all live on boats. Where they live afloat, they are dispersed; the boats move and follow no regular pattern. Boats registered at this port go up river to Nanping, Jian'ou and Shaowu, or down river to Lianjiang and Changle, or even to Shanghai. On a short trip, they might return within half a month, but on a long trip, not even in half a year. Steam ferries and ships from other ports also come and go frequently. Their dialects are complex, and they do not belong to the Marine District. This is a situation that is difficult to control.[23]

Reports on the district written in the few years after its establishment were full of examples of the difficulties the government had to face.

For example, the same report noted that although many people were enthusiastic for the new administrative arrangement when it was first set up, as their livelihood did not improve in the years immediately following, their enthusiasm rapidly waned. For that reason, participation in the elections to the residents' committee was disappointing: three of the five residents' committees failed to elect a chairperson, all the chairpersons and deputy chairpersons were given temporary appointments, and only 38 members, or 27 per cent of the total elected positions, were elected to the committees. Second, the rivers and inlets making up the marine district did not fit easily into the districts that were to be established under the residents' committees, and so there were incessant disputes on how the designated number of households might fit into a district, and even after registration, some households were totally left out. Third, although government emphasized that the elections should seek out "active participants" (*jiji fenji*), as supporters to the regime were called, the

Going beyond pariah status: the boat people of Fuzhou 149

result of the elections was that "good and bad people were mixed together" (*haohuai xianghun*), meaning that some *baojia* headmen who had held office from before Liberation were also elected. This last observation should be understood in the context of the political climate of the day, during which the standoff with the Guomindang government on Taiwan was creating a great deal of tension. Fuzhou, as internal documents of the time noted, was located on the frontline of the standoff, and the mobility of the boat people, it was thought, made them easy targets of manipulation.[24]

Moreover, there was the question of Roman Catholicism. The government tried different means of propaganda and education to bring "religious work" into the routine of the boat people's daily lives, such as by combining such work with poverty alleviation or by introducing propaganda through songs, theatre, storytelling or popular fiction. However, none of its efforts brought any obvious result. A report noted that some people held the view that "the country is very good, but we are hungry". Others wavered between remaining believers and becoming cadres, and sought to go to church in secret. Some young people might have been losing their enthusiasm for religion, but they were not going over to the government. They were "merely afraid of having to kneel for a long time during church service". Besides, many believers were suspicious of the government's policies on religion, while most had only a hazy idea of what the government's policies were on Roman Catholicism. Some people believed the priests, who said that even Joseph Stalin must have been a believer to adopt the Roman Catholic name "Joseph". Few understood the difference between life before and after Liberation, the Guomindang and the Chinese Communist Party, old and new China, or that imperialism was the cause of the present difficulties in people's livelihood.[25]

Certainly, the boat people or even the Church did not totally negate the state's efforts. A record compiled in 1956 of "model deeds' (hygiene, learning to read, bomb awareness) carried out by Roman Catholics in Fuzhou included instances of participation by boat people such as transport workers, ferrymen, a stoker and a pilot. Social mobilization conducted by the local government and its agencies gave much scope to political participation, and boat people, just as other people in Fuzhou, took part in it, whether or not they were Roman Catholics.

The people of the marine district, nevertheless, were subject to an experience that was very different from that of their counterparts who had settled on reclaimed land. Nantai island splits the Min river into two branches. The branch of the river that flows to the north of the island, known as the Bailong river, incorporated the marine district, but the branch to its south, known as the Wulong river, was delineated outside it. The banks of the Wulong river were subject to land reform and, because the rivers criss-crossed reclaimed land and river banks in this area, land reform in 1951–1952 encountered many problems posed by the continuum of settlement from dwelling in lineage villages, to living in sheds and to living on boats. The draft plan for land reform in the Fuzhou suburb drawn up in 1951 stated the problems very clearly. The

150   *Huang Xiangchun*

population was large relative to available agricultural land, the class structure was complex, many people having become wealthy by their engagement in a wide range of jobs; agriculture was highly commercialized, the income of all classes was affected by the market and subject to rapid changes; rent was high and tenancy relationships were extensive.

Because the boat population had always been held in low social status, and because most were quite poor, they were looked upon as exploited classes. The local government recognized that while there were fishermen who depended for their livelihood on fishing, most boat people had been engaged in different ways in agriculture, and that both farming and fishing interests had to be looked after. It ruled that all land that had been held privately or communally by landlords was to be redistributed to occupying peasants and fishermen.[26] On that basis, many boat people were given the status of "hired poor peasants" (*gu pinmin*). As such, they were given land and, thereby, won the right to live ashore.

Actual practice was much more complicated than the regulations had allowed for. Those complications were brought home to the present writer in an interview by someone who took part in the land reform at Nangang:

> In our training class, we were told we had to look after the fishing people, because most of them were very poor, had no land and lived on boats. Nevertheless, some of them were quite rich, richer than us peasants. Some of them managed trawlers outside the district, and, like the Zheng family at Xiangxia who moored at Yangqi, they had bought land during the Republican period over at Liufeng which they rented to outside boat people. So, during land reform, their land was also distributed. Also, although some fishing people might live here, they had land in other districts, and people in those districts might not agree to give them land. Moreover, there wasn't enough land to distribute; there wasn't enough even for peasants, and if you had boats, at least you could make a living from the boats. Some fishing people received land, but not all of them. Some were not yet living on land at the time of land reform, and so their households were not registered in this district, but in a special marine district. For that reason, they did not take part in land reform in this district. They did not take the opportunity to come on shore, and many might not have wanted to come on shore; or even if they did, they did not know how to farm. They came on shore only if they were very poor, when they had no money to pay for a boat or fishing tools, or when their boats were damaged and they could not afford to repair them, or if they couldn't catch enough fish, or carry enough cargo. When they did come on shore, they brought their boat up to the shore at some fixed location, and then they hired themselves out as labourers or farm workers. They had no roof above their heads and no floor under their feet. They lived like that for generations. Only those who made it to land that way and were engaged in some farming were given land at the time of land reform.

Going beyond pariah status: the boat people of Fuzhou   151

> That was fortunate for them, for otherwise, how could they own land? If other people let them some land, they were fortunate enough.[27]

The description of boat people settled in one location and working on land in another was exasperated by the division of neighbouring reclamations into new districts. The phenomenon of the "flying sediments" (*feizhou*) was well-known during land reform: grouping neighbouring reclamations together favoured people living in the neighbourhood and severed the connection between land and its developers, such as the boat people who did not live nearby. In reality, many boat people who were not given land continued to be registered in the marine district, and were looked upon as being primarily engaged in fishing or transportation.

Along with land reform, the question of the boat people's ethnicity came to the fore. It is not at all clear if any ethnic distinction applied to the boat people prior to the twentieth century, but the question was increasingly posed in the 1920s and 1930s – even if often answered in the negative – whether the boat people known as the Dan made up an ethnic group. In the scholarly literature from imperial times, the word "Dan", which possibly originated in Guangdong, was frequently applied also to the boat people in Fujian and so, by association, the same question applied to the Fuzhou boat-living people. A Fuzhou municipal government report of 1952 discussed the pros and cons of recognizing the boat people as an ethnic minority, and was concerned that such recognition might amount to affirming the boat people's pariah status. A study in 1953 by the Fuzhou municipal government, nevertheless, recognized that that there were significant "ethnic characteristics" (*minzu tedian*) among the boat people, including a physique that had been shaped by boat-living; special customs in communal singing after New Year and at Mid-Autumn Festival, dress and hairstyles, and marriage customs such as the lack of a taboo on widow remarriage. It recognized that the boat people did not have a common language, that they were not educated and that they were not adept to the lineage traditions commonly found among land people; that is to say, they barely knew the names of their forebear beyond three generations, had no ancestral halls and maintained no written genealogies. On their personalities, the report noted that the boat people, having been long exploited by the land people, felt inferior to them ("we boat people cannot become officials" was a common sentiment, the report noted), and so a common "ethnic sentiment" (*minzu ganqing*) was shared.[28]

In 1954, an authoritative report was submitted by Professor Chen Bisheng of Xiamen University to the Fuzhou municipal government on the ethnic nature of the boat people that answered the questions raised in the 1953 study. He concluded that most of the characteristics of the boat people were similar to the land people and that the differences could be explained in lifestyles. Their dark skin and bent legs, and even their hairstyle, came from boat-living and their wedding ceremonies were similar to those of land people, although boat-women "enjoyed more social liberty and widows did not remain single".

152   *Huang Xiangchun*

The songs they sang were found all over Fuzhou. He concluded, therefore, that under Stalin's guidelines for ethnic differentiation, because the boat people did not have a common language, did not occupy the same territory, did not share a common economic life and because they never had a common culture, they did not share an "ethnic personality" (*minzu xingge*) or "ethnic consciousness" (*minzu guannian*).[29] A similar argument appeared in 1956 in the report of the working group on the ethnic character of the Dan people in Guangdong and, with the conclusion that the Dan were ethnically Han, the ethnic question for the Fuzhou boat people was also closed.[30]

Just as the city government was determining whether the boat people should be considered an ethnic minority, one of the most bizarre incidents in recent Fuzhou history occurred. Panic spread in Fuzhou in 1953 and 1954 from the belief that fearful spirits were about. The incidents related to the panic were taken seriously by the government and were, therefore, well recorded in government documents, which are now available in the city archives.

In July 1953, just as Fuzhou people were preparing the many offerings for gods and spirits typical for this time of the year, members of the People's Liberation Army (PLA) swimming in the Asia Swimming Pool in the marine district discovered a "monkey spirit" (*houjing*), which they initially took for a spy. They captured it and sent it to the Xiehe Hospital. After that incident, there were other sightings of "monkey spirits": four of them had heads covered in long hair, were as tall as teenagers, exhibited long teeth and were said to have come into the Asia Swimming Pool seeking refuge from the typhoon. Two of them were shot by the PLA as they came on land; the other two were killed by the people and had their bodies hung from a tree, for it was said they devoured people and were responsible for the death of several people at the swimming pool. It was said that one of them grabbed a PLA soldier by the ankle and said: "I have to go into my next incarnation; I have already found five replacements for myself." Then it was said on 10 July, a frog was caught in Cangshan district, who, when stones were thrown at it, said: "I am General Frog, very powerful." A pregnant woman heard that and realized that was why her alarm clock fell down from the table even when no one had touched it, and the two sons of a person bound over for surveillance (*guanzhi fenzi*) died of gastroenteritis. A boat person who had formerly worked as a medium said the frog general had descended upon him, and predicted that there would be cholera epidemic unless it was offered a feast and performance by a storyteller. On 13, the storytelling was offered, and a feast was to be offered on 15 July, but the director of the propaganda department at Cangshan district came to know about it, confiscated the frog and "educated" the public against superstition.[31]

A year later, in August 1954, the rumour came about that there were sightings of ghosts. They took place in the fourth residents' committee as the propaganda work for the draft national constitution had just started. The fourth residents' committee had been identified as a testing ground for propaganda, and so the ghost sighting proved quite distracting for the

Going beyond pariah status: the boat people of Fuzhou   153

propaganda effort. The residents of the district included many Roman Catholics and, at the time of the sightings, the local Roman Catholic church had promoted evening prayers at home for a programme known as "a month of peace" (*taiping yue*). The local priest had to conduct exorcism for more than ten households, and all those activities competed with the government's call for meetings to discuss the draft national constitution. The government report of the time indicates that the government believed that the church was the instigator of the rumour with the aim of disrupting its activities. It investigated the incident and after anti-superstition education, claimed that peace was restored.

It is quite possible to see in the government reports that the supposed rumour and panic could have been rooted in popular beliefs. The monkey and frog were among the animals that commonly represented two of the five gods of pestilence that Fuzhou people sacrificed to. By 1953, moreover, Roman Catholic missionaries and even believers were being accused of collusion with forces outside China. Contemporary government files document the popular reaction to government measures in those years. They indicate that many people felt that despite the prevalence of belief in the existence of ghosts and gods of pestilence, they also believed that the government had singled out the boat population in its propaganda. They also note the arrest of missionaries among them contributed to a Roman Catholic reaction.[32]

In other words, the household registration in 1952–1953 was conducted in the midst of considerable tension, the tension being revealed in the sightings of ghosts and spirits. The excitement died down after a while, and religion, along with boat status, seemed to have passed into history.

The tenacity of tradition

One day in February 2001, on the 11th day of the second lunar month, at Guocuoli village, Cangshan district, the villagers held their annual ceremony to invite the Great King god at the village temple into the village. As in previous years, preparation for the visit began from the first day of the lunar year, when the managers of the Hongshan temple, the reputation of which was known over a large part of Fuzhou, posted their notices to invite the villagers to make their offerings and to parcel out responsibilities for dealing with the god's regalia for the occasion. The god would be carried out of his temple in a sedan chair and paraded around the village for the sake of good fortune. The Guo surname in the village took care of the entire ceremony. Their elders served as managers for the festival, villagers of the Guo surname donated money, prayed for blessings, laid out offerings and received the god during the parade. Ostensibly, villagers of the Jiang and Bian surnames in the village took no part. Even though the parade would pass by the houses of the Jiang and Bian surnames, not only did they not lay out offerings to receive the god but also, when the parade passed through, every family closed its door as if they wanted to keep a clear distance from the god. They did that

154   *Huang Xiangchun*

because they were known as boat people. Unlike people of the Guo surname, the Jiang and Bian surname people were Roman Catholics.

The Jiang and Bian surname households numbered about 40. It was said they came ashore during the Republican era but it was only after Liberation that they settled as villagers. Before they came ashore, they moored on the river by the Guo surname village. They worked as ferrymen, fishermen and haulers of timber, but they were on good terms with the Guo surname land people, who were fruit and vegetable gardeners. According to people of the Guo surname, children belonging to the land people were frail and needed to be cared for by the boat people and, for that reason, at the major festivals, it was the custom for elderly boat people of good fortune to give a bowl of rice to land children to bless them. The land people returned the kindness by offering the boat people home-made New Year cakes. Customs signifying dependency such as these balanced the "insider/outsider" relationship between the land and boat people.

However, as the Jiang and Bian boat people came to settle in the Guo surname's village, and especially after 1956 when the marine district was abolished, the newcomers and the incumbents continued to keep themselves quite apart. Not only was it widely known that the Jiang and the Bian surnames had been settled on boats, their religion also segregated them. The Guo surname villagers sacrificed regularly at the local temples and thought of their villages in the context of those temples. The Jiang and Bian surname people had been Roman Catholics for several generations. They used to hang a picture of the Virgin Mary on their boats and attend service at the Fanchuanpu church every Sunday. After they came ashore, they built a small church in the midst of their houses. Yet, because the area now occupied by the Jiang and Bian surnames fell within the territory that sacrificed to the Great King god of Hongshan temple, the parade must, as a matter of course, go by their houses. However friendly their relationships with the Guo surname, as long the ceremony continues, the Jiang and the Bian surnames will be known to be outsiders.[33]

It now seems a long time ago that boat people inhabiting the foreshore of Fuzhou were kept in a pariah status. The *baojia* registration in the Republican period, household registration and land reform in the 1950s, the expansion of Fuzhou city and even the spread of Roman Catholicism among the boat people all made an impact on changes to their status so that they no longer seem as peripheral as they once did. Without any doubt, their living standard has also altered immensely. Many people no longer live on boats. On the banks of the Wulong river, many boat people moved ashore at the time of the land reform of the 1950s, and made their living not only from fishing in the river but also from agriculture and fish culture. As a result of their move ashore, on the banks of the river were established many new villages under names ending in "island" (*zhou*), "share" (*fen*), "mount" (*dun*) and "dyke" (*dang*). Below Nantai island, thanks to fishery reforms in the 1960s, the boat people had also moved ashore into "fishing people's new villages" (*yumin xincun*). They now

Going beyond pariah status: the boat people of Fuzhou   155

specialize in deep-sea fishing. As for the boat people who had lived on the Bailong river – that is to say, on that stretch of the river lying between Nantai Island and Fuzhou city – although they were incorporated into the marine district from the early 1950s and were, therefore, considered to be included within Fuzhou municipality, compared to their fellow boat people elsewhere, their process of moving ashore had been fraught with difficulties. Well beyond the year 2000, many of their households could still be seen in the winding rivulets of the Taijiang and Cangshan districts, set against a background of houses that had been built for them by the municipal government since the 1990s. It may be said that the descendants of the Fuzhou municipal boat people enjoyed the same rights to education, jobs, social security and welfare as other urban residents, whether they lived in farming or fishing villages, and whether or not they lived in the city, but in the eyes of the local governments and many land people, they remained underprivileged, requiring special care, support and reform. As late as 2004, the Fuzhou municipal government had to declare that the "last batch" of boat people had moved ashore. Whether or not they did, the image of the boat person remains, and attached to that image are the many stories of livelihood on the boats, their origins, customs and practices, even their physique, ready to be revived periodically. In 2009, the *Fuzhou Evening Post* newspaper announced that the local government was to clear the houseboats, and in 2010 it reported that measures of control had been completed, including the destruction of 96 houseboats.[34] Nevertheless, that is unlikely to be the end of the road for the boat people. As long as many among both land and boat people can still recall where the boat people had moored, come ashore and settled, and as long as they think they know who they were, the image of the impoverished people living forever on boats will continue even when boat and land people are no longer distinguishable.

Notes

1 Zheng Zhenman, *Family Lineage Organization and Social Change in Ming and Qing Fujian*, trans. Michael Szonyi, with Kenneth Dean and David Wakefield, Honolulu: University of Hawaii Press, 2001; Kenneth Dean and Zheng Zhenman, *Ritual Alliances of the Putian Plains: Vol. 1: Historical Introduction to the Return of the Gods; Vol. 2: A Survey of Village Temples and Ritual Activities*, Leiden: Brill, 2010; Michael Szonyi, *Practicing Kinship: Lineage and Descent in Late Imperial China*, Stanford: Stanford University Press, 2002.
2 *Minxian xiangtu zhi* (Local history of Min county), Fuzhou: Fuzhou shi difangzhi bianzuan weiyuanhui, 1906, reprinted 2001, pp. 156–162, 176–179.
3 "Chongxiu Longtan Shangshu miao tijuan bei" (Record of donations for the repair of the Shangshu temple at Longtan), 1880, seen by author; Zeng Xiangrong, "Fuzhou Longtan yizang she" (Charity burial association at Longtan, Fuzhou), *Taijiang wenshi*, 1989, 5, pp. 34–38.
4 "Fujian sheng shuishang jingchaju zhun yi zai jianzhu Fuzhou zhan qizhong zhunxu Qingmeng dao chuanhu zai Hudie dao tingbo you" (Memorandum on permission given by the Fujian province marine police for boat households of the Qingmeng district to moor at Butterfly Creek), 1949, Fujian provincial archives, 86-1-529.

156   *Huang Xiangchun*

5 Fujian sheng difangzhi bianzuan weiyuanhui (ed.) *Fujian sheng zhi: gong'an zhi* (Fujian province gazetteer: public security), Beijing: Fangzhi chubanshe, 1997.
6 Deng Huaxiang, "Fujian lidai hukou guanli" (Household registration in different periods in Fujian), *Fujian shizhi*, 2000, 2, pp. 41–46.
7 "Minhou xian zhengfu chengbao benxian chuanhu wei guanli bianli zengshe chuanhu chuanpai qinghe beiyou" (Memorandum on the request by the Minhou county government for boat household registration for the sake of convenience of control), 1943, Fujian provincial archives, 11-7-4805; "Fujian sheng shuishang jingchaju xiezhu jiaqiang chuanhu guanli banfa" (Methods for Fujian province marine police to assist in strengthening control of boat households), 1948, Fujian provincial archives, 11-11-1138.
8 Like the word "Dan", nobody quite knows how "*keti*" or "*quti*" should be written, and all discussions on their literary origins are speculative. For other variations of the term, see Wu Gaozi, "Fuzhou danmin diaocha" (Survey of Dan people in Fuzhou), *Shehui xuejie*, 1930, 4, pp. 141–155; Chen Bisheng, "Guanyu Fuzhou shuishang jumin de mingcheng, laiyuan, tezheng yiji shifou shaoshu minzu deng wenti de taolun" (Discussion concerning the name, origin, special characteristics of the boat people of Fuzhou and whether they are minorities), *Xiamen daxue xuebao*, 1954, 1, pp. 115–126
9 Lin Zengcheng, "Taijiang danmin shenghuo de kunan shi" (A history of the lives of poverty of Taijiang dan people), *Taijiang wenshi*, 1989, 5, pp. 43–48.
10 Min haiguan Xiadou zhisuo (Xiadou branch office, Fujian Customs), "Beiwang lu" (Memorandum), 20 September, 1944, Fujian Provincial Archives, 68-7-17.
11 Interviews by the author on 23 July 2002, at Lujia village, Xiangqian township, Minhou county. Lin Sen died in 1943, well before the establishment of the People's Republic.
12 Fujian sheng shehui chu, "Wei cheng qinzhan liquan xunyu quti bing zhun yu paiyuan yifa chengle qigou huifu bentu guyou shengye yimian xiedou you" (Memorandum on the abolition of usurpation of property rights and permission to appoint an official to oversee the return to established organizational purpose in order to curb armed feuds), 1946, Fujian Provincial Archives, 11-9-579.
13 "Juqing chuanqing zhunyu chiling pingdi yi su shuishang qiongmin you" (Proposal for permission to issue order for cheap sale of rice to relieve the poor people), 1947, Fujian Provincial Archives, 6-4-1499.
14 Eugenio Menegon, *Ancestors, Virgins and Friars: Christianity as a Local Religion in Late Imperial China*, Cambridge, MA: Harvard University Asia Centre, 2009, describes the history of Roman Catholicism from the seventeenth to the nineteenth century in the nearby county of Fuan but does not seem to have detected a boat people's connection there.
15 Fujian Provincial Government Religious Affairs Office, "Fuzhoushi shuishangqu Tianzhu jiao gongzuo qingkuang baogao" (Report on the conditions of the Fuzhou city waterborne district Roman Catholic Church), 21 May 1953, Fuzhou Municipality Archives, 37-1-2.
16 Rao Wusheng (ed.), *Fuzhou zongjiao zhi: Tianzhu jiao* (A history of religion in Fuzhou: Roman Catholicism), Fuzhou: Fujian renmin, 2000, p. 135.
17 Nogami Eiichi, *Fukushū kō*, Taibei: Fukushū Tōei Gakkō, 1937, p. 75. Nogami was headmaster of the Fukushū Tōei Gakkō, that is, the Fuzhou Japanese School.
18 Xu Tiantai, "Fujian hunsang xiqing jiusu suotan" (Miscellanies of old customs in marriage, funeral, and other celebrations), in Fujian sheng zhengxie wenshi ziliao weiyuanhui (ed.), *Wenshi ziliao xuanbian* (Selections from literary and historical sources), Vol. 2, Fuzhou: Fujian renmin, 2001, p. 133.
19 Interview by the author on 17 February 2003 at Xindang village, Xiangqian township, Minhou county.

Going beyond pariah status: the boat people of Fuzhou 157

20 Fuzhou Marine District People's Government, "Fuzhou shi shuishangqu minzhu zhengquan jianshe gongzuo qingkuang baogao" (Work report on the Fuzhou Marine District democratic government construction), October 1953, Fuzhou Municipality Archives, 34-1-31.

21 Fuzhou Municipality People's Government, "Guanyu benshi shuishangqu jianzheng gongzuo zongjie" (A conclusion on the work of political construction in the marine district of this city), March 1951, Fuzhou Municipality Archives, 34-1-4.

22 Fuzhou Marine District People's Government, "Fuzhou shi shuishangqu minzhu zhengquan jianshe gongzuo qingkuang baogao" (Report on work related to the establishment of democratic government in the Fuzhou city marine district), October 1953, Fuzhou Municipality Archives, 34-1-31.

23 Fuzhou Marine District People's Government, "Fuzhou shi shuishangqu minzhu zhengquan jianshe gongzuo qingkuang baogao".

24 Fuzhou Municipality People's Government, "Guanyu benshi shuishangqu jianzheng gongzuo zongjie".

25 Fujian Provincial Government Religious Affairs Office, "Fuzhoushi shuishangqu tianzhujiao gongzuo qingkuang baogao" (Report on work related to the Roman Catholic Church in the Fuzhou city marine district), 21 May 1953, Fuzhou Municipality Archives, 37-1-2.

26 "Fuzhou shijiao tudi gaige ruogan juti wenti de chuli banfa" (Procedures for handling actual problems arising in land reform in the Fuzhou suburb), 1951, Fuzhou Municipal Archives, 27-1-92. "Guanyu benshi xiaqu nei Minjiang ganzhiliu zhoutian shadi deng guiding," (Regulations on mud and sand banks on the distributaries of the Min river under the purview of this city), December 1954, Fuzhou Municipal Archives, 34-1-31, also shows that boat people who were registered in the marine district were given more ready access to newly formed land than other people.

27 Interview conducted by the author at the Yangqi Shangshu ancestral temple at Gaishan township, Cangshan district, Fuzhou municipality on 30 July 2001.

28 Both citations in this paragraph are taken from Fuzhou Municipality People's Government, "Fuzhou shi shuishang danmin qingkuang baogao" (Report of an investigation into the marine Dan people of Fuzhou Municipality), 1953, Fuzhou Municipal Archives, 34-1-17. The concern that the recognition of ethnic distinction might affirm the boat people's pariah status was apparently known to the boat people. An interviewee recalled: "My father said, during the land reform, the government wanted to define us as an ethnic minority. Many people objected, saying that if we were so defined, we would be more bullied by the land people" (Mr Jiang Bingyin of Xindang village, Xiangqian district, 17 February 2003).

29 "Guanyu Fuzhou shuishang jumin de mingcheng, laiyuan, tezheng yiji shifou shaoshu minzu deng wenti de taolun" (Discussion of the name, origin, characteristics of the Fuzhou boat people and the question of whether they are a minority ethnic group), 1954, Fujian Provincial Archives, 138-1-1145, and published with amendments under the same title in *Xiamen daxue xuebao* as noted in footnote 8.

30 Huang Guangxue and Shi Lianzhu, *Zhongguo de minzu shibie* (Ethnic classification in China), Beijing: Minzu chubanshe, 1995, p. 291.

31 "Fuzhoushi renmin zhengfu gonganju baogao guanyu 'haihou', qingwa da jiangjun qingkuang you" (Report of the Fuzhou Municipal Public Security Department on the "sea monkey" and the frog general), 21 July 1953, Fuzhou Municipal Archives, 27-1-182.

32 Fuzhou Municipal Public Security Department, "Wei shuishangqu fasheng naogui yaoyan de zuiyao gongzuo baogao" (Report on tracking down rumours of ghost sightings in the marine district), 14 September 1954, Fuzhou Municipal Archives, 37-1-5.

158 Huang Xiangchun

33 Field observations on 3 February 2001 at Guocuo *li*, Hongguang village, Jianxin township, Cangshan district, Fuzhou. For a further discussion of the insider/outsider distinction as exhibited in festival participation, see Huang Xiangchun, "Difang shehui zhong de zuqun huayu yu yishi chuantong: yi Minjiang xiayou diqu de 'shuibu shangshu' xinyang wei zhongxin de fenxi" (Group discourse and ritual tradition in local society: an analysis of the cult of the minister of water in the lower reaches of the Min river), *Lishi renleixue xuekan*, 2005, 3(1), pp. 115–154.

34 *Fuzhou wanbao* (Fuzhou evening post), 4 December 2009 and reports available on Fujian dongnan xinwen wang (www.fjsen.com), such as www.fjsen.com/d/2009–12/30/content_2576767_3.htm (accessed 1 September 2012).

11 From sheds to houses

A Dan village in the Pearl river delta in the twentieth century

Zeng Huijuan

The word "Dan" used on people living in the Pearl river delta denotes not only people who lived on boats, but also people who lived on land reclaimed for cultivation but who were deemed to have no rights for living there, as research by Helen Siu and Liu Zhiwei has demonstrated.[1] Prior to their research, works on the Dan described them as "boat people", and indeed some were.[2] This chapter describes a Dan village in which the majority of its members had for some generations lived on land. They were characterized not by their boats, but by their sheds. By the 1950s, when, after the land reform, they were given right to land, sheds gave way to brick houses. By the 1980s, as in much of the Pearl river delta, the policy of "reform and opening" (*gaige kaifang*) brought to the village a new economic order. By the time I interviewed its inhabitants, in 2012, not only shed-living but the early days of the recent wave of economic reform had passed into memory. Much of the history of the transformation of the village in the twentieth century has to be presented in the light of that memory, but from what was said, it is still possible to reconstruct changes to the social structure and the relationship of the land-living Dan with their boat-living counterparts.

Big Cloud village

Big Cloud village is located in Panyu district of Guangzhou city, on the side of the Shawan river, one of the distributaries of the Pearl leading to the sea. Across the river is Shawan, studied by Helen Siu and Liu Zhiwei. From the eighteenth century, the area on which the village stands underwent the sort of land reclamation that they had written about. Very much like the He surname ancestral trusts that, from the sixteenth century, registered for tax stretches of the mudbanks along the rivers, built dykes to keep out flood water and recruited tenants to work on the land so formed, the Su surname ancestral trusts from Bijiang village in Shunde, from the eighteenth century, had built the Good Luck Embankment at the location where the village was to be located and recruited tenants. Today, Big Cloud village has a population of 4,276 people, and its neighbour, Stone Bank village, also within the embankment, a population of 3,500.

160　*Zeng Huijuan*

Within the embankment, farmland was, and is, criss-crossed by four streams leading into the Shawan river. Settlements were concentrated on the embankments on their sides, so that if one could take a bird's-eye view of them, they would appear as ribbons along the streams. Big Cloud village is the collective name of the settlements along those streams, conveniently named Big Cloud stream, Second Cloud stream, Third Cloud stream and Fourth Cloud stream. No direct evidence exists of when the settlements at Big Cloud village came about. Nevertheless, it was common knowledge that the Dan lived in sheds on the embankments along the rivers. The stilts on which the sheds were built were commonly noted as their characteristic, as indicated in the names given to them, such as *shuilan* (houses on stilts at the water) or *danpeng* (Dan people's sheds). Their houses were said to be shaped like a boat, with a somewhat rounded roof and compartments as one might find on their boats.[3]

Long-settled villages in the Pearl river delta are usually made up of brick houses. They are laid out in rows and some among them are finely adorned both on the roof and on the outer walls. Some of those houses are demarcated for special ritual purposes as temples and ancestral halls, and those houses tend to be built with intended signs of grandeur: stone steps leading up to the front entrance, which is raised on a platform and flanked by pillars. Houses built to demarcate permanence are located on land that had been opened to cultivation long before the mid-Ming dynasty (say the fifteenth century), unlike the alluvial land that had been opened for cultivation since. To people who live in long-settled villages in the older parts of the Pearl river delta, the people living on the alluvial land, known as *shatian* (sandy land), are shed-living Dan. They think of the shed-living Dan as drifters, poor people who did not own the land they farmed and could ill-afford the rent they owed their landlords, and who, succumbing to debt, including some accumulated from gambling as might be expected of such mean people, would drift on.

The image of the drifter is not true of the shed-people. In speaking to me, the shed-people emphasize the permanence of their abode. I have from my notes the impression I gathered from Mr Chen, then aged 86 years, who was born in 1925 and who grew up in Stone-banked village:

> When he was small, aside from Net-Sunning Quarter and the Sandy Nose, people also lived on the Big Mound, on the side of Shawan Creek. Big Mound had a lot of land and no rent was asked for it, but not many people lived there and nobody wanted the land.

He had heard from older people that

> A long time ago, the Shawan people came over here to farm. They built the Big Mound here which is higher than the surrounding land so as to use it as a shelter when the typhoon came. Every evening, after finishing the farm work, they left their boats there and ferried across the river to Shawan. After they made enough money, they returned to the "inside"

From sheds to houses: a Dan village in the Pearl river delta   161

(that is, back to Shawan). The Big Mound belonged to the Shawan people. But after they left, they had no-one looking after it, and so the land was left fallow. It was just overgrown. Because the land was higher, it was hard to irrigate. So, when our ancestors came, they did not choose to settle there. Nevertheless, some other people came later than we did. They were very poor; maybe they owed a lot of debt, they farmed on the Big Mound rent-free.

When these people farmed the land [abandoned by the Shawan owners], they had to carry irrigation water from "outside" at the Stone Bank Stream. And they had to go up the mound to irrigate their fields. It was hard work farming there. The fields were also exposed to typhoons. So they frequently went hungry.[4]

The description is highly indicative of how the "shed people" might think about segregation. There were the landowners from Shawan, who lived on the "inside" and the very poor who farmed the land they abandoned who gathered water from the "outside". People who were very poor frequently went into debt, farmed land that was hard to irrigate and often went hungry. In between, there were the people who lived in sheds. They had settled earlier than the very poor.

If the inhabitants of Stone Bank thought they had settled earlier than the very poor on Stone Mound, Mr Feng of Big Cloud thought Big Cloud was settled even earlier than Stone Bank, and for that reason, the land belonging to Stone Bank was more sandy and less fertile. More than that, he said, Stone Bank was also located nearer to the people of Net-Sunning Quarter. Of the people of Net-Sunning Quarter, he said:

They were professional fishing people. They came from a fish port in Zhongshan county, and they sold their fish there. In the old days, there was no periodic ban on fishing, and so those people put stakes in shallow water and put seine nets round them. Fish were caught on the nets. Those seine nets were longer than 10 *zhang* [approximately 11.3 feet]. Those people seldom went into the village. They stocked up their fish and then sold it onshore. When there was no fish, they went to Zhongshan, because there was a big fishing port there. They grew some vegetables, also hired people to carry fish for them, but usually not people from the villages. They thought that village people did not know enough about the ways of the water.

They were fishing people. They drifted on the water, caught fish for a living and they came and went. We have for generations lived on land and farmed. Occasionally, we have fish and shrimps with our meals, but we usually live in sheds on land, unlike those people who drift all the time.[5]

The stages of settlement are reflected succinctly in the ethnological classification as seen in oral reports. The fishing people of Net-Sunning

162 *Zeng Huijuan*

Quarter were drifters, and were different from the villagers of Stone Bank and Big Cloud. Of the two villages, Stone Bank came under suspicion because it was located near Big Mound. For the land villager, it was access to land that provided stability and familiarity.

On another occasion I was told Net-Sunning Quarter was inhabited by three brothers, known as Seine Bo, Seine Tian and Siener. Nobody knew their surname. They worked with seine nets and so the net became their identifier. They lived in sheds. They fished from the Shawan river during the day and went back to their sheds in the evening. They made a lot of money from fishing, a seine net being as expensive as a cow.[6]

Sheds as homes, the making of Big Cloud

Access to land allowed a sense of stability because sheds, like houses, were regarded as being bound to a location. This is how Mr Guo, who was 79 years of age at the time of my interview, described Big Cloud village:

> When he was small, that is to say, in the 1950s and earlier, there were embankments on both sides of the river. Until 1964, the water level was quite high and so the river was wider than what it is now by 1 to 2 metres.

> The sheds were built on the banks. A metre away from the sheds, there was the embankment, which we called the jetty (*butou*). Every family had its own jetty, made of stone or brick. The sheds were made of dried sugar-cane. They were about as big as a duck cage. The entire "monkeys' den" comprised no more than two to three *zhang* [approximately seven to eight square metres]. There was only enough room to sleep in. Wealthy families would have had a partition separating the parents from their children, but poor families did not have the partition. Anything worth money was left in the house known as the "big shed" [*daliao*]. The big shed faced south. Its entrance faced the kitchen, located on the edge of the stream. Because of the danger of fire, it was located several metres from the big shed. When meals were cooked, they were eaten at the kitchen. In between the kitchen and the big shed was the jetty, where things might be washed.

> The latrine was located behind the big shed, that is to say, opposite the embankment. Each family had its own latrine. There was a big vat in there to store manure for the vegetable plots, but it was not used for paddy. Every family had the equivalent of 8 to 10 square metres of garden plots for daily vegetables. They also raised chickens, ducks and geese. Ducks and geese wandered into the streams, the chicks ran around everywhere. On the side of the kitchen, they put up chicken and duck coops. Aside from the fowls and the vegetables, their entire property consisted of a frying pan, eating utensils, bed boards and some blankets. As for farm tools that they used when they worked for other people, they had

From sheds to houses: a Dan village in the Pearl river delta 163

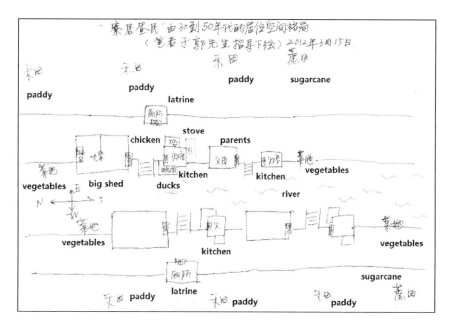

Figure 11.1 Houses near Mr Guo's big shed from the 1930s to 1950s (credit: Zeng Huijuan).

their own hand shovel, water lily shovel, rice transplant board, straw rain jacket, rice granaries and seedling transplant boat, while other farm tools and oxen belonged to the landlords.

Elderly parents' sheds were usually located nearby. They lived in a small shed with its own kitchen. If they were in poor health, they would eat in the big shed and in that case, there was no need to give them a separate shed.[7]

Under Mr Guo's guidance, I produced a diagram of the houses near his big shed from the 1930s to the 1950s (see Figure 11.1). What was very clear from his description is that although the family did not live under a single roof, their sheds being small, he had a clear sense of who lived where and what belonged to them. Sheds might be rebuilt periodically, but the locations they occupied were stable. From the location sprang a clear sense of a community that was grounded at a place.

Ancestors and gods

Like the land population, people living in sheds in Big Cloud village not only believed in the powers of their ancestors and their gods, but ancestors and gods were demarcated at specific locations on land. Their funeral ceremonies

164   *Zeng Huijuan*

were identical to those conducted in the land villages in the Pearl river delta. The corpse had to be cleaned as soon as the deceased expired, his or her descendants mourned, the mourning process, like elsewhere in the delta, consisted of hiring professional mourners to "wail" in front of the corpse. The same village daoists who officiated for land villages officiated for the shed people. With proper ceremony, the body was dispatched by boat to the hills near Shiqiao city where it was buried. Grave land might be had only by paying the people who looked after the hill land over there. Like the village people, after the body was buried, the family brought back the spirit of the deceased to the shed where a spirit altar had been set up. In a practice not previously reported of funerals on the delta, the daoist would have prepared a spirit tablet also for "companions as ordered by the Lord Laozi on high" at the altar. These were "guests" who had accompanied the spirit of the deceased and who, by being placed at the altar, took part in the offerings made to the deceased's spirit. Again, like the land villagers, mourning clothes were regarded as carriers of bad fortune, and had to be discarded with the help of the daoist. For three weeks after the deceased had expired, the daoist was also invited to say prayers every seven days. After 21 days, mourning was regarded as having been served, and on the 100th day after death, a meal was served for all who had attended the funeral.[8]

When the land population thought of the boat people as being without roots, they often thought that the boat dead were discarded summarily and burial sites were not remembered. But what I heard from them was totally different. The shed people of Big Cloud practised periodic sacrifice at the graves at the Qingming festival. Annual sacrifice was made at the graves of the newly dead continuously for three years. These were known as the "new graves" (*xinshan*) and had to be sacrificed to before sacrifice was offered to the "old graves" (*jiushan*). Among the old graves, sacrifice at the pivotal ancestors attracted a procession of more than 100 people every year and money had to be paid to the local people on the occasion. After the sacrifice to the pivotal ancestor, sacrifice would be made to individual household ancestors. Sacrifice was also offered to ancestors at ancestral tablets installed on domestic altars. The domestic tablets were offered food daily and during periodic celebrations. They were notified of births, examination results, and weddings. Daughters-in-law were given the duty of offering them water every morning and evening.[9] The symbolic importance of the domestic spirit tablet was most marked at the time of family division. Mr He, the village cadre, said of his personal experience:

> My elder brother was ten year older than I. When he married, my father contributed money and personally helped to build him a shed to live in. The new shed was located near the big shed. We also built him a kitchen behind the shed. Nevertheless, we continued to eat together.
>
> When I was 20 *sui* [19 years old], I married. Until I married, the family was not divided at meals. After my brother married but before I did, the

From sheds to houses: a Dan village in the Pearl river delta   165

incense [*xianghuo*] on our domestic altar was kept in my father's house and undivided. The word "incense" here refers to the ash in the incense holder on the altar. When all the sons in the family had married, the incense had to be divided. Each son would take a little ash to his own home and put it into the incense holder on his own domestic altar. The altar in the father's house was not moved, but, when every son had gathered his incense, offerings would no longer be made to the ancestors at the father's domestic altar and the tablet there would be burnt. Every son would make a tablet for the repose of the ancestors' spirits to be deposited on his own domestic altar.

Daughters played no part in the division of incense. If the family had only daughters and no sons, when they had all married, there would be no one left to take care of ancestral worship. The incense was then said to be "broken" [*duan*]. Some people in such a situation would adopt a son, often from the street. Sons abandoned on the street often had the hour and date of their birth kept in their clothes and they would continue the incense.[10]

The families were male-centred. At marriage, the daughter was sent away and the daughter-in-law was received into the family. A clear indication of that relationship was that mothers who saved up for valuables (such as gold bracelets) kept them for their daughters-in-law but not their daughters.[11] Weddings made use of very much the same ceremonies as might be found in land villages, except for the fact that because the bride had to be fetched by boat, she was rowed over by women of her own family and received by the bridegroom's boat, whose entourage consisted only of men. As was common practice in the Pearl river delta, her friends and relatives would go separately to the groom's house with a prepared meal, to indicate that the bride did not depend on her nuptial partner's largesse, and on the third day, would take her back to her natal family, where she would live for the next year or more, appearing only in the groom's house during her parents-in-law's birthdays or weddings of other members of the groom's family. This was the practice of the now well-described "delayed transfer marriage" (*buluo jia*).[12]

Children had to be protected by the "little old ladies" (*pozai*), whose spirits were installed under the domestic altar. They were sacrificed to especially on the second day of the second month, on the occasion known as "the old ladies' festival" (*apo dan*), on which occasion they were offered dough fingers mixed with sugar (dough rolled into strips and cut to the length of a finger). When the last child in the family married, he or she had to make a final offering to the ladies, after which their collective portrait would be removed from the house.[13]

There were other gods of the family and the sheds. Daily sacrifice was offered to the dragon god near the river, the earth god at the jetty and at the doorways of the sheds, the kitchen god, and heaven. The shed people also took part in pilgrimages and processions of the major temples in the vicinity.

166   *Zeng Huijuan*

Nevertheless, they did not have ancestral halls. That was the biggest difference between the shed people and many land villages.

Community

Before Liberation, sheds were loosely clustered on the streams leading into the principal river, the Shawan. Each cluster was made up of a common surname, often closely related as families. The Guo and the He surnames were the most numerous, and other surnames included Chen, Feng and Liang. They had relatives outside the village and they often described lineage affinities with other groups in the surroundings. Mr He, the village cadre, described his family background to me in the following terms:

> My father's generation consisted of six sons and a daughter. In my father's times, he and two younger brothers lived over here, but my grandfather did not. We lived on the Third Stream. Our brothers and sisters were everywhere, at Yuwotou, Lingshan and Shunde. Many lived in Yuwotou. In the village, many people are my distant relatives. My close relatives live in Yuguotou. We all help one another, cutting and gathering grass. My Yuwotou relatives did not have their own land, but worked on other people's land, unlike my two uncles who lived here and rented some land.
>
> I was born in 1927 in Stone Bank village. My uncles lived in Big Cloud. I lived most of the time with them. I had two uncles, and they had some land, maybe 100 *mu*. This was rented land. We often worked as farm-hands for the landlords and went hungry.
>
> In the old society, a *mu* produced three to five piculs of paddy. Rent cost one to two piculs and so you were left with three piculs. Out of that, 70 to 80 catties had to be paid as protection money on the sands, and several tens to the government for self-defence. So altogether you paid four piculs and had only one picul left. Then there were other expenses, such as the introductory fee for renting the farmland. You had less than a fifth of the grain you grew for yourself. When we didn't have enough to eat, we went to work in the sugarcane fields. Many people looked for help in those days and so nobody starved. There were 20 to 30 big landlords around, 20 on our stream alone, including my second uncle. We were relatives and so I came over to Big Cloud to help him.
>
> Our ancestors came from Daliang in Shunde county. We had a He surname ancestral hall there. They had a written genealogy to show that our ancestors were there. In those days, every so often, people in charge of the ancestral hall in Shunde would come over. Before Liberation, they came once every year, to see if any of us had given birth to a son. If a son was born to you, you had to pay birth-of-son money. After you had paid, they gave you a share of pork every year.

From sheds to houses: a Dan village in the Pearl river delta   167

The Shunde people came with the genealogy. Once they had distributed their pork and collected money, they left. We didn't go to the ancestral hall at Daliang. We only sacrificed to our own grandfather. They came here, we didn't go over. After Liberation, they came over twice. People of the He surname in Big Cloud have mostly come from the Daliang ancestral hall, so have those of Stone Bank village. But the people of the Guo surname, as the second biggest surname, have largely come from Pingshan or Zhong *cun*.[14]

The house clusters were by no means closed to the óutside world. Family, marriage, lineage and religious connections were invoked to create a sense of community and to see why that should be, it is necessary to understand the importance of the rivers in linking up the shed clusters. Big Cloud village resembled more Kaixiangong in the Yangzi delta, as studied by Fei Xiaotong, than the lineage villages described by Liu Zhiwei and David Faure.[15] Boats going on the streams and the river provided the principal transport and the trading relationships. Trade was coordinated even if not concentrated at two locations, one of which was the Net-Sunning Quarter, near Shawan river, where boat people had gathered, and the other was the little sandbar along the river known as the Sandy Nose. There was a general store, and a butcher and fish stalls at both places. There were also several barbers, tailors and doctors. Business, however, was not transacted only at the shops, for goods were gathered there and brought back for sale at the village. When the pork gathered at the village stall was not totally sold out during the day, the hawkers put it in their boats and rowed upstream to look for customers. People living in the sheds did not often go to market themselves. More often, they entrusted their purchases to boatmen who provided regular transport service along the streams, much in the fashion described by Fei Xiaotong for Kaixiangong village. Nevertheless, the marketplaces provided mooring for boats going up- and downstream and so were regarded as social centres. The local opium shop was located at Net-Sunning Quarter, and the gambling stalls and teahouses were opened daily at both, as were a few other markets. There were also two schools at Net-Sunning Quarter, one of which Mr He, the cadre, attended. He recalled that many fishing people's children attended school. In the light of what the published literature says about the fishing people's lack of education, that was a rather surprising remark.[16]

A great deal of work required coordination that cut across family boundaries. Land devoted to paddy needed careful irrigation control, and sluice gates were maintained to regulate the amount of water entering into the fields. The sluice gates were privately owned and the owners charged a fee for the use of irrigation water. By the 1920s, this part of the delta was given over to the cultivation of sugarcane. Harvesting sugarcane not only provided work for many, but there were also eight sugarcane presses scattered among the shed settlements. These heavy ox-driven stone presses were housed in sheds that had to be rebuilt every year. Sugar cane was collected from landlords. The

168   *Zeng Huijuan*

oxen were provided every year by their keepers at Stone Bank village. Each press required the service of some 100 people. They were hired after the paddy harvest and they included not only local people but also workers coming from other counties. There was also a sugar refinery that employed modern machinery. It was located in Net-Sunning Quarter and owned by the notorious gangster Li Longji, whose considerable influence stretched from here to as far as the county city at Shiqiao.[17] Not all sugarcane was pressed. White cane was sold unprocessed. It fetched a much better price than the black cane that was pressed for juice, but it required a heavier outlay because fertilizer was needed. Cane was sold at the two markets at Net-Sunning Quarter and the Sandy Nose for export to Guangzhou or Hong Kong. Sometimes the boats came into the streams to collect cane, and sometimes villagers went themselves to Guangzhou to make their sale.[18]

As in other places of the Pearl river delta, territorial relationships were reflected in temple networks. The major temple in the area was the God of Agriculture temple at Net-Sunning Quarter. Mr Chen of Stone Bank village, 85 years old, recalled vividly life focused around the temple:

> The temple consisted of four compartments. People from Stone Bank, East Guide village and Big Cloud came here for the opera. They donated incense money. Donors of incense money then stayed to have a meal together in the big shed nearby. On the day of the god's festival, only vegetarian food was served, no meat. Near the temple were many general stores, and they came to life during the festival.

> The God of Agriculture was kept in the temple. The figure was made of wood. Above his head [was a plaque] bearing the characters "Peace to the people, and plenty for all things". The 22nd day of the seventh lunar month was his birthday. On that day, a big shed was built for the opera. The operatic company was hired by wealthy people from Guangzhou or Shunde out here. [He used the term "*kailai*", signifying that the company had come from "inside" the area to the "outside".] There was also lion dancing. Many people came ... A lot of firecrackers were let off. We children went over to pick up [unexploded firecrackers] from the debris.

> One of the activities on the day of the festival was the "water float" [*you shuile*]. For that, the village daoist priests [known locally as the *nanmo*] would go on a boat and travel on all the streams in Stone Bank and Big Cloud. But they did not go to the Sandy Nose stream. They threw paper offerings into the stream as they chanted their prayers. They also threw in edible buns. Because the God of Agriculture looked after our production, the daoists threw the buns into the water to "nourish the fish, shrimps and paddy fields". On that day, every family had to burn paper and offer buns outside its place. Children would stand ready by their

From sheds to houses: a Dan village in the Pearl river delta   169

sheds. When the boat with the priests came along, they jumped into the water to salvage the buns.[19]

Further afield, some people went to temples outside the area. They could not take part in the annual parade of the Northern Emperor at Shawan, but they went to see it as an entertainment. The big cane growers went as far as the Dragon Mother's temple at Zhaoqing to seek her blessing. Some people also went to the Guanyin temple of Nanhai to seek better fortune, boys were taken there at the ages of three, six and nine *sui* (two, five and eight years of age respectively) and girls at two, five and eight *sui* (one, four and seven years of age).[20] Unlike the annual ceremony at the God of Agriculture's temple, they went to those temples with their peers and not as a group representing their villages.

Conclusion

Since the establishment of the People's Republic in 1949, many changes came to Big Cloud and nearby villages, but despite land reform, communization and considerable economic prosperity since the 1980s, the village structure remained quite stable. Since the 1980s, industry has moved into Big Cloud and its surrounding villages. Some 27 factories are located there and workers from the outside swarm the area. From the 1960s, the sheds gave way to permanent brick houses, many of two floors. The Guo surname of Big Cloud now attend ancestral worship every year at Pingshan and believe that, like reputable lineages on the Pearl river delta, their ancestors had moved to Pingshan from Zhuji *xiang* in the northern parts of Guangdong. Mr Guo, the current deputy party secretary, finds attending lineage banquets in Pingshan a very convenient way to meet more people.[21] The fishing people of Net-Sunning Quarter are still there. They live in brick houses but still have some sheds, where spirit tablets are still found on the domestic altar. During land reform in the 1950s, they were also allocated to a production brigade, and so came under separate accounting from the villages nearby. They had fishing boats and were not given any land, but fishing provided them with a larger income than the land people.[22] Another indication of a continuation from the past is a notice posted in 2012 reporting the dividend payable to Big Cloud villagers from land rented out by the village. The notice records 15 personal names, less their surnames. No doubt, the villagers knew one another's names and, like a lineage village, had no need of a surname demarcation. In a village where no ancestral hall exists to demarcate lineage boundaries, the surname probably matters little.

In many ways, Big Cloud is very similar to Big Stream Mouth village on the other side of the Shawan river, which I also studied.[23] Big Stream Mouth, like Big Cloud, was made up of sheds, the inhabitants of which fished in nearby waters. They paid a tax to some powerful overlord for the right to fish, and

170 *Zeng Huijuan*

lived in the shadow of a wealthy Shawan village. They worked for landowners in Shawan at harvest time, and some held an adoptive relationship with Shawan villagers: the shed people were said to be able to endure a tough life and so the people "inside" – that is to say, villagers living on the older parts of the delta – had them ritually adopt their children to offer spiritual protection. This sort of ritual adoption was common all over the Pearl river delta, and akin to adoption of children by local gods or even the spirits of trees and rocks. Interestingly, ritual adoption from the people "inside" never extended to people living on boats, who were thought to have been too intractable. Like the people of the land villages, Big Stream Mouth had earth gods and arrangements to provide regular sacrifice to them. Despite their proximity to Shawan, they were not part of the procession of the Shawan protective deity, the Northern Emperor. They took no part in the procession, and the procession never visited their village. From the point of view of the Shawan people, Big Stream Mouth belonged to the "outside".

Helen Siu and Liu Zhiwei, writing about the Dan of the Pearl river delta, and distinguishing their research from previous scholarship, said of their experience:

> The contrast between labels imposed by others and self-identification is striking. In Chaolian *xiang* of Jiangmen municipality, residents of established lineage communities assert repeatedly that a lineage community at the southern edge of the island is of Dan origin. When asked, the latter vehemently deny such categorization. They point to the fisherfolk further down the river instead.[24]

Denying the Dan status for oneself and passing it to the next village down-river is exactly what I found at Big Cloud and its surrounding villages or at Big Stream Mouth. That is, indeed, one of the reasons why it has been so difficult to study the Dan. Indeed, the word "Dan" is often used for the people of the Pearl river delta by scholars, by newspapers and even by people who live there themselves. As a pariah status, it is one to get out of. My experience in Big Cloud and Big Stream Mouth shows that whether or not one gets out of the status to the satisfaction of people who live upstream, it is possible for people downstream to map the practices of people upstream onto their own style of life. People upstream notice the impermanence of wooden sheds, but people downstream who live in them see them as fixed abodes. Access to fishing, farming and trade downstream would have contributed to boom and bust in the same way as such activities would have upstream. In her work on Xinhui county, Siu describes the financial collapse even of big landlords in the 1930s.[25] There must have been mobility in and out of the Dan status. Nevertheless, sheds remained until they were replaced full-scale in the 1950s and 1960s, and the architecture reified the ephemeral concept of Dan-ness, so that it would be said, almost of eternity, that on the Pearl river delta there were the Dan, who lived on boats and, if found on land, lived only in sheds.

From sheds to houses: a Dan village in the Pearl river delta   171

Notes

1 Helen F. Siu and Liu Zhiwei, "Lineage, market, pirate, and Dan, ethnicity in the Pearl river Delta of South China", in Pamela Kyle Crossley, Helen F. Siu and Donald S. Sutton (eds.), *Empire at the Margins, Culture, Ethnicity, and Frontier in Early Modern China*, Berkeley: University of California, 2006, pp. 285–310; Helen F. Siu, *Agents and Victims in South China: Accomplices in Rural Revolution*, New Haven: Yale University Press, 1989.
2 Liu Zhiwei, "Lineage on the sands, the case of Shawan", and Helen F. Siu, "Subverting lineage power: local bosses and territorial control in the 1940s", in David Faure and Helen F. Siu (eds.), *Down to Earth: the Territorial Bond in South China*, Stanford: Stanford University Press, 1995, pp. 21–43 and 188–208.
3 Guangdong sheng minzu yanjiusuo (ed.) *Guangdong danmin shehui diaocha* (A social survey of the Dan people in Guangdong), Guangzhou: Zhongshan daxue chubanshe, 2001, p. 43.
4 Mr Chen, aged 86 *sui* at time of interview on 1 March 2012, was born in 1925 and grew up in Stone Bank village.
5 Mr Feng, aged 78 *sui* at time of interview on 28 February 2012.
6 Mr Chen of Big Could village, 1 March 2012. Mr Chen was born in 1925 in Stone Bank and grew up in that village
7 Mr Guo, aged 80 *sui* at time of interview of 25 February 2012.
8 Madam Chen of Big Cloud village, aged 82 *sui* at time of interview on 17 March 2012.
9 Madam He, approximately 50 *sui* who was born and married in Sansha village, interviewed on 5 March 2012.
10 Interview with Mr He, who was born in Stone Bank village and had moved to Big Cloud and built a shed there when he married around 1949, interviewed on 3 March 2012.
11 Mr He of Big Cloud village, 3 March 2012.
12 Madam He, 5 March 2012. On the delayed-transfer form of marriage, Helen F. Siu, "Where were the women? Rethinking marriage resistance and regional culture history", *Late Imperial China*, 1990, 11, pp. 32–62.
13 Interview with Madam Liang on 18 March 2012. Madam Liang was born in Big Cloud village and was 84 *sui* at the time of the interview. The "little old ladies" were also described to me as the "12 milk ladies", commonly found in temples all over the Pearl river delta to offer protection for children.
14 Mr He of Big Cloud village, 19–26 March 2012. Pingshan and Zhongcun were neighbouring villages quite close to Shawan. Many boat people in Panyu claimed that their ancestors had come from Pingshan,
15 Fei Hsiao-tung (Fei Xiaotong), *Peasant Life in China: A Field Study of Country Life in the Yangtze Valley*, London: Routledge, 1939; Ke Dawei (David Faure) and Liu Zhiwei, "Zongzu yu difang shehui de guojia rentong – Ming-Qing Hua'nan zongzu fazhan de yishi xingtai jichu" (Lineage and the identification of state with local society – the ideological foundations of lineage development in Ming and Qing south China), *Lishi yanjiu*, 2000, 3, pp. 3–14.
16 Interviews with Madam Feng of Big Cloud village, 21 March, 2012; Madam Chen of Big Cloud village, 17 March 2012; Mr He of Big Cloud village, 3–7 March 2012.
17 Mr He of Big Cloud village, 24 March, 2012. On Li Longji, see Han Guang, "Wo suo zhidao de 'Shiqiao huangdi' Li Longji" (Li Longji, the king of Shiqiao I know about), *Guangdong wenshi ziliao*, 1965, 14, pp. 120–146.
18 Mr He of Big Cloud village, 27 March, 2012, who learnt about cane farming from his elder brother. Mr He's elder brother was a cane-farmer for 30 years.
19 Mr Chen of Big Could village, 17 March 2012. Mr Chen was born in 1925 in Stone Bank and grew up in that village.

172   *Zeng Huijuan*

20 Madam Liang, aged 55 *sui*, Big Could village, 6 March 2012
21 Mr Guo, aged 50 *sui*, 25 March 2012.
22 Mr He of Big Cloud Village, 18 March 2012.
23 Zeng Huijuan, "Cong piaoyi dao dingju – Qingmo Minguo shiqi Panyu Dachongkou 'liaoju shushangren' yanjiu" (From drifting to settlement – the "shed-living boat people" of Dachongkou village in Panyu county from the late Qing to the Republic), *Tianye yu wenxian*, 2012, 69, pp. 7–13.
24 Siu and Liu, "Lineage, market, pirate, and Dan," p. 288.
25 Siu, *Agents and Victims in South China.*

12 The recent history of the fishing households of the nine surnames, a survey from the counties of Jiande and Tonglu, Zhejiang province

Sato Yoshifumi

This chapter is based on research conducted by the author from 2007 to 2010 at Jiande county in Zhejiang. Jiande county is located 80 miles inland from Hangzhou. It is on the Xin'an river, which joins with the Lanjiang river to become the Fuchun river, flowing into the sea at Hangzhou Bay.[1] People known as the "fishing households of the nine surnames" (*jiuxing yuhu*) have historically inhabited the stretch of the river from Jiande to Hangzhou.[2] Hangzhou generated a great deal of traffic on the river, being a major city since the ninth century and the Southern Song capital for most of the twelfth and thirteenth centuries.[3] The term "fishing households of the nine surnames" implies that the people to whom it applied made their living by fishing, but it should be remembered that the same area was agriculturally fertile and commercially active, giving rise to farming and transport in which they might easily also have engaged.

Historical texts describe the fishing people of the nine surnames as having been engaged in entertainment and prostitution. Nevertheless, our interviews show that the fishing households of the nine surnames were engaged primarily in fishing and transport. They have long been known for using cormorants in their fishing.[4] That became a subject that I could discuss with the fishing people I met.

Talking to descendants of the "fishing households of the nine surnames"

At a fishing village in Sandu township, near the confluence of the Xin'an and Lanjiang rivers, I spoke to an elderly man born in 1929 who had lived on a boat before Liberation. He owned three to four small boats from which he fished and he lived on a large house boat. This is a record of my conversation with him:

Q: What did you fish with before Liberation?
A: Cormorants.
Q: When you went elsewhere to fish in winter, did you do that collectively?
A: Collectively.

Plate 12.1 Fishing village of the "fishing households of the nine surnames", also providing for tourist leisure (credit: Sato Yoshifumi).

Q: Did you all fish with cormorants?
A: Some with cormorants, but there were other means, including nets.
Q: When you fished in winter, what was the most common means of fishing?
A: In the old days, cormorants. Later, the cormorants were destroyed, and other methods were used, including nets.
Q: What sort of people went to fish? Did the boats that moor over here all go?
A: They all went.
Q: How many boats went to fish together in winter?
A: Many, as many as 50 to 60 boats, coming from all over.
Q: Not only from Sandu township, is that right?
A: No, not only from Sandu, fishing people from Lanxi, Jinhua and Quzhou all came.
Q: Where did they go to fish?
A: They all went to Qililong. The water was deep at Qililong and fish gathered there.
Q: Is Qililong the spot where fish was most plentiful around here?
A: Yes, it was most plentiful, especially in winter.
Q: With so many people around, did they fight over the fish?
A: No.

The recent history of the fishing households of the nine surnames 175

Q: How did the cormorant recognize you as its home?
A: It knew.
Q: How did it know?
A: It knew better than we did. When you were on the boat, it swam over
   to you.
Q: Did you tie a string around its neck when it fished?
A: Yes, you had to do that. If you didn't, it swallowed the fish.[5]

A fisherman born in 1933 also from Dayang township, upriver from Sandu, told me that in spring, they used to fish at Xiaya township at Jiande, and in winter on the Fuchun or Lanxi rivers, or even as far as Hangzhou. They used both cormorants and fishing nets. They had a house boat and two to three small fishing boats. He said on the Lanxi river or at Xiaya in Jiande, there were 30 to 40 fishing boats that fished with cormorants. Each fishing household had from seven to 16 of those birds. Marks of red, black or white were painted on the feathers for identification.[6]

At Dayang township, another former fisherman born in 1935 told me that he also fished with cormorants. He also told me his family background: his father married into his mother's family. At the time of the marriage, his father and two younger brothers worked on his maternal grandfather's boat. They usually moored that boat by the river bank and fished from smaller boats. His maternal grandfather and his uncles (his father's brothers) all fished with cormorants until the time of the Cultural Revolution in the 1960s. Later on, they fished with nets. His uncles' sons often went as far as Anhui province, on the upper reaches of the Xin'an river, to fish. By the end of the season, they returned to Jiande. In winter, as many as 400 to 500 boats fishing with cormorants went from as far away as Quzhou to the Xin'an and Lanjiang rivers to fish.[7]

On their engagement in transport, the fisherman at Dayang who was born in 1935 had the following to add:

Q: Did your boats have to transport salt?
A: Yes, they did.
Q: Did you have to pay tax on the salt you transported?
A: The Guomindang fined you if they found salt being smuggled under your
   cargo. They beat the palm of your hand. There was an office at Tonglu
   county [down-river from Sandu] that dealt with that.
Q: They beat the palm of your hand?
A: Yes, when you were caught carrying things, you would lose money and also
   be beaten. When I was young, I was once caught at Tonglu.
Q: How did the tax-boats collect tax? How much did they charge?
A: I don't know how much, but it was collected by the Guomindang
   government. They would charter a boat, carry a gun to drive fear into
   you, and then come alongside. I don't know what taxes they collected.
   Because it was not convenient for boats to stop at Tonglu or Fuyang,

176　*Sato Yoshifumi*

the tax-boats came out to collect from us one by one. Elsewhere, the tax station was located in fixed places.

Q: Before Liberation, what did you carry in your cargo?

A: Firewood and charcoal for Hangzhou. Most boats carried firewood to sell to the timber and firewood shops in Hangzhou. There were gangsters in Hangzhou who extorted money from the boats. They were everywhere. In the old days, land people were press-ganged to join the army but not the boat people. On land, they took away two out of every three men, or even one out of every two. Rich people bought able-bodied men to serve in their stead. They paid for that with sacks of grain.

A 61-year-old former manager of a shipping company confirmed to me that in the 1970s, before the dam was built across the Xin'an river, the "fishing households of the nine surnames" carried firewood, timber and tea from Jiande to Hangzhou, and shipped back manufactured products. When his company was set up in 1968, they carried firewood and charcoal to Hangzhou, and brought seafood, sugar, salt, cotton cloth, rice wine and soy sauce to Jiande.[8]

I probed for their experience as the "fishing households of the nine surnames". The fisherman at Dayang township born in 1933 told me:

Q: When your father went ashore, he was not allowed to wear shoes. Is that right?

A: That is right.

Q: Aside from not wearing shoes, was there anything else that marked them out from the land people?

A: When I was small, the elders said they were exposed for working for the revolution and so they were brought down [*da xialai*]. All three of them, Chen, Qian and Xu were brought down. [Author's note: The informant was using terminology acquired in recent years. By "revolution", he did not mean the series of events leading to the establishment of the People's Republic, but rebellious activities in dynastic times.]

Q: What happened when they were brought down?

A: They were told to fish. For that reason, they were not allowed to wear shoes.

Q: Not allowed to go ashore?

A: Going ashore was allowed, but they were not allowed to wear shoes.[9]

The same man also told me that if they went ashore in shoes, some people were bound to take notice.

The fisherman at Dayang born in 1935 added:

It was hard not being allowed to wear shoes when you went on shore. You could only sell fish on the river bank. You could not go into the market. You were dressed in a short outer jacket with buttons in front, tied up

The recent history of the fishing households of the nine surnames 177

with a belt on the waist, and you went barefoot, because you were not allowed to wear shoes.[10]

I had the chance to speak to people living on land for their reaction on the fishing households. They were quite indifferent. I did not gain the impression that they were apprehensive of the fishermen's presence.[11]

Were there really nine surnames? The elderly fishermen I spoke to mentioned Chen, Sun, Qian, Xu, He, Li and Ye. They seemed to be concentrated separately in different stretches of the rivers. Transport operators owned their own jetties on the river and were referred to as "boat people's headmen" (*chuanjia zhang*). Nevertheless, I was not given the impression from my interviews that fishing rights to any part of the rivers were exclusively held by particular surname groups. It seemed that fishermen could take their fish to wherever they thought it was profitable. Did the people who spoke to me know all along they were descended from the fishing households of the nine surnames? One person told me the story that someone realized that only after he had heard stories about the ancestors in a teahouse in Hangzhou on a trip delivering cargo.[12] Nevertheless, when they spoke to us, they said they were their descendants. How they all came to think so remains a subject that needs further consideration.

A history from records and reminiscence

One of the best descriptions that may be found of the "fishing households of the nine surnames" comes from documents written in 1866 related to the remission of taxes for which they were held responsible. Yanzhou prefect Dai Pan, who initiated that effort, produced various reports that described what he knew of the people so described. Along with tax remission, the provincial governor, on Prefect Dai's advice, also abolished the pariah status of the "nine surnames". Those reports are invaluable for comparison with what I encountered in interviews. For that reason, they deserve careful consideration.[13]

Prefect Dai explains why he took an interest in the "nine surnames". He was magistrate of Tonglu county near Jiande in 1854, when, on a visit to the area bordering Anhui province, the owner of the boat on which he travelled asked him to alleviate the sufferings of the boatmen. He said he would if he was ever appointed to Yanzhou prefecture. In 1865, he was, and he was as good as his word in seeking the reform.

According to Prefect Dai, legend had it that the "fishing households of the nine surnames" were descendants of followers of Chen Youliang, who was defeated by Zhu Yuanzhang before Zhu became the founding Ming dynasty emperor. For siding with Chen, they were castigated into boat living and making their living by fishing (*bianru zhouju*), a term implying that they were not allowed to settle on shore or take up positions that were not demeaning. In time, he said, many became transporters. Originally, 2,031 boats were

178 *Sato Yoshifumi*

registered, on which each man was levied a tax of 0.5 tael of silver, and each woman 0.41 tael. The tax was paid to Jiande county, where the Yanzhou prefectural government was located. By the 1850s, they numbered more than 1,000 people.

It is, of course, possible that the prefect had had access to administrative records, but the facts he cited are readily available in the 1828 edition of the Jiande county gazetteer. There, it is noted that the "boat households" (*chuanhu*) of nine surnames and occupying 2,031 boats, large and small, were held liable for the head tax for 507 males and 108 females, at rates recorded in the "boat household registry" (*chuanzhuang ce*) only slightly varying from rates Prefect Dai cited. The gazetteer also notes that the "fishing households of the nine surnames" did not intermarry with people living on shore, even though some land people took their women as concubines. It also notes that in time, some fishing households had settled ashore, and thereby "the good and the mean have become blurred and household registration is made inaccurate" (*liangjian huxiao, huji cuoza*). At the time that entry in the gazetteer was written, the pariah status of the "nine surnames" had not broken down, and so it notes that officials had imposed policing to ensure that the occupational segregation was followed.[14]

Prefect Dai noted in his petition to his superiors that the amount recorded in the "boat household registry" had, since 1727, been merged into the land tax and, therefore, had disappeared by the time he was writing. Nevertheless, aside from the head tax, boat households had also to pay charges to various government offices, on which, according to the prefect, they expended half of their income. The main thrust of the prefect's initial petition to his superiors was to request that those tax charges be removed.

Yet, the same petition laid out other reforms that he wanted to conduct. By the time Prefect Dai wrote, the "nine surnames" had branched into the transport business. Dai noted that the boats they used were referred to as "Jiangshan boats", named after Jiangshan county on the upper reaches of the Lanxi river. Those were passenger boats, the refined ones in particular being favoured by wealthy merchants going up and down the river. The same boats, however, were known for prostitution, such a service not being offered by women of the "nine surnames" but by women who were purchased by boat-owners for the purpose. Dai proposed, and his superiors accepted, a three-pronged approach: tax remission, emancipation from the pariah status and a reminder that prostitution was against the law and had to be given up on pain of punishment. Moreover, citing as precedence imperial rulings made in 1770 and 1771 that emancipated people of lowly status in numerous provinces in which the "fishing households of nine surnames" of Zhejiang were also mentioned, Prefect Dai noted that four generations after emancipation, descendants of people of lowly status might rightfully sit for the imperial examination. On that basis, his superiors demanded that he compile a list of all emancipated households, and that the prefect did, appending a list of 196

The recent history of the fishing households of the nine surnames 179

names of household heads who had registered under the "fishing households of the nine surnames".

Prefect Dai Pan's reforms in 1866 put my interviews in 2012 into perspective. Nevertheless, it is necessary to note changes that had intervened between then and my visit to Jiande county. In 1927, the Zhejiang provincial administration under the newly unified Republican government implemented reforms afresh. Reports from the counties reveal that the term "fishing households of the nine surnames" had survived in the counties in the vicinity of Jiande. Nevertheless, the numbers cited in county reports show how small the population so described was: taking into consideration government and newspaper reports, contemporary writer Tong Zhenzao reckoned there were 1,700 people scattered in seven counties.[15] Some of them were noted as having already settled on shore, but others continued to live on boats. They seem to have been characterized by specific locations in the county known to have been inhabited by people of their kind. Many were fishermen, but some were transporters (the transport of timber being particularly noted in one instance), a minority consisted of sedan-chair carriers and, as noted in four counties, there were prostitutes found among them. In 1927, the provincial government reiterated essentially the approach that had been advocated by Prefect Dai Pan in 1866; that is, tax removal, emancipation and banning prostitution. Interestingly, reports from the counties suggest that quite a few of the fishing households of the nine surnames were "quite wealthy". The Hang *xian* county magistrate reported:

> According to Shen Zhenqian, member of the self-government committee of Jianggan district, there used to be boats of the "fishing households of the nine surnames" in the district, but the people have long settled ashore and are no different from ordinary people.

The Qu county magistrate wrote:

> Such people were despised upon by society in the Qing dynasty and came under much restriction. Since the 1911 Revolution, many changes had come about. Some of them have savings or are engaged in other trades [other than fishing], and so are wealthy and hold property. Some have graduated from civilian and military schools and taken public office. They are scattered all over the villages, towns, and cities. They don't acknowledge their origin, and they intermarry with other people, just like ordinary people. There are not many of them.

The provincial government promoted *baojia* policing and even fishery associations among the fishing households, even though it is not clear how effective those measures were.[16]

Since the late 1960s, the numbers registered as fishing households had dwindled: in Jiande, there were only 149 fishing households in 1983, consisting of 597 people, of whom 151 lived by fishing on the river (the others being engaged in fish farming and other activities), and in nearby Tonglu county in 1985, there were 164 fishing households, consisting of 394 persons. The fishing population in Tonglu at earlier times was 879 persons in 1935, 517 persons in 1949 and 792 persons in 1958. In Jiande and Tonglu from 1967, with government assistance, the fishing households had also given up living on boats and settled ashore in fishing villages (*yuye cun*). They were organized into "fishing brigades" (*dadui*) during the commune movement of the late 1960s and 1970s, and in the 1980s became villages (*cun*). In 1959, a hydroelectric dam was built across the Xin'an river, thereby creating the Qiandao (literally, "thousand island") lake, which by the 1980s became a popular tourist attraction. Since that time, the "fishing households of nine surnames" have come to be looked upon as a cultural heritage. By then, cormorant-fishing had been banned.[17]

What, therefore, do interviews conducted in the twenty-first century tell us about the continuation of the "fishing households of the nine surnames"? Do they confirm the continuation, by adoption or birth, generation after generation, of descent lines that originated in the Ming dynasty belonging to people of demeaned status who lived on boats? Or, do they lend support to the continuation of a historical term, and the ideas it was associated with, as applied to people who lived on boats, whether or not their ancestors were held in demeaned status?

Certainly, for centuries, there had been fishing people and transporters on the rivers near Jiande county and, likewise there was prostitution servicing the wealthy merchants who travelled on transport boats. They were not all of them "fishing households of the nine surnames". In the 1920s, so few were found when the provincial government declared their emancipation once again, that little was said about descent among the cases reported.

We might assume that at different times, self-admission provided support for the belief in the continuation of the "nine surnames", which was, indeed, what I witnessed in my interviews. Nevertheless, oral history is limited by the lifespan of the people who can be interviewed. An 80-year-old person interviewed in 2012 would have been born in 1932, and what he or she remembered witnessing would have occurred no earlier than the mid-1930s. By then, experience under the Qing dynasty would have been no more than a memory passed down by word of mouth.

How fluid, indeed, was social life on the rivers? The reports that came of reforms conducted in 1866 and 1927 acknowledged that many people who lived on boats had moved ashore, and that many women were purchased from outside the boat-living community to serve as prostitutes, just as they also acknowledged that a popular view of the people living on boats associated them with a menial status. Just about all that we can be certain about is that the notion of the "fishing households of the nine surnames" had survived in memory and was appealed to time and again in reforms directed at tax,

The recent history of the fishing households of the nine surnames   181

prostitution and status emancipation. Equally certain is the lively economic life on the rivers, providing a living for the many who lived or worked on boats, and who incorporated the collective memories of the past to create their own history.

Notes

1 The research for this chapter was conducted by a research group consisting of the author, Professor Ota Izuru of Hiroshima University and Professor Wu Tao of Sun Yat-sen University and organized within the framework of the project on "Maritime cross-cultural exchange in east Asia and the formation of Japanese traditional culture: interdisciplinary approach focusing on Ningbo" headed by Professor Kojima Tsuyoshi of the University of Tokyo. The group spent a total of 35 days in the four years between 2007 and 2010 to interview 42 people for this project. It was generously helped by local scholars and keepers of the temple at which descendants of the "fishing households of the nine surnames" worshipped. By their reports, their identity as descendants of the nine surnames may be traced to similar claims made to them by their elders.

2 Feng Xunzhan, "Shemin, duomin, jiuxing yuhu kao" (A study of the She people, the fallen people, and the fishing households of the nine surnames), *Dixue zazhi*, 1914, 11, pp 75–78. For background on the pariah status in the Qing dynasty, including the fishing households of the nine surnames, see Kishimito Mio, "Yoseitei no mibun seisaku to kokka taise: yosei gonen no shokaikaku o chusin ni" (The status policy of the Yongzheng emperor and the structure of the state: a focus on the various reforms in the fifth year of Yongzheng) in Chugoku shigakukai (ed.), *Chugoku no rekishisekai: togo no shisutemu to tagenteki hatten* (The historical world of China: the system of unity and multi-centred developments), Tokyo: Tokyo toritsu daigaku shuppankai, 2002, pp. 269–300; Kiyama Hideo, "Settō 'damin' ko," (Study on the fallen people of Zhejiang), *Shakaishi kenkyū*, 1984, 4, pp. 61–116; Anders Hansson, *Chinese Outcasts, Discrimination and Emancipation in Late Imperial China*, Leiden: Brill, 1996, pp. 133–139.

3 Li Zhao, *Tang guoshi bu* (Supplement to the history of the Tang dynasty), c. ninth century, reprinted Shanghai: Shanghai guji, 1979, p. 62.

4 Berthold Lauffer, *The Domstication of the Cormorant in China and Japan*, Chicago: Field Museum of Natural History, 1931; Kane Hiroaki, *Ukai* (Raising cormorants), Tokyo: Chuko ronsha, 1966.

5 Report of Q.ZE on 24 August 2007.

6 Report of C.ZK on 23 August 2007.

7 Report of L.BX on 19 and 20 August 2007.

8 Report of T.YQ on 24 August 2007 and 18 August 2008; Jiejiang sheng Jiande shi jiaotong ju (ed.), *Jiande shi jiaotong zhi* (History of transport in Jiande municipality), Beijing: Haiyang, 1996, pp. 17–19.

9 Report of C.ZK on 23 August 2007 and 18 August 2008.

10 Report of L.BX on 20 August 2007 and 15 August 2008.

11 For example, report of L.ZQ on 16 August 2008.

12 Report by C.LG on 28 August 2009.

13 Dai Pan, "Cai Yanjun jiuxing yuke lu" (A record of the abolition of the fish tax for the nine surnames of Yanzhou prefecture), in Dai Pan, *Dai Pan sizhong jilue* (The papers of Dai Pan in four postings), 1868, no publisher, separately paginated, reprinted in Wang Youli (ed.), *Zhonghua wenshi congshu* (Books in Chinese literature and history), Vol. 48, Taibei: Huawen shuju, 1969.

14 *Jiande xianzhi* (Gazetteer of Jiande county), 1828, 4/15b and 21/13b.

182 *Sato Yoshifumi*

15 Tong Zhenzao, "Qianjiang jiuxing yuhu kao" (A study of the fishing households of the nine surnames on the Qiantang river), *Lingnan xuebao*, 1931, 2(2), pp. 4–50. Tong was a reputable bibliophile resident in Hangzhou who took an interest in local history.

16 Jiande xian yuhui (Jiangde county fishery association), "Guanyu zuzhi chengli de baogao, xunling, zhangcheng, huiyilu, mingce, yuye jiuji tongzhi" (Report, instructions, statutes, minutes of meetings, name registries and fishery relief on establishment), Jiande Municipality Archives, 1810-1-21; "Jiande xian zhengfu guanyu diaozheng baojia, xuanju shuishang baozhang ji fucha hukou wenjuan" (Jiande county government documents on the adjustment of *baojia*, election of *bao* headmen among the boat population and re-checking of household registration), Jiande Municipality Archives, 1808-6-106.

17 *Jiande xianzhi* (Gazetteer of Jiande county), 1986, pp. 225–231; *Tonglu xianzhi* (Gazetteer of Tonglu county), 1991, pp. 155–159; Ota Izuru, "Renka gyosen kara rikujou teikyo he: taiko ryuiki gyomin to gyogyouson no seiritsu" (From houseboats to settlement on shore: the fishing people of Tai lake and the establishment of their fishing villages), in Sato Yoshifumi, Ota Izuru, Inada Seiichi and Wu Tao (eds.), *Chugoku noson no shinko to seikatsu: Taiko ryuiki shakaishi koujutsu kirokushu* (Religion and Livelihood in Chinese villages: an oral record of the social history of the Tai lake region), Tokyo: Kyuko shoin, 2008, pp. 47–67.

Appendix 1

The religious festival of the Liu-wang-wei, 19 May 1877, *North China Herald*

Friday, 12 May, the day of the Chinese third moon, was the opening day of the annual religious Liu-wang-wei (Liuwang *hui*), a faithful minister of the Sung (Song) Emperor, Wei-sung (Huizong), who reigned towards the end of the troublesome times of the Sung dynasty, which preceded its final subjugation by the Mongols. Weisung's reign seems to have been further troubled by internal disaffection, and Ching (Jin), described as a usurper, having taken him prisoner, he is said to have committed suicide – whereupon Liu, his faithful minister, to show at the same time his loyalty and devotion, committed suicide also. Liu received posthumous honours, being deified and ordered to be worshipped under the name of Ming-jaou (Ming *chao*), and the popular belief ever since has been that he is acting as prime minister to the Emperor Wei-sung in the Chinese Hades. These things happened about 700 years ago, and temples have been erected in all parts of the country to the memory of this doubly-devoted servant. During later years these have multiplied enormously; and at and around our neighbouring village of Kong-wan (Jiangwan) several of them are to be found. So great has the fame of Liu become, that there are many other gods deemed subservient to him, and his effigy, which represents rather a jolly Bacchanalian than a prime minister given to suicide, is in some of the temples surrounded by a perfect Walhalla of civil, military and naval deities-the former being those whose supernatural care is believed to be chiefly exercised in the care and promotion of the local crops – they are in fact a body of male Ceres'. Be all this as it may, the 28th day of the Chinese third moon is Liu's great anniversary; several subsequent days being, however, also devoted to the worship of his subordinates. For nearly six centuries has this interesting ceremony been performed at Kong-wan and elsewhere throughout the Empire – affording an apt illustration of the all-pervading teaching of the Chinese in matters ancestral.

Extremes sometimes meet, and that extremes met on this occasion at Kong-wan is irrefutable. On the one hand, thousands of country-people flocked to the village on foot, by boat, or by wheelbarrow, some from distances of from 80 to 100 *li* (32 to 40 miles), to take part in a religious ceremonial just as their fore-fathers had done for centuries before them; – on the other hand, thousands more proceeded, by railway, from Shanghai, and the

184 *Appendix 1*

villages around, bent on the same errand. One of the triumphs of modern civilization and science, was for once made subservient to the observance of an antiquated sacred rite, the real origin and meaning of which was to the great majority of the devotees as obscure, if not as totally unknown, as the sound of the steam whistle which they heard during their journey.

At Kong-wan, there are two larger and smaller temples, all dedicated wholly or in part, to Liu – the latter having been erected by private believers, who, probably, had either been fortunate in their crops, or in trade, or considered themselves in some way benefitted through the god's influence. Between the two larger temples lay the track of an annual procession of devotees, the priests of course insisting that, to be thoroughly efficacious, offerings must be made, and incense and joss-paper burnt, before the shrines in both places. However, for the first the procession was now omitted – the track lay across the railway, and the native authorities, fearful of accident, forbade its taking place. Last year, we are assured, on credible authority, the procession numbered many thousands, being in fact a procession simply between the two buildings which are only about half a mile apart – the people on arriving at the second temple breaking off to give place to their successors, who formed up at the first temple, and thus proceeded in a seemingly never ending stream for three or four hours, bearing their offerings in their hands, and walking to the sound of music. Many of these offerings were tawdry but picturesque, and when seen altogether in large quantity, must have had a peculiarly pleasing effect. Much preparation had been made as usual for the purpose, the Magistrate of Paoshan (Baoshan) issued a proclamation, in which he was supported by the Taotai of Shanghai, forbidding the procession, and three of the Taotai's officials were on the spot to see it enforced. The people bore their disappointment quietly, and consoled themselves with burning their offerings, together with incense and paper sycee in the large bronze urns at each joss-house, and then wandering about, or sitting in groups conversing, in the neighbouring villages and fields, all seemingly happy and contented. To say that the surrounding district was like a fair would give but an imperfect idea of the scene presented. People were here, there, everywhere, not in sparse groups, but in masses; and the priests must have been great gainers, for at nearly all the joss-houses, the chinking sound of cash thrown into the baskets placed to receive them, was almost incessant.

The native officials tried to induce the Railway authorities to cease running the trains, but it was thought unadvisable to do so, and the result was that the line also reaped a rich harvest. From about eight o'clock in the morning till one, the traffic from Shanghai was great; but from that hour till dusk double trains had to be put on, as many as 308 passengers crowding at a time into the six carriages forming one train. They actually fought and struggled for places, and men, women, and children, were at times packed so closely that breathing seemed impossible and comfort was abolished. There was not sitting room for them – the carriages were alike crowded with standers as sitters, and for some hours after each train left the platform, sometimes hundreds

Appendix 1 185

and always scores, were left behind till the next arrival and departure. When it is remembered that this went on for hours throughout the day, some idea of the animated scene presented at the station may be obtained, as well as an approximation of the number of persons carried. Never since the line was opened has there been such a scene, and the greatest care had to be exercised by the several station-masters, engine-drivers and conductors to prevent accident. Mr Morrison superintended the arrangements in person, and as it was soon seen that the people could not be kept off the rails, especially in the neighbourhood of Kong-wan, where they surged to and fro like a troubled sea, he detached twenty permanent-way men to act as watchmen, and the great traffic was conducted without a single hitch or accident throughout the day.

There was no real reason why the procession should not have been held – the trains might have been so arranged as to have prevented all probability of accident or interference with the procession, but this did not seem to strike the Mandarin mind, and so on this occasion, as they could not stop the trains in favour of the procession, they autocratically stopped the procession in favour of the trains; and thus caused a ceremony honoured by observance of centuries to give place to the mighty emblem of modern progress. Can this be regarded as another instance of China awakening from her ancient conservatism?

Appendix 2

Mechanization, market and moving ashore

He Xi and David Faure

Living on boats as a style of life came to an end towards the end of the twentieth century. Its demise can be traced to three broad changes: mechanization, the market and boat people moving ashore. The first had to do with technological changes on boats, trawling and fishing; the second had to do with the capitalization of marketing, which effectively centralized urban fish markets; and the third with government policies on urban planning, hygiene, education and the timeless and vague notion that mobility without registration was socially dangerous. Although many of those changes came to be noticeable in the early years of the twentieth century, it took the entire century for them to take hold over many parts of China.

Background

In the early years of the twentieth century, a new approach to fishing was signalled by the innocuous term "fishing industry" (*yuye*). The term was obviously used in earlier times in Chinese history, but as the Qing dynasty committed itself to political and economic reform in its last years, it signalled no longer a livelihood but – along with agriculture, manufacturing and mining – a sphere of economic exploitation of natural resources. The technological impact was realized in Japan before it was in China. In China, ideas for reform were mooted in 1904 when the up-and-coming scholar-cum-industrialist Zhang Jian proposed that fishery companies be set up, that steam boats be introduced that were capable of deep-sea fishing, and that government acknowledge that it had jurisdiction over coastal waters so that it might provide them with policing and protection. The combination of technology, business practice and jurisdiction characterized reports and public discussions on fishery for the rest of the century.[1]

By the end of the twentieth century, the terms of the discussion in the early 1900s were fully realized on all the three scores of technology, business practice and jurisdiction. For most of the first half of the century, however, reality mostly did not match up to the rhetoric for change. Changes quickened by mid-century, and by the century's end, few people living on the coast maintained the lifestyle their grandparents had. That is not a very remarkable

Appendix 2 187

observation: it would have been true of the great majority of China's population, whether or not they lived on the coast.

Mechanized boats

The introduction of mechanized boats into deep-sea fishing in the first half of the twentieth century, for example, was far from a success story. The most comprehensive descriptions of coastal fishing are given in a paper written by Wang Zongpei in 1932 and two volumes by Li Shihao both in 1936.[2] Wang was working in the investigation department of the Zhejiang Bank in 1931, and Li worked for the Department of Industry in the Ministry of the Interior.

Table A2.1 summarizes statistics cited by both authors as estimates of the fishing population and the number and variety of boats used. As late as perhaps 1930, fishing boats outside strongly Japanese-dominated Liaoning and Shandong were not mechanized. In Dairen and Port Arthur, for example, Li reported that including Japanese-owned boats, 199 steam boats were in operation, but he made no mention of them in Liaoning outside that area. Hence, the 133 noted in the table for Liaoning were Chinese-owned but based at the Japanese-dominated ports. In Shandong, he noted 150 mechanized vessels, mostly based in Qingdao, Yantai (Chefoo) and Weihaiwei. Chinese boats based in China-controlled ports were all listed under Jiangsu. On the exact number, his various reports differ. The source cited for Table A2.1 records that 25 mechanized boats were in use, but in his other report, written in the same year, Li says that by 1930, only three were operational, and into the 1930s, there were only about a dozen more.[3] Steam boats were used in the Shanghai surroundings primarily for fishery research, but the many descriptions of fishing methods in the 1920s and 1930s suggest that technology remained mostly traditional. Aside from coastal or inland fishing (on rivers and lakes), where nets and traps might be set up in shallow water, fishermen went out in sailing junks to their fishing grounds, many still operating in pairs for trawl-net operations. In terms of numbers, whether of boats or the populations of fishing people, reports from Wang are substantially different from Li. This is not surprising, because the data are quite impressionistic.

Wang provides reports for the relative importance of fishing in the different coastal provinces in 1917, reproduced here in Table A2.2. They show that the number of boats credited to the province was associated with income from fishing. Zhejiang and Guangdong, with the largest number of boats, reported the highest value in their annual catches. Yet, it must also be realized that Shandong caught up very rapidly, not by having more fishing junks but by having more mechanized boats. By 1933, the *Shenbao Annual* reported that the income from fishing in Shandong amounted to 20 million yuan. Li estimates that a mechanized boat could fetch 30,000 yuan per year, compared to 600 for a sailing junk and so, although Li thinks the *Shenbao Annual* figure grossly exaggerates, it can be seen that an increasing number of steam fishing boats was producing an effect on income. Li's figures conflict substantially

Table A2.1. Fishing population and boats

	Wang Zongpei, 1932				Li Shihao, 1936			
	Population	Households	All boats	Mechanized	Population	Households	All boats	Mechanized
Liaoning	40,200	11,800	11,000	n/a	23,005	9,282	6,155	133
Hebei	n/a	n/a	n/a	n/a	40,000	n/a	4,000	n/a
Shandong	19,000 plus	n/a	1,536	n/a	46,838	n/a	8,043	150–160
Jiangsu	23,000	n/a	1,800	n/a	20,000–30,000	n/a	4,000	25
Zhejiang	350,000	n/a	23,000	n/a	n/a	n/a	12,710	n/a
Fujian	n/a	n/a	n/a	n/a	n/a	n/a	3,500 plus	n/a
Guangdong	n/a	n/a	n/a	n/a	n/a	n/a	11,790	n/a

Source: Li, *Zhongguo haiyang yuye xianzhuang jiqi jianshe*, pp. 11–140; Wang, "Zhongguo yanhai zhi yumin jingji", pp. 100–102.

Appendix 2 189

Table A2.2. Monetary value of fishing in 1917 (million yuan)

Liaoning	1.6
Hebei	2.1
Shandong	8.7
Jiangsu	9.8
Zhejiang	10.7
Fujian	2.3
Guangdong	13.5

Source: Wang, "Zhongguo yanhai zhi yumin jingji", p 100.

with Wang's, as will be seen below, but the income differential between mechanized boats and sailing junks must still hold.

The impression that changes from the early 1900s to the 1930s to the fishing industry were driven more by the market than by technology is attested to in studies on Zhoushan, arguably one of the most important fishing ports in coastal China. Zhao Yizhong, a compiler of the detailed *History of Zhoushan Fishery*, carefully documented the critical changes there in the fishing industry.[4] Since the Song dynasty, there had been record of fishing villages on the Zhoushan islands as well as the gathering of fishing boats coming from as far as Fujian in the fishing seasons. Business must have grown as the village of Shenjiamen grew into a major port through the second half of the nineteenth century and the early twentieth. Fujianese junk owners set up the Fujianese guild there in 1863, and by 1925, five other fishing associations were set up there. Comparing two texts written about local fishery at Zhoushan in 1882 and 1906, and noting how very similar their descriptions of local fishery were, Zhao concluded that little had changed in the last decades of the nineteenth century, and ascribed mounting growth to the discovery of new fishing grounds for the small yellow croaker in the 1910s further out to sea than traditional grounds. Yet, fishing boomed from the 1910s to the 1920s. By 1919, some 2,500 small trawlers (*tuochuan*) with capacity of 5,000–6,000 catties of fish came annually from Taizhou every season for the yellow croaker, and 600 large trawlers with capacity for 30,000–40,000 catties came from Ningbo. In addition, hundreds of boats came from other coastal areas, including fishing ports in the Zhoushan archipelago itself.[5]

Nonetheless, the mechanization of fishing boats made up only part of the history of boat mechanization in China. The mechanization of transport boats developed more rapidly in the coastal traffic from the second half of the nineteenth century. On that subject, a ready summary of the documentation, drawn primarily from Chinese Maritime Customs reports, is available from Wiens.[6] The impression given in his data is that the junk trade was rapidly declining through the first few decades of the twentieth century but was by no means negligible as late as the 1930s. He notes that in the two most prosperous ports, that is to say, Shanghai and Dalian, respectively 14 and 8 per cent of all trade in 1930 was carried by junks. Tianjin was the exception where

190   *Appendix 2*

only 1 per cent was. In the smaller sea ports, such as Fuzhou and Shantou, it was respectively 33 and 21 per cent. Wiens excluded Hong Kong, which, for its colonial status, would not have appeared in the Maritime Customs' statistics. For comparison, it may be noted that the Hong Kong Harbour Office reported for 1930 that the trade carried by junks into and out of Hong Kong (1.3 million tons) was nearly twice that carried by steamers (0.7 million tons).[7]

Many people who made a living from transport were also involved, not in inter-city trade, but in the provision of very localized ferry services.[8] As bridges and roads were built, such provision came to be phased out. Yet the replacement of the village ferry again took place over a very long stretch of time. As an indicator of the magnitude of change, it may be noted that in 1949, 1979 and 2009, China had respectively 50,000, 550,000 and 2,400,000 miles of highway.[9] Many contemporary accounts show that ferry boats were widely in use until the 1960s.

Changes in fish marketing

Contemporary reports describe two ways by which fishing boats were owned. Some were owned by proprietors who did not themselves put to sea, so all hands on board were hired. Nevertheless, other boats were collectively owned by the fishermen themselves. Whichever way the boats were owned, the fishermen operated in protected gangs mostly of people who came from the same home county. In the Republican period, the gang-like networks were formalized as "fishing associations" (*yuhui*) and levied charges for the protection that they offered. The Republican government by 1922 began to regulate their activities.[10] Some of the protection was genuine, as piracy – a term that no doubt included territorial disputes between gangs – was rife, but there were also complaints of extortion by the associations.

Wang Zongpei goes into the question of fishing boat financing in some detail, concentrating apparently on boats operating near Zhoushan. His reconstruction of a budget for a pair of trawlers shows that 520 yuan was paid in annual boat rental, 360 yuan as interest on loan, 140 yuan for various fees and charges on the catch, 567 yuan for food, 1,270 yuan for other costs (nets, tools, religious celebrations, payments for use of small boats, etc.) and 2,230 yuan for wages. Set against catches worth 6,000 yuan, the profit was quite marginal. He also cites a study by a fishermen's association at Zhoushan that shows an income from fishing of 2,000 yuan and expenditures of just about the same amount. Interestingly, the expenses include repairs for three houses, an indication that boat owners did not only live on boats.[11]

The fishermen sold their fish to dealers who were likewise organized in gangs. It is not clear many dealers collected fish at sea, but at least in a thriving fishing ground such as Zhoushan, some dealers operated ice boats to purchase the fishermen's catches. As an indication of the scale of ice-freezing, it may be noted that in 1933, of 708,000 piculs of fish imported into Shanghai, 634,000 piculs were frozen.[12] In a study on Ningbo published in 1936, it was

Appendix 2 191

found that credit for the 40 ice boats that plied in the river nearby was provided by eight major dealers, who, by providing loans, had the right to purchase the catch. Apart from the need for capital, the loans from the dealer enabled the peculiar arrangement by which ice boats paid fishermen for their catches. The ice boats carried no ready cash when they sailed out to sea to purchase from the fishermen. Instead of cash, they paid with promissory notes, the flags that they flew indicating the dealer they were associated with who provided credit for the notes. The report states specifically that this arrangement worked only for established dealers. Fishermen did not trust new dealers, and guarantee from the native banks was needed if a new dealer was involved.[13]

Reformers of the fishing industry, who believed in government direction of reform efforts, lamented the protective nature of local gangs and the unwieldy character of fish-marketing through layers of intermediaries. Likewise, they poured scorn on the loans that fish dealers advanced boat-owners in anticipation of their catches. For both reasons, they supported the setting up of fishery cooperatives and open auctioning of daily catches at well-financed government-approved fish markets.

Fishing cooperatives were part of a wider cooperative movement that was promoted by the Republican government from the last years of the 1920s as a measure to alleviate rural poverty. The movement was also backed by the modern banks. That was why Wang Zongpei, working for the Zhejiang Bank, would have conducted a study into fishery and devoted considerable scope to the fishermen's budgets.[14] When the town of Shenjiamen at Zhoushan petitioned the provincial government for setting up a fishing cooperative in 1935, its application was granted on the understanding that it would be capitalized at 600,000 yuan, half of which was to be provided by the fish dealers in the town, and the other half to be borrowed from banks that the provincial government would identify. The bank loan, moreover, was to be fully guaranteed by the fish dealers.[15]

The auction system was implemented as a novelty when the Shanghai Fish Market was opened in 1936. The market was highly successful. By early 1937, monthly transactions went well above one million yuan.[16] When war with Japan broke out by July 1937, trading was interrupted because the puppet government set up its own alternative fish market in Shanghai. The Japanese military, having taken over the Zhoushan archipelago, was able to divert all fishing boats to the new market.

On market trends, until the Ministry of Industry collected supply statistics in Shanghai, there can only be hazy impressions of the trading volume in fish and other aqua-products (fish, molluscs, seaweeds). Nevertheless, the rapid growth of coastal cities, not only Shanghai, but also Tianjin and Hong Kong, must have provided an expanded market and, therefore, the pull factors behind the search for new fishing grounds and the thriving scene in marine fishing. The sense of intense activity may be found not only in marine fishing, but also on the rivers and lakes, and in the development of fish farming. Table A2.3 shows that from 1933 supply increased quite substantially into the

192   *Appendix 2*

Table A2.3. Supply of aqua-products to Shanghai, 1933–1948 (000 tons)

	Marine products	Fresh-water products	Salted and dried products	Total
1933	33	8	10	51
1934	39	8	19	66
1935	35	9	20	64
1936	38	12	11	61*
1937–1939	n/a	n/a	n/a	n/a
1940	42	13	17	72
1941	41	13	20	74
1942	27	3	8	38
1943	25	3	14	42
1944	37	8	18	63
1945	7	3	2	12
1946	35	9	13	57
1947	39	14	10	63
1948	46	13	12	71

Source: Shanghai yuyezhi bianzuan weiyuanhui (ed.), *Shanghai yuyezhi* (A history of the fishing industry in Shanghai), Shanghai: Shanghai shehui kexue chubanshe, 1998, p. 242, citing *Shuichan yuekan*, 1946.

*Missing reports for March and April

Table A2.4. Import and export of fish and sea food, 1912–1928 (Annual averages, million Haikwan taels)

	Export	Import
1872–1881	0.07	1.62
1882–1891	0.26	3.00
1892–1901	0.98	4.78
1902–1911	1.18	9.30
1912–1921	1.68	15.41
1922–1931	2.34	24.73

Source: Li and Qu, *Zhongguo yuye shi*, pp. 175–176.

war years of the 1940s. A similar trend may be detected in import and export statistics from the Maritime Customs Service, for Table A2.4 shows that a very persistent export deficit expanded over the years that was of concern to the Republican government, especially in the 1930s. However, more relevant to the state of the fishing industry in China is that, despite the imbalance, Chinese exports were also increasing. Contemporary reports indicate that by the mid-1930s, fishermen in Zhoushan felt the impact of the depression that was settling into China's major cities, especially Shanghai, but such was not the case until then.

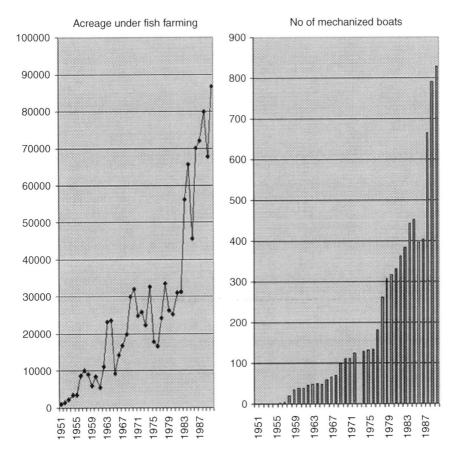

Figure A2.1 Acreage under fish farms and number of mechanized boats in Leqing county, 1951–1990.
Source: Leqing shi shuichanju (ed.), *Leqing xian shuichan zhi*, pp. 80, 98.

Not a great deal has been written about the fishing industry during the war years. The data beyond the establishment of the People's Republic in 1949, however, are clear and straightforward. The process of mechanization continued, as is illustrated in Figure A2.1 from data available regarding Leqing county, in the Wenzhou area, with a long-established fishing industry. Despite the annual fluctuations, it can be seen that the number of mechanized boats took off from modest beginnings only in the late 1950s, but expanded enormously after 1979. The same may be said for acreage under fish farming. Products from fish-farming, as measured by weight, grew from 12 per cent of overall aqua-products to 61 per cent.[17]

194   *Appendix 2*

Moving ashore

The slow pace of change in mechanization and market development up to the 1970s and its very rapid escalation from then on is reflected also in the migration of boat people ashore. The boat-living way of life in Guangdong could be documented in some detail in as late as the 1940s, and in Hong Kong as late as the 1950s.[18] All of China (but, obviously, not Hong Kong) came under the changes that were brought by socialism from the 1950s to the 1970s. The experience of Leqing county was typical. As early as 1951, as land reform was carried out, fishermen were assigned their class status. By 1952, the fishing households joined fishery collectives. By 1954, they were grouped into 26 primary cooperatives that by 1956 were grouped into 19 upper-level cooperatives; in 1958, as communes were formed, the 19 cooperatives became integral parts of the eight communes in the county. All the while, the fishing households retained their fishing household status. By the end of the Cultural Revolution, there were 23 fishery brigades. By 1979, under Deng Xiaoping's reform policy, contracts between fishery teams and the brigade became possible, and from that beginning very successful private enterprise emerged.[19]

Available data on the fishing population as presented in Table A2.5, there-fore, reflect the household registration of the 1950s. The table shows that the fishing population, as registered, amounted to approximately four million for most of the 1950s to 1980s, that they were registered in approximately one million households, lived in 4,000–5,000 fishing villages and were grouped into about 300–400 fishing districts (*xiang*). The statistics available do not

Table A2.5. Fishing districts, villages, households and population, all China, 1950–1988

	Districts	*Villages*	*Households (million)*	*Population (million)*
1952				4.2
1974	323	4,601		3.72
1976	304	4,408	0.81	3.80
1977	323	4,601	0.83	3.96
1978	311	4,063	0.83	3.94
1979	319	4,141	0.87	4.01
1980	316	4,132	0.90	4.05
1981	324	4,191	0.93	4.06
1982	331	4,369	0.99	4.25
1983	329	4,674	1.03	4.36
1984	354	4,571	1.08	4.48
1985	400	4,730	1.13	4.70
1986	366	4,799	1.14	4.43
1987	388	5,006	1.23	4.99
1988	386	5,125	1.26	5.16

Source: Zhonghua renmin gongheguo nongyebu shuichan si (Aqua-products Department, Ministry of Agriculture, People's Republic of China) (ed.), *Zhongguo yuye tongji sishi nian* (Forty years of fishery statistics in China), Beijing: Haiyang chubanshe, 1991, p. 4.

Appendix 2   195

indicate how many among them lived on boats. Nor should it be assumed that people who lived on boats were necessarily registered as fishing households. Over the centuries, when the historical literature refers to boat-living, it has associated it not only to fishing and transport as occupations, but also to pariah status, in particular to urban slums and to the pleasure quarters of sing-song girls. Household registration in the early 1950s privileged fishing as an occupational status category. Boat-living households that did not make that occupational claim would have fallen within other categories.

The category known as the "shed household" (*penghu*) in Shanghai is a case in point. These were slum-dwellers who lived in very makeshift sheds and broken boats. Of the boats it was said that they had ferried many a refugee from the countryside who continued to live in them after they arrived in Shanghai. In time, many were broken and towed ashore, continuing as dwellings until their owners moved out into sheds. Surveys in the 1950s show that their inhabitants were absorbed into the lowest-paying jobs in Shanghai and by then such slum houses were gradually rebuilt. With good reason, living in a Shanghai slum was not thought of as boat-living. In Shanghai, the bottom rungs of society were said to be occupied by people from northern Jiangsu (Jiangbei), as the surveys found to be the case. Yet, moved to a different context, in Guangzhou and Fuzhou, the urban boat population had long given up fishing and would not have been noticeably different from the Shanghai slum-dwellers.[20]

In the Shanghai suburbs and in Jiangsu province (of which Shanghai was a part before 1949), data are available on the process by which boat dwellers were moved to shore. Recently compiled gazetteers argue that the impetus came in the early 1960s, in the aftermath of the Great Leap Forward. The Chengdong commune of Jiating county, which continued to manage its fishery resources collectively as distinct from the relaxation in reaction to the Great Leap that characterized developments elsewhere, declared in 1963 that in recognition of central government policy to conduct "socialist re-education", it would implement the moving of the boat people to shore. As a result, all the 48 fishing households of the team moved to houses built for them. Among the counties in the Shanghai suburb, the move to living on shore took place in earnest during the Cultural Revolution: 1,918 households living on shore by 1966, 3,858 by 1971 and 6,290 by 1975, when the total fishing households in 1965 amounted to only 5,716.[21] In Jiangsu province, which claimed 40 per cent of all boat-living households in the entire People's Republic, the centrally directed movement began in 1966 and was fully implemented by 1967, with resources also provided by the central government. By 1978, of the 63,370 households of fishing people living on boats (*lianjiachuan yumin*), 53,407 (84 per cent) were living on land.[22] The dating of the move ashore to the 1960s is not absolute. Even in Jiangsu, a reference to the Hongze lake, possibly written during the Great Leap in 1958, claimed that 4,872 households (90 per cent of all boat-living households) were moved to shore in that year.[23] The momentous change also affected other provinces in different ways. On

Zhoushan (Zhejiang province), boat-living was uncommon, a survey in 1948 noting that of the 224 fishing households, most lived in sheds. From 1964 to 1972, the sheds were replaced by houses. After economic reform in 1978, within three years, most (906 houses) were rebuilt into two-storey houses.[24] In Guangdong and Fujian, reports were not forthcoming about the moving of boat people ashore in the 1960s, but post-2000, it has been reported that the last boat-living fishing households were being moved ashore.[25] In inland Anhui province, it was found by survey in 2008 that 15,285 households lived on boats, making up 51 per cent of all fishing households.[26]

Economic changes since 1979 that brought rural migrants to the cities also brought outsiders to the fishing towns and villages. Lin Guangji reports that among 4,820 people working in fishery in Wuyu village in Fujian province, 2,960 came from outside, outnumbering the 1,850 local people by 60 per cent. The local people were defined by him as people who had held fishing as an occupation before the reforms began in 1978. The outside people, who had come from elsewhere in Fujian and from Anhui, had come to work on boats and the floating fish farms that the local people owned and operated. Some outside people had also come to work in the factories and workshops, servicing boats, dealing with ice storage, making nets and so on. Moreover, some local people had also migrated out to the cities.[27]

Moving ashore involved much more than residence. It had to do with very major changes in ways of life, just as education, hygiene and other amenities came to make an impact. Interviews within a single family conducted by Tang Guojian in Shandong in 2009 demonstrate some salient elements of intergenerational differences brought about by changes to education and career opportunities over time.[28] The grandfather interviewed recalled living on the boat and making a living from fishing. The son was born in 1957 and started work at 17 years of age in the commune. He started working on a boat in 1976, and by 1980, took advantage of the new economic policies to purchase his own boat, hire a helper and work independently. In 2002, his business began to accumulate a loss. He gave up independent work and was employed on a ship. The grandson was born in 1978. He graduated from high school (*gaozhong*) in 1996 and worked at odd jobs. At the time he was interviewed, he worked in an internet café in the town. He had remained unmarried and lived with his father and grandfather. He had never been to sea. Although anecdotal, the experience of the three men indicates a pattern by which the fishing family loses its independence and is either merged into larger fishing operations or detached altogether from fishing. Another report in 2006 notes that in Nantong (Jiangsu), 906 households of boat-living people had come from Huoqiu county in Anhui, who altogether had an estimated 3,000 children who needed to attend schools but were not able to enter the regular local schools.[29] The two reports add up to a gloomy picture of the fishing family going into underemployment or unemployment, and the migrant family producing the next generation who would be poorly educated. They underline the danger of a new underclass being produced to

Appendix 2 197

replace an earlier underclass, which had really been a long-established trend among the boat-living people.

Notes

1 Micah S. Muscolino, *Fishing Wars and Environmental Change in Late Imperial and Modern China*, Cambridge, MA: Harvard University Asia Center, 2009; Li Yushang, *Hai you fengqian, Huang Bo hai de yulei yu huanjing bianqian (1368–1958)* (Rich and poor harvests from the seas: fishes of the Yellow and Bohai seas and environmental changes, (1368–1958)), Shanghai: Shanghai jiaotong daxue, 2011.
2 Li Shihao, *Zhongguo haiyang yuye xianzhuang jiqi jianshe* (The present conditions of marine fishery in China and its construction), Shanghai: Shangwu, 1936; Li Shihao and Qu Ruoqian, *Zhongguo yuye shi* (A history of fishery in China), Taipei: Shangwu, 1965, first published 1936; Wang Zongpei, "Zhongguo yanhai zhi yumin jingji" (The economics of fishery on the China coast), *Jingji xue jikan*, 1932, 3(1), pp. 97–154.
3 Li and Qu, *Zhongguo yuye shi*, pp. 153–165.
4 Zhao Yizhong, "Zhoushan yuye fazhan shi chutan" (A first exploration of the history of the development of fishery in Zhoushan), *Zhongguo shehui jingjishi yanjiu*, 1984, 2, pp. 104–114; Zhoushan yuzhi bianshe zu (ed.), *Zhoushan yuzhi* (History of Zhoushan fishery), Beijing: Haiyang chubanshe, 1989.
5 *Daishan zhenzhi* (Gazetteer of Daishan township), 1919, pp. 5/4a–7a.
6 Herold J. Wiens, "Riverine and coastal junks in China's commerce", *Economic Geography*, 1955, 31(3), pp. 248–264.
7 "Report of the Harbour Master for the Year 1930", in Hong Kong Government, *Hong Kong Administrative Reports for the Year 1930*, Hong Kong: Government Printer, 1931, p. 6.
8 Fei Xiaotung, *Peasant Life in China, a Field Study of Country Life in the Yangtze Valley*, London: Routledge & Kegan Paul, 1939, pp. 249–256, provides a vivid example.
9 Zhongguo guojia tongjiju (ed.), *Zhongguo tongji nianjian 1985* (China statistical yearbook 1985), Hong Kong: Xianggang jingji daobaoshe, 1985 p. 385; Zhongguo guojia tongjiju (ed.), *Zhongguo tongji nianjian 2011* (China statistical yearbook 2011), Hong Kong: Xianggang jingji daobaoshe, 2011, p. 616.
10 Li and Qu, *Zhongguo yuye shi*, p. 96.
11 Wang, "Zhongguo yanhai zhi yumin jingji", pp. 114–122.
12 Yun Pu, "Minguo ershier nian fen Shanghai shi jinkou haichan xianyu zhi guancha" (Observations on the import of fresh fish into Shanghai city in 1933), *Shuichan yuekan*, 1934, 1(1), pp 5–7.
13 Lin Moucun and Wu Yuqi, "Yinxian yuye zhi diaocha" (Investigation into the fishing industry of Ningbo), *Zhejiang sheng jianshe yuekan*, 1936, 10(4), pp. 30–54.
14 The Zhejiang Bank was among 12 banks that formed a syndicate in 1936 to finance the fishing industry. The banks were to provide 800,000 yuan and the Ministry of Industry 200,000 yuan to make up a one million yuan fund. (*North China Herald*, 11 November 1936). On the background of the cooperative movement, see Fang Xianting, "Zhongguo zhi hezuo yundong" (The cooperative movement in China), in Fang Xianting (ed.), *Zhongguo jingji yanjiu* (Studies of China's economy), Changsha: Shangwu, 1938, pp. 413–432.
15 "Shenjiamen choushe yuye hezuo she" (Organizing a fishery cooperative at Shenjiamen) *Hezuo yuekan*, 1935, 7(10–11), p 76.
16 "Shanghai yushichang minguo ershiliu nian yiyuefen yingye shu'e tongjibiao" (Statistical table showing business volume in January 1937 at the Shanghai Fish Market), *Shuichan yuekan*, 1937, 2–3, pp. 80–82.

198   *Appendix 2*

17 Leqing shi shuichanju (ed.), *Leqing xian shuichan zhi* (History of aqua-products of Leqing county), Hangzhou: Zhejiang renming, 1999, pp. 80, 98.
18 Chen Xujing, *Danmin de yanjiu* (A study of Dan people), Shanghai: Shangwu, 1946; Wu Ruilin, *Sanshui danmin diaocha* (A survey of Dan people in Sanshui), Guangzhou: Lingnan daxue Xinan shehui jingji yanjiusuo, 1948; Barbara E. Ward, "A Hong Kong fishing village", *Journal of Oriental Studies*, 1954, 1(1), pp. 195–214.
19 Leqing shi shuichanju, *Leqing xian shuichan zhi*, pp. 175–180.
20 Chen Zhiliang, "Shanghai de danmin" (The Dan people of Shanghai), *Hua'an*, 1934, 2(7), p. 9; Xiao Yu, "Shanghai de danmin" (The Dan people of Shanghai), *Renren zhoubao*, 1947, 6, p. 12; Zhang Shaochuan, *Jindai Shanghai Zhabei jumin shehui shenghuo* (The social life of Zhabei residents in Shanghai in modern history), Shanghai: Shanghai cishu chubanshe, 2009, pp. 271–287; Zhang Xinghua, Wan Yulin and Zheng Chuanrui, "Shanghai shi Penglai qu de bufen penghu jumin shenghuo diaocha" (A study of the livelihood of some shed-household residents in the Penglai district of Shanghai city), *Shanghai weisheng*, 1951, 1(7), pp. 61–64; Shanghai shehui kexueyuan jingji yanjiusuo, chengshi jingji zu, *Shanghai penghu qu de bianqian* (Changes in the shed districts of Shanghai), Shanghai: Shanghai renmin, 1962.
21 Shanghai yuyezhi bianzuan weiyuanhui (ed.), *Shanghai yuyezhi* (A history of fishery in Shanghai), Shanghai: Shanghai shehui kexue chubanshe, 1998, p. 74–76.
22 Jiangsu sheng shuichanju shizhiban (Jiangsu province aqua-products bureau history office) (ed.), *Jiangsu sheng yuye shi* (History of fishery in Jiangsu), Nanjing: Jiangsu kexue jishu chubanshe, 1993, p. 145.
23 Feng Jianmin, "Hongze xian zuzhi bulao yumin lushang dingju" (Hongze county organizes fishermen to settle ashore), *Zhongguo shuichan*, 1958, 13, p. 21.
24 Zhoushan yuzhi bianshe zu, *Zhoushan yuzhi*, pp. 406–407.
25 "Xinhui Sanjiang gongshe yuye dadui xincun" (New village for Xinhui county Sanjiang commune fishery brigade), *Jianzhu xuebao*, 1975, 3, p. 44; "Weimin yuye dadui xincun" (Weimin fishery brigade new village), *Jianzhu xuebao*, 1975, 3, pp. 43–44, report that the two fishing villages in Guangdong were built in 1967.
26 Qian Dongfang, Zhang Jun and Xu Zhao, "Anhui sheng 'lianjiachuan' zhuanye yumin shengchan shenghuo xianzhuang, wenti ji duice" (The present living conditions and problems of professional 'houseboat' fishermen in Anhui province and a policy to deal with them), *Zhongguo yuye jingji*, 2009, 6(27), pp. 32–36.
27 Lin Guangji, "'Yumin, yuye, yucun' luoji yu beilun – yi Longhai shi Wuyu cun yuye diaocha wei li" ("The logic and mistaken theory of 'Fishing people, fishing and fishing villages' – the case of a survey of fishery in Wuyu village of Longhai city), *Zhongguo yuye jingji*, 2010, 4(28), pp. 5–17.
28 Tang Guojian, "Cong danmin dao 'shimin': shenfen zhi yu haiyang yumin de daiji liudong" (From "Dan" to "citizen": the status system and intergenerational mobility among fishermen), *Xinjiang shehui kexue*, 2001, 4, pp. 129–135.
29 Ling Bugui and Sun Mingxiong, "Zhenyang luoshi Nantong chuanmin zinu jiaoyu?" (How to implement education for boat people's children in Nantong?), *Jianghai zongheng*, 2006, 2, p. 56.

Glossary of Chinese characters

ba	霸
baihua	白话
Bailing	百龄
baimaochang she	白茅枪社
bannong banyu	半农半渔
bao	保
Beigang	北港
bianru zhouju	贬入舟居
Bing, Song Emperor	昺, 宋帝
Botou	泊头
buluo jia	不落家
butou	步头
buzhu	埠主
caishendou	财神斗
chacao weibiao	插草为标
chaidi	柴地
Chang *he*	长河
chang jiaqian	唱家前
chang shenge	唱神歌
Che *yuanshuai*	车元帅
Chen Youliang	陈友谅
chengguan	承管
chijiu	吃酒
chili ce	赤历册
chishou	池首
choushen	酬神
chu laozu	出老祖
Chu, Prince of	楚王
chuanchang	船长
chuanhu	船户
chuanjia zhang	船家长
chuanzhuang ce	船庄册
chun yumin	纯渔民

200 Glossary of Chinese characters

citang	祠堂
cun	村
da xialai	打下来
da zongci	大宗祠
dadui	大队
dagu	大股
Dai Jing	戴璟
Dai Pan	戴槃
daliao	大寮
dan (Taihu religious ceremony)	賧
Dan, *dan*	蛋
dang	垱
dangjia zuo zhuren	当家做主人
danjia	蛋家
danpeng	蛋棚
Daqu *shan*	大衢山
dashen	大神
dawang	大王
daxian (temple)	大仙庙
Da-Xiao Deng	大小嶝
Daxie	大榭
daxing	大姓
dian	佃
Diaocha, lake	汈汊湖
Dongting (lake)	洞庭湖
Dou (surname)	窦
dou	斗
du	都
duan	断
duangong	端公
dun	墩
duomin	堕民
Erlang, god	二郎神
Fang Guozhen	方国珍
feizhou	飞洲
fen	份
fuju caowu	浮居草屋
fuye	副业
fuzhu	福主
gaige kaifang	改革开放
gang	港
gangji	港籍
Gao Zhu	高翥
gaoshi bei	告示碑

Glossary of Chinese characters 201

gong'an ju	公安局
gongsuo	公所
gongzi she	公子社
gu pinmin	雇贫民
Gu Yanwu	顾炎武
gu	罟
guan	管
Guangzhao Taishan Kanghuang, great emperor	广兆泰山康皇大帝
guanye	管业
guanzhi fenzi	管制分子
guding	罟丁
gupeng zongli	罟棚总理
gupeng	罟棚
guzhang	罟长
haizhu	海主
Hao Liangtong	郝良桐
haohuai xianghun	好坏相混
hebosuo	河泊所
hiashang eshao	海上恶少
Hongwei	红卫
houjing	猴精
Hu'an	湖案
Hualin	华林乡
huan fumu xiao	还父母孝
Huang Dalai	黄大来
Huang Gan	黄干
Huang *gong c*i	黄公祠
Huang Hao	黄灏
Huang *sigong*	黄四公
Huang Xiaoyang	黄萧养
Huang Zongxi	黄宗羲
hufen	湖分
huitou	会头
huizhu	会主
huke	湖课
hukou maoyi	糊口贸易
humaozi	湖猫子
Hunan *yuye gongsi*	湖南渔业公司
huzhu	湖主
Ji, Prince of	济王
jia	甲
jiachuan	家船
jianzui yu	尖嘴鱼

202 *Glossary of Chinese characters*

jiaodai	交代
Jiaoshou *keng*	脚手坑
jiashen	家神
jiatang zhouzi	家堂軸子
jiating jisi	家庭祭祀
jiji fenji	积极分子
jing	境
Jing, Prince of	景王
jingli	经理
jingshen	敬神
jingzhu	境主
Jinqian	津前
Jintang	金塘
jiushan	旧山
jiuxing yuhu	九姓渔户
jizu	祭祖
jumin xiaozu	居民小组
jun	军
junzhu	军主
kaiguang	开光
kaikou ren	开口人
kailai	开来
Kaixiangong	开弦弓
Kang *yuanshuai*	康元帅
keti	科蹄
laili	来历
lan (fishing)	罱
Laoti	老蹄
laoye	老爷
laozu	老祖
Li Shihao	李士豪
Li Sizu	李思祖
Li Tong	李侗
Li Zhenyi	李震一
Li Zicheng	李自成
liangjian huxiao, huji cuoza	良贱互淆, 户籍错杂
lianjiachuan yumin	连家船渔民
Liannan *xiang*	蓼南乡
Liansi (marshes)	莲泗荡
Liaohua *chi*	蓼花池
Liaohua *zhen*	蓼花镇
lijia	里甲
Liu Meng	刘猛
Liu Zhensheng	刘贞升
Liuwang *chan*	刘王忏

Glossary of Chinese characters 203

Liuwang *hui*	刘王会
Liuwang	刘王
Lu Xiufu	陆秀夫
Lu, Prince of	鲁王
lushang de liumang dipi	陆上的流氓地痞
ma	祃
Mazu	妈祖
Miao *gang*	庙港
Miao Sui	缪燧
min	民
minghuan ci	名宦祠
mingtang	明堂
minzu ganqing	民族感情
minzu guannian	民族观念
minzu tedian	民族特点
minzu xingge	民族性格
moushi sandai zongqin	某氏三宗亲
Nan Juyi	南居益
nan tianmen jiujie	南天门九姐
Nangang	南港
Naozhou	硇洲
nongmin	农民
Pan Lianggui	潘良贵
penghu	棚户
pengzailao	棚仔佬
pengzaizhu	棚仔猪
pozai	婆仔
qianhai	迁海
qisan she	旗伞社
Qu Dajun	屈大均
Qu Yuan	屈原
quti	曲蹄
Sandu	三都
sanyue po	三月坡
Shangfang (hill)	上方山
Shangguo Pingtian	上国平天
shangjie shen	上界神
shangli	上礼
shatian	沙田
Shawan	沙湾
shen jinpeng	神进棚
shen	神
Shenbao	申报
Shenjia *tangmen*	沈家堂门
shequ	社区

204 *Glossary of Chinese characters*

shoufen	收分
shoushi	首事
shuike fei	水稞费
shuilan	水栏
shuishang qu	水上区
shuishang ren	水上人
Shuixian	水仙
su	素
suku	诉苦
Tai (lake)	太湖
Taihu *yuye guanli weiyuanhui*	太湖渔业管理委员会
Taijiang	台江
Taijun (temple)	太君庙
taiping yue	太平月
taiqin hui	太亲会
taiye she	太爷社
Tang *chuan*	唐船
Tang *shen hui*	唐神会
tangmen	堂门
tantou	坛头
tiandi sanjie	天地三界
Tianhou	天后
Tianzhu *jiao*	天主教
Tong Zhenzao	童振藻
tu	图
tuochuan	拖船
Wang Guozuo	王国祚
Wang Shu	汪忓
Wang Yangming	王阳明
Wang Zongpei	王宗培
wangchuan gui	网船鬼
wangchuan hui	网船会
Wangjiangjing	王江泾
wangming bucheng zhi tu	亡命不逞之徒
wangzhu	网主
Wei (village)	微村
Weishan (lake)	微山湖
weisuo	卫所
weiyang lutou	圍養路頭
Wen Tianxiang	文天祥
wokou	倭寇
Wu Jun	吴郡
Wuxing tang Shenshi zupu	吴兴堂沈氏族谱
Xia Shidong	夏时栋
xiajie shen	下界神

Glossary of Chinese characters 205

xianfeng	先锋
Xiang (surname)	项
xiang	乡
xianghuo	香火
xiangshe	乡社
xiangshe	香社
xiangtou	香头
xiangxian ci	乡贤祠
xiangyou qian	香油钱
Xiaoli tan	小里潭
Xiaya	下涯
Xie Taijiao	谢泰交
Xinglong *she*	兴隆社
xinshan	新山
xu jiapu	续家谱
Xujia *gongmen lao* Xinglong *she*	徐家公门老兴隆社
Xujia *gongmen*	徐家公门
yamen	衙门
Yang Hanzhao	杨汉昭
yang	阳
yaopai	腰牌
yemin	业民
yi	夷
yin	阴
yitang laozu	一堂老祖
you shuile	游水乐
yu	渔
yuanshou	缘首
yuhu	渔户
yuhui	渔会
yuke	渔课
yumin gongshe	渔民公社
yumin shehui	渔民社会
yumin xincun	渔民新村
yumin	渔民
yuye cun	渔业村
yuye renkou	渔业人口
yuye	渔业
zanshen ge	赞神歌
zao	灶
Zhang Huangyan	张煌言
Zhang Shiche	张时彻
Zhang xing qu yuzhou	张姓取鱼舟
zhang	丈
Zhao Gongming	赵公明

206 *Glossary of Chinese characters*

zhaoguan	照管
Zheng Chenggong	郑成功
Zheng Jing	郑经
Zheng Xiao	郑晓
Zhengyi	正一
Zhou Chen	周忱
Zhou Di	周氐
Zhou Shenghua	周圣化
zhou	洲
Zhoushan	舟山
Zhu Xi	朱熹
Zhu Yuanzhang	朱元璋
zhuanye	专业
Zhuji *xiang*	珠玑巷
zongzu lishihui	宗族理事会
zongzu	宗族
zoudeng	走灯
zu	祖

Index

adoption of children 23, 102, 105, 121
altar heads 125, 126, 128
altars, domestic 12, 15, 16, 25, 89plate, 91, 115; as genealogical record 110; and sacrifice 13, 90, 164
ancestral spirits *see* spirits
anchorages 12, 83 *see also* Northern Anchorage; Southern Anchorage; Temple Anchorage
animal husbandry 162
anti-superstition education 152, 153
army pressgangs 144, 145

Bailong river 149, 155
Beijing 45, 47
Big Cloud village 159–70; ancestors and gods 163, 164–5, 166; funeral ceremonies 163, 164; patriarchal 165; self-identification 170; sense of community 163, 167; trade and shops 167
Big Stream Mouth village 169, 170
"boat household" registration 5, 144, 145
boat-and-shed living 1–27; and ethnicity 23; identity and ritual 11–20; pariah status 1, 2–3, 4, 151, 157 n. 28, 170; registration 4–11
boat ownership, types of 190app
boat people ethnicity 151–2; lack of education 52; oppression 147; pariah status 142, 145; religion 146; rights and privileges 146; settlement on land 155; status 146, 150; uprisings 5
boat registration 6, 7, 37–9, 40, 64
brick houses 76, 98, 159, 160, 169
British East India Company 45, 48
Bureau of Fishery 64

Chen Bisheng, Professor 151
Chen Hansheng 22
Chen Juncai 101
Chen Youliang 177
Chengdong commune 195
Chinese Communist Party 104, 149
Chongqing 140
Chu, prince of 70, 71
coastal evacuation 7, 38, 41, 47–8
collectivization 101, 105, 122, 194app
common worshipping 13
commune movement 12, 14, 76, 101, 104–5, 180, 194 *see also* Chengdong commune; Tai Lake commune
Communism, suppression of 144
conscription 144
"continuing the genealogy" ceremony 17–19, 120, 122, 127plate, 128–30
cormorants, fishing with 23, 173, 174, 175
corvee service 6, 35, 36, 68, 144
crab farming 101, 105, 106
"crimson registries" 10, 11
cross-holding of property 8
Cultural Revolution 23, 58, 129, 194app, 195app
Cunningham, James 8, 52–3
customs stations 40, 45, 51

Dai Jing 37
Dai Pan 177–9
Dan people 1–3; ethnicity 151, 152; household status 6; move to land 22; registration 5; status 36; tax registration 33, 34 *see also* Big Cloud village
Danzhou (Hainan) 34
Davis, Sir John Francis 8, 53

208 *Index*

Daxie island 46
deep sea fishing 96–8, 155, 187app
deity scrolls 17, 18, 122–5
Deng Xiaoping 194app
Diaocha lake 67–79; "lake shares" 68–9;
  litigation 70–6; lake records 9, 10
Dinghai city 52, 53
Dongting lake 135–41; annual catch 137;
  fishing people living on boats 136–7;
  fishing people settled on land 137–8;
  peripheral communities 135, 136;
  social class 20, 21, 139–41
Dou Zhenbiao 88, 89
dowries 10, 68, 69
dragon boat races 92
Du Zhen 86
dykes 21, 22, 67, 73, 74, 75

education 41, 50, 64, 104, 149, 155
  see also anti-superstition education;
  literacy
emperor Bing 87, 89
entertainment 21, 105, 169
ethnography 2, 11–20
exploitation 138, 140, 147, 150, 151

"fallen people" 54
family planning 105
famine 77, 126, 129
Fanchuanbu 146
Fang Guozhen 5, 45
farming 9, 21, 24, 53
Fei Xiaotong (Fei Hsiao-tung) 13, 14,
  21, 22, 167
ferry boats 143, 190app
festival of the Liu-wang-wei 183–5app;
  see also King Liu temple festivals
fish tax 6, 10, 34–5, 40, 67, 72–3, 139
fishing associations 190app
fishing cooperatives 64, 104–6, 191app
fishing households: commercialization
  of 3; localization of 17; registration
  14; status 6; as subsidiary
  occupation 63
fishing households of the nine surnames
  2, 173–81; emancipation of 2,
  24, 178–81
fishing industry, reforms 186app,
  191app, 194app
Fishing People's Association 63
fishing permits 64, 105
fishing rights 5, 9, 11, 57–65, 72–3
floating nets 138
flooding 67

foraging rights 26, 36, 76, 77
foreshore rights and taxation 35–6, 38
Foshan 84
Fu Yiling 24
Fuchun river 24
Fujian 7, 37, 40, 41
Fuzhou: boat people 142–55; boat
  registration 147; clearance of
  houseboats 155; ethnicity 22–3;
  geography and history 142, 143–7;
  household registration 143–5, 147,
  148; land-or boat-dwelling status
  ambiguous 145; marine district, land
  reform and ethnicity 147–53; marine
  office 147–8; migration ashore 23, 143;
  oppression 149, 150; spirits and mass
  hysteria 152–3; residents' committees
  148; Roman Catholicism 146–7, 149,
  153, 154; tenacity of tradition 153–5;
  urbanization 143

Gao Zhu 4
Gaozhou city 13
genealogy *see* lineage
Ghost Festival 50
God of Agriculture temple 168
grain transportation 45, 74
Grand Canal 17
Great King Temple 97
Great Leap Forward 195app
Gu Yanwu 35
Guangzhou city 159
Guomindang 147, 149, 175

Hall of Local Notables 50
Hall of Reputable Officials 50
Hanchuan 67, 68
Hangzhou 24
Hansson, Anders 2
Hanyang 4, 74
Hao Liangtong 47
Hong Kong 1, 190app, 191app, 194app
Hongwei 11, 12
household registration: avoidance of
  22, 35; *baojia* (mutual responsibility)
  7, 8, 22, 37, 39, 52, 60, 86–7, 102,
  142–5, 154; "crimson registries" 10,
  11; documentation 178; early 37;
  failure of 41, 50; fishing household
  status 6; Ming government 33, 35, 41;
  in People's Republic 11, 14, 23, 143–5,
  147, 148, 153, 154, 194app, 195app;
  Qing government 41, 143; saltern
  households 36; Song government 5

Index 209

Huang Dalai 48, 51
Huang Gan 4, 5, 8, 9
Huang Xiaoyang rebellion 3
Huang Zongxi 47

identity papers 39
imperial examination 49, 50
Imperial Library 49
imports and exports 51, 192t app
incense associations 15, 101–11, 104
incense head 15–17, 109, 113–19
irrigation 75, 161, 167

Japan, technological advances 186app
Japanese occupation 140
"Japanese pirates" 6, 37
Jiangwan 14
Jinagxi Normal University 65
Jing, prince of 70, 72
Jinqian Tianhou temple 84
Jintang island 46
junks 1, 12, 38, 39, 40

Kaixiangong 13
Kangxi period 49, 74
Keti Hill 147
King Liu temple festivals 14–16
Knotweed pond 8, 57, 58–63
Kong-wan 183–5app; *see also* Jiangwan

"lake cats" 121
lake records 10, 69, 72
lake shares 67, 68–9
Lan Li 50
land, registration of 6, 7, 35, 41
land, usurpation of by princes 70
land grant 70, 72
land reclamation: Big Cloud village
  159–60; Fuzhou 142; group
  reclamation 151; litigation 75;
  provision of work 21, 50, 77, 105;
  reduction of lakes 67, 139; and
  restriction on settlement 6, 22
land reform 23, 57, 63, 98, 149–50
land rights 138; arbitration 74
land taxation 50, 75, 140
land-based status 3
landlessness 2
language 20, 98
Li Jingui 109
Li Shihao 187app
Li surname 61, 70
Li Tong 48, 51
Li Zhenyi 138, 139–41

Li Zicheng 47
Liaoning 187app
Lin Guangji 196app
Lin Sen 145
lineage 8, 18, 19, 78–9; depiction 122–4;
  Diaocha lake 68; lineage management
  committee 125; status defining 3;
  Weishan lake 120–31
literacy 2, 19, 20, 104, 129
Literary Temple 49
litigation, property rights 69, 76–9;
  documentation 72; Ming dynasty
  70–2; Qing dynasty 72–5, 76; threat 25
Liuwang (Prince Liu) temple 110
livestock 53
local administration 70–1
local histories 143
Long river 8, 57, 59, 60
Lu, prince of 47, 70
Lu Xiufu 92
Lujia island 145
Luozhou 142
Luxu village 116

marine police 147
market reforms 101
marketing 190–3app
Martyrs' Temple 49
mechanization of boats
  187–90app, 193app
Menegon, Eugenio 146
Menggang village 93
Miao Sui 8, 49, 50, 51–2, 53, 54
migration to land 20, 23, 101, 194–7app
military stations 10, 33, 51, 54, 74–5
Min river 143, 147, 149
Ming dynasty: documentation 10, 11;
  economic development 77; evacuation
  47; fishing households 1, 2; fishing
  industry 3, 33–42; princely patronage
  78; registration 6–7, 33; settlement
  ban in Shousan 45–6; taxation 35
modernization 142, 143
"monkey spirit" 152
mud-ski 53

Nan Juyi 46
Naozhou island 83–99; ceremonies 94–5;
  circulation of gods 90–5; coastal
  evacuation 83; control of sedan-chairs
  88; deities 12, 13; documented
  history 83, 84; domestic altars 90,
  91; Gangtou (Port Head) village
  85; Hongwei village 95, 96–7, 98;

210 *Index*

Jinqian Tianhou temple 94, 98; land people 86–90; language 98; military garrison 88; temples 94; three statues of the Mazu 94; Xianglong Academy 86 *see also* Northern Anchorage; Southern Anchorage
net-fishing 136, 139
"new fishing people's villages" 64
New Fishing village, Luxu township 117
New Year 17, 58
Ni Chunbao 116, 117
Ni Gaoming 116
Ningbo 49, 50, 190app, 191app
Nogami Eiichi 146

Old Prosperity Association 110
Opium War 8, 22, 53

paddy 167, 168
Pan Lianggui 4
pariah status 1, 2–3, 4, 24, 27, 177, 179
patronage 50, 51, 78
Pavilion for Promoting the Examination 48
Pearl river delta 2, 3, 6, 22, 24, 36, 159–70; community 166–8; shed-living 162–3
pearl-fishers 2
"peasant" status 64
peasants 22, 23, 63, 105, 139, 140, 150
People's Republic of China: boat-and-shed living 22–3; commune movement 76; and incense 115; registration 11, 14, 23, 143–5, 147, 148, 153, 154, 194app, 195app
Pingtian temple 93
Pingwang village 116
piracy 7, 37, 41, 52, 190; Japanese 45, 46
poetry 4
policing (*baojia*) 7, 22, 37, 39, 52, 60, 86–7, 142–5
political participation 149
"pond headman" 9
port headmen system 39
portraits 15, 17, 102, 109, 117–18, 122
Portugal 45
poverty 50, 126, 149, 191
Poyang lake 57–65
precinct committees 23
private enterprise 64, 105, 122
property rights, Diaocha lake 67–79; "lake shares" 68–9; litigation 70–6; lake records 9, 10

protection networks 6, 7, 37, 190app
purity 26
Putuoshan 47, 48

Qing dynasty 3, 6, 7, 10; economic development 77; fishing industry 33–42; household registration 143; land and fishing rights 61; reforms 186app; taking of Zhoushan 47–8; taxation 40–1; troops on Naozhou island 12; water rights 57; Zhoushan island customs station 45
Qu Dajun 35

railways 14, 184app, 185app
reed collection 73, 75
"reform and opening" policy 159
religion: banning of 129; revival of 105; as seditious 19; segregation 153–5 *see also* Roman Catholicism
repopulation of islands 50, 51
Revolution 1911 179
ritual and identity 12–20
river mooring stations 6, 33–4, 35
Roman Catholicism 22, 23, 146–7, 149, 153, 154
Royal Asiatic Society 52

sacrifices: ancestral 1, 17–18, 120; animal 128; banning of local 106; to circulating gods 90, 91, 94; daily 13, 165; domestic altars 115; funeral 164, 165; government attitude towards 19; incense associations 102; revival of 105; and scrolls 122–5
salt 8, 33, 36, 40–1, 45, 51, 53
salt tax 41, 48, 175
scrolls, ancestral 17, 18, 122–5, 127–30
sea walls 50, 51
secret societies 147
seine nets 137, 138, 139, 162
settlement ban 51–2
shad fishing 136, 137
Shandong 187app, 196app
Shanghai 189app, 195app
Shanghai Fish Market 191app
Shawan people 24
She Kanglue 17
shed-dwelling 11, 52, 95app, 97, 160–1; on stilts 96, 160
Shen Fuxiang 115
Shen Quandi 116, 117
Shen Ruisheng 117, 118

Index 211

Shen Xiaolin 113, 114, 115, 117
Shenjiamen 191app
Shuixian temple 93, 97
silver 6, 35, 37, 60, 74, 178
"single-whip reform" 35
sinking nets 138
Sino–Japanese War 140, 191app
Siu, Helen and Liu Zhiwei 36, 159, 170
slum dwelling 195app
smuggling 3, 5, 47
social identity 3, 20, 21
social mobilization 149
"socialist re-education" 195app
Song dynasty 1, 2, 4, 5, 6, 87
"songs of praise to the gods" 113–15,
   116, 117, 118
spirit masters 17
spirits: evil 126, 128; funeral practice
   164–5; mass hysteria 23, 152–3; and
   misfortune 106; representations 15,
   25, 109, 117, 122; rituals 17–18, 50,
   110, 118, 127, 128; spirit tablets 54, 90,
   93, 169
Stalin, Joseph 152
Stone Bank village 159, 162
subsistence fishing 8
sugarcane 166, 167, 168
Szonyi, Michael 142

Tai Lake 101–11; fishing cooperatives
   104–6; sacrifices 18; small-boat fisher
   families 102–3; uprising 5; Wang
   family 103–4
Tai Lake Commune 103
Taiping Rebellion 3, 9, 59
Taiwan 39, 47
Tang (goddess) 122
Tang Guojian 196app
tax amnesty 35
taxation: cultivated land on foreshore
   51; goods in transit 51; household
   registration 144; land registration 6;
   landowners 20; local 70; loopholes
   5; Qing dynasty 40–1; rent charges
   8; river anchorages 61; tenants 34
   see also fish tax; salt tax
technological advances 20
Temple Anchorage 14, 101, 102–4, 106,
   107, 108
temple worship and travel 169
Terada Hiroaki 68
territorial rights 41, 42, 145
Tianhou goddess 93

Tianjin 189app, 191app
Tong Zhenzao 179
torture 70, 71, 138
trade, sea-borne 8, 143
trade associations 145
transport boats, mechanization of
   189app, 190app
Treaty of Nanjing 22, 142
tribute grain, transport of 5

village festival, account of 14

Wang Shu 37, 46
Wang Yangming 2, 24
Wang Zongpei 187app,
   190app, 191app
Wangjiangjing 14
Wanzi lake 138, 139
water rights 21, 57, 138
Wei Qingyuan 47
Wei village 121–2
Weishan Lake 120–31; ancestors and
   gods 122–5; "continuing the family
   genealogy" ceremony 125–30;
   ethnography 19; "lineage committee"
   129; localization 17; poverty 129;
   rituals 18; settlement on land
   121, 122
Wen Tianxiang 93
whitebait fishing 136, 137, 138, 139
women 116, 117, 126
written records 4–11
Wu Jun 8
Wu Three-Seven 97
Wuchang 70
Wucheng city 57
Wuchuan 86

Xiamen University 151
Xin'an river 180
Xu Bin 10, 11
Xu Family's Hall 101, 107
Xu family's Prosperity
   Association 106–11
Xu Guanming 106, 107, 109, 110
Xu Guixiang's hall 118
Xu Zhenglong 110

Yangzi river 4, 5, 13, 15
Yuan dynasty 3, 5, 45, 68

Zhang Huangyan 48
Zhang Jian 186app

212 Index

Zhanjiang city 83
Zhao Yizhong 189app
Zheng Chenggong 7, 37, 38, 47, 83
Zheng family, protection network 7
Zheng Jing (son of Zheng Chenggong) 48
Zheng Xiao 45
Zhentian temple 84
Zhou Chen 5
Zhou Di 135–8, 140

Zhoushan archipelago 45–54; county administration 48–53, 54; fishing 7, 8, 13, 189–92app; impact of depression 192app; military stations 46; Ming settlement ban 45–6; Qing dynasty 47–8; shed-living 196; social structure 12
Zhu Delan 47
Zhu Xi 4
Zhu Yuanzhang 5, 45, 177

Printed in the United States
by Baker & Taylor Publisher Services